THE WILD DUCK

A NEW TRANSLATION

THE WRITING OF THE PLAY

CRITICISM

A NORTON CRITICAL EDITION

HENRIK IBSEN

THE WILD DUCK

A NEW TRANSLATION
THE WRITING OF THE PLAY
CRITICISM

Translated and Edited by

DOUNIA B. CHRISTIANI
WISCONSIN STATE UNIVERSITY AT EAU CLAIRE

W · W · NORTON & COMPANY · INC · *New York*

Contents

vi · *Contents*

Criticism

Preface

A first reading of *The Wild Duck* may well leave the student as perplexed as the play's earliest reviewers—more so, indeed, since he knows it to be an acknowledged masterpiece and cannot, like them, dismiss it as a failure. It should reassure him to learn that even a critic like Sarcey found it "obscure, incoherent, intolerable." Only Shaw and Rilke apprehended its magnificence from the start. Although *The Wild Duck* gained early recognition as the most masterfully constructed of Ibsen's prose dramas, its innovative combination of farce with tragedy and of realism with symbolism has only rather recently won the sort of appreciation that is based on acute critical analysis. Placing before the student the full range of background material and studies in criticism which represent every extant approach to the play, this edition aims to inform his judgment while furnishing both substance and models for independent essays in criticism.

The Note on Translation accounts for minor departures from the original text, while the Notes on Interpretation deal with the correspondence between various characters and their mode of expression, along with other problems of meaning.

The critical views cited in this volume reflect the full spectrum of opinion, from Strindberg's paranoid delusion that *The Wild Duck* was a personal attack on him—that it cast doubt on the paternity of his eldest child, for one thing—to its comparison by M. C. Bradbrook with *Hamlet*. However, as our intention is not to recapitulate a success story but to survey the progressive elucidation of *The Wild Duck*, the emphasis is on critical studies which, taken together, constitute an authoritative analysis of the play in the context of Ibsen's total production and its influence on the development of modern drama. Furthermore, these critiques are outstanding examples of the various critical approaches to literature, from Downs's leisurely explanation of the play to Reinert's detailed study of its sight imagery and Thompson's digest of extant psychoanalysis of its characters, from Forster's impressionistic response to the poetry in Ibsen to Valency's penetrating inquiry into the nature of his symbolism. Mary McCarthy's and Robert Adams' spirited essays, which attest to the abiding vitality of Ibsen, cannot fail to arouse a keen interest in all the master's work.

As to the selections from Ibsen's notes and drafts, there is hardly a point in debate among critics of *The Wild Duck* which they cannot illuminate in some way. What strikes one first of all is how remote the rudiments of the play are from the eventual finished work; vestiges of *A Doll's House* and *An Enemy of the People* and foretokens of *Rosmersholm*, *The Lady from the Sea*, and *Hedda Gabler* jostle the theme of the sybaritic do-gooder, the Ur-Gregers of *The Wild Duck*. Ibsen apparently started out to write another thesis play such as his public expected, but the slowness with which his materials fell into shape suggests how little the project inspired him. Then something happened. The self-congratulatory good Samaritan "K-d" modeled on Alexander Kielland turned into a demanding idealist resembling Kierkegaard* and, what is astonishing, into a caricature of the crusading playwright himself. Small wonder that Ibsen's contemporaries were nonplused when *The Wild Duck* appeared; far from rearranging his familiar ideas into a new configuration, he turned them topsy-turvy. Today, instructed by such scholars as Valency, we can see how Ibsen's early critics measured the play by what they anticipated and understood. But even for us the fairly complete drafts reprinted in this volume are an instructive index to the immense difference between standard playwriting and the genius of the achieved work of art that is *The Wild Duck*.

There is reason to suspect, too, that the "psychoanatomist" who is moved to assess the effect on Ibsen of his youthful transgression (see p. 176) will find his most pregnant clues in the genesis of *The Wild Duck*: the change in direction which theme and plot take from Ibsen's original intention, the personal elements of Ibsen not only in Gregers and Hjalmar but in Relling, Hedvig, and Molvik, Hedvig's death on her fourteenth birthday, and Gina, for whom Ibsen could not have encountered a model in all his years abroad. Even the literary critic who shuns psychoanalysis of authors or fictional characters cannot but be struck by Ibsen's unique attachment to this play, his joy in working on it once its characters came alive and his reluctance to part with it. Something in all this suggests the operation of a subconscious force in the creative process which, dis-

---

* Why does Gregers Werle think his name is hideous? True, it started out as *Walle*, which is cognate with English *wall-eyed*—an interesting variation on the play's theme of flawed vision, by the way. But there is nothing hideous about "Gregers Werle." The name Søren, however, is a euphemism for Satan popularly used as a mild swearword, while *Kierkegaard* means "Churchyard." Incidentally, Kierkegaard, whose ideas on marriage and on Christianity are echoed in Ibsen's jottings for *The Wild Duck*, was, like the character "K-d," the son of a wealthy father and indulged himself lavishly in the creature comforts.

cerningly traced, may provide the answer to why *The Wild Duck,* the most sordid and pessimistic of Ibsen's plays, is also the most genial.

I am deeply indebted to Mr. Erik J. Friis, editor of the American-Scandinavian Foundation publications, and to Professor Maurice J. Valency for their careful scrutiny of my translation and many valuable comments and suggestions. Mr. D. Austad, cultural attaché at the Royal Norwegian Embassy in London, and Mr. Erling Grønlund, Head Librarian of the Norwegian Department at Universitetsbiblioteket, Oslo, whom I bombarded with queries about Norway in the 1880's, responded with utmost generosity. Mrs. Evelyn Derouin and Mr. Maynard Bjorgo of the Wisconsin State University–Eau Claire library assisted me with unfailing good will and dispatch. To all of them, my thanks!

DOUNIA B. CHRISTIANI

The Text of

The Wild Duck

Translated by Dounia B. Christiani

Characters

HÅKON WERLE, *businessman, industrialist, etc.*
GREGERS WERLE, *his son*
OLD EKDAL
HJALMAR EKDAL, *his son, a photographer*
GINA EKDAL, *Hjalmar's wife*
HEDVIG, *their fourteen-year-old daughter*
MRS. SØRBY, *housekeeper to Håkon Werle*
RELLING, *a doctor*
MOLVIK, *a one-time theological student*
PETTERSEN, *Håkon Werle's servant*
GRÅBERG, *Håkon Werle's bookkeeper*
JENSEN, *a hired waiter*
A FLABBY GENTLEMAN
A THIN-HAIRED GENTLEMAN
A NEARSIGHTED GENTLEMAN
SIX OTHER GENTLEMEN, *Håkon Werle's guests*
SEVERAL HIRED SERVANTS

The first act takes place at the home of HÅKON WERLE; *the four following acts at* HJALMAR EKDAL's

Act One

At HAKON WERLE's *house. The study, expensively and comfortably appointed; bookcases and upholstered furniture; in the middle of the room a desk with papers and documents; subdued lighting from lamps with green shades. In the rear, open folding doors with portières drawn back reveal a large, elegant drawing room, brilliantly lit by lamps and candelabra. Front right in study, a small baize-covered door to the office wing. Front left, a fireplace with glowing coal fire. Farther back on left wall, double doors to the dining room.*

PETTERSEN, WERLE's *servant, in livery, and the hired waiter* JENSEN, *in black, are putting the study in order. In the drawing room, two or three other hired waiters are busy arranging for the guests and lighting more candles. The hum of conversation and the laughter of many voices can be heard from the dining room. Somebody taps his wine glass with a knife to signal he is about to make a speech; silence follows; a toast is proposed; cheers, and again the hum of conversation.*

PETTERSEN [*lights a lamp on mantlepiece and sets shade on*]. Say, will you listen to them, Jensen. That's the old man on his feet now, making a long toast to Mrs. Sørby.

JENSEN [*moving an armchair forward*]. Do you think it's true, what they're saying—that there's something between them?

PETTERSEN. Devil knows.

JENSEN. I guess he must've been quite a lad in his day.

PETTERSEN. Could be.

JENSEN. They say he's giving this dinner for his son.

PETTERSEN. That's right. His son came home yesterday.

JENSEN. I never even knew old Werle had a son.

PETTERSEN. Oh, yes, he's got a son all right. But you can't budge him from the works up at Højdal. He's never once been to town in all the years I've worked in this house.

A HIRED WAITER [*in doorway to drawing room.*] Say, Pettersen, there's an old fellow here . . .

PETTERSEN [*grumbling*]. Oh damn. Who'd want to come at this time!

[OLD EKDAL *appears from the right in drawing room. He is dressed in a shabby overcoat with high collar, and woolen mittens. He has a stick and a fur cap in his hand; a parcel wrapped in brown paper under his arm. Wears a dirty reddish-brown wig and has a little gray mustache.*]

PETTERSEN [*going toward him*]. Good God! What are you doing here?

EKDAL [*in doorway*]. Absolutely must get into the office, Pettersen.

PETTERSEN. The office closed an hour ago, and . . .

EKDAL. They told me that at the gate, old man. But Gråberg's still in there. Be a good sport, Pettersen, and let me slip in through here. [*Points to baize door.*] Been this way before.

3

PETTERSEN. Well, all right then, go ahead. [*Opens door.*] But just be sure you go out the right way. We've got company.

EKDAL. Know that—hm! Thanks, Pettersen, old chap! Good old friend. Thanks. [*Mutters to himself.*] Ass! [*Exit into office.* PETTERSEN *shuts door after him.*]

JENSEN. Does he work in the office?

PETTERSEN. No, they just give him some copying to do at home when they're rushed. Not that he hasn't been a somebody in his day, old Ekdal.

JENSEN. Yes, he looked like there's something about him.

PETTERSEN. Yes, indeed. I want you to know he was once a lieutenant.

JENSEN. Go on—him a lieutenant!

PETTERSEN. So help me, he was. But then he switched over to the timber business, or whatever it was. They say he's supposed to have played a dirty low-down trick on Mr. Werle once. The two of them were in on the Højdal works together then, you see. Oh, I know old Ekdal well, I do. Many's the time we've had a bitters and beer together down at Ma Eriksen's place.

JENSEN. Him? He sure can't have much money to throw around?

PETTERSEN. Lord, Jensen, no. It's me that stands treat, naturally. Seems to me we owe a little respect to them that's come down in the world.

JENSEN. Oh, so he went bankrupt?

PETTERSEN. Worse than that. He was sentenced to hard labor.

JENSEN. Hard labor!

PETTERSEN. Anyway, he went to jail . . . [*Listening.*] Sh! They're getting up from the table now.

> [*The dining room doors are thrown open from within by two servants.* MRS. SØRBY *comes out, in conversation with two gentlemen. The rest of the party, among them* HAKON WERLE, *follow shortly thereafter. Last come* HJALMAR EKDAL *and* GREGERS WERLE.]

MRS. SØRBY [*to the servant, in passing*]. Pettersen, will you have the coffee served in the music room, please.

PETTERSEN. Very good, Mrs. Sørby.

> [*She and the two gentlemen exit into drawing room and thence off to right.* PETTERSEN *and* JENSEN *exit the same way.*]

A FLABBY GENTLEMAN [*to a* THIN-HAIRED ONE]. Whew! What a dinner! *That* was something to tuck away!

THE THIN-HAIRED ONE. Oh, with a little good will it's incredible what one can manage in three hours' time.

THE FLABBY GENTLEMAN. Yes, but afterwards, my dear sir, afterwards!

A THIRD GENTLEMAN. I hear the coffee and liqueurs are being served in the music room.

THE FLABBY GENTLEMAN. Splendid! Then perhaps Mrs. Sørby will play something for us.

THE THIN-HAIRED ONE [*in an undertone*]. As long as Mrs. Sørby doesn't play something *on* us, one of these days.

THE FLABBY GENTLEMAN. Oh, I hardly think so. Berta isn't the type to cast off her old friends. [*They laugh and exit into drawing room.*]

WERLE [*in a low, depressed tone*]. I don't think anybody noticed, Gregers.

GREGERS [*looks at him*]. Noticed what?

WERLE. Didn't you notice either?

GREGERS. What was I supposed to notice?

WERLE. We were thirteen at table.

GREGERS. Really? Were there thirteen?

WERLE. [*with a glance toward* HJALMAR EKDAL]. As a rule we are always twelve. [*To the others.*] In here if you please, Gentlemen!

[*He and the remaining guests, except* HJALMAR *and* GREGERS, *exit rear right.*]

HJALMAR [*who has heard what was said*]. You shouldn't have sent me that invitation, Gregers.

GREGERS. What! This party is supposed to be for *me*. And I'm not to invite my best, my only friend?

HJALMAR. But I don't think your father approves. I never come to this house any other time.

GREGERS. So I hear. But I had to see you and have a talk with you. Because I expect to be leaving again soon.—Yes, we two old school chums, we've certainly drifted far apart, haven't we. It must be sixteen-seventeen years since we saw each other.

HJALMAR. Is it as long as all that?

GREGERS. It is indeed. Well now, how are you getting along? You look fine. You've put on weight, you're even a bit stout.

HJALMAR. Hm, stout is hardly the word. But I suppose I do look a bit more of a man than I did in the old days.

GREGERS. Yes, you do. Outwardly you don't seem to have suffered much harm.

HJALMAR [*in a gloomy voice*]. But inwardly, Gregers! That's a different story, believe me. You know, of course, how terribly everything collapsed for me and mine since we last saw each other.

GREGERS [*more softly*]. How are things now with your father?

HJALMAR. Ah, let's not go into that. Naturally, my poor unfortunate father makes his home with me. He hasn't anyone else in the world to turn to. But look, it's so desperately hard for me to talk about this.—Tell me instead how you've been, up there at the works.

GREGERS. Delightfully lonely, that's how I've been. Plenty of opportunity to think about all sorts of things.—Come over here; let's make ourselves comfortable.

[*He sits down in an armchair by the fireplace and draws* HJALMAR *into another beside him.*]

HJALMAR [*with sentiment.*] I do want to thank you, all the same, Gregers, for asking me to your father's party. Because now I can see you don't have anything against me, any more.

GREGERS [*in surprise*]. Whatever gave you the idea I had anything against you?

HJALMAR. Why, you did have, you know, the first few years.

GREGERS. What first few years?

HJALMAR. After the great disaster. And it was only natural that you should. After all, it was only by a hair that your father himself missed being dragged into that ... oh, that terrible business!

GREGERS. And because of that I'm supposed to have a grudge against you? Whoever gave you that idea?

HJALMAR. I *know* you did, Gregers. Your father told me himself.

GREGERS [*startled*]. My father! Oh, I see. Hm.—Was that the reason I never heard from you afterwards—not a single word?

HJALMAR. Yes.

GREGERS. Not even when you went and became a photographer.

HJALMAR. Your father said it would be better not to write you about anything at all.

GREGERS [*absently*]. Well, well, maybe he was right, at that. —But tell me, Hjalmar—are you pretty well satisfied now with things as they are?

HJALMAR [*with a light sigh*]. Why, yes, on the whole I can't complain, really. At first, as you can imagine, it was all pretty strange. My whole world shot to pieces. But then, so was everything else. That terrible calamity of Father's—the shame and disgrace, Gregers ...

GREGERS [*shaken*]. I know. I know.

HJALMAR. Of course I couldn't possibly think of continuing my studies. There wasn't a penny left. On the contrary, there were debts—mostly to your father, I believe.

GREGERS. Hm ...

HJALMAR. Well, so I thought it best to make a clean break, you· know—drop my old life and all my connections. It was your father especially who advised me to do that; and since he put himself out to be so helpful to me ...

GREGERS. My father did?

HJALMAR. Yes, surely you know that? Where could *I* have got the money to learn photography and equip a studio and set up in business? Things like that are expensive, let me tell you.

GREGERS. And my *father* paid for it all?

HJALMAR. Why sure, didn't you know? I understood him to say he'd written and told you.

GREGERS. Not a word about its being *him*. He must have forgotten. We've never exchanged anything but business letters. So it was my *father* ... !

HJALMAR. It certainly was. He never wanted it to get around, but it was him, all right. And of course it was also he who put me in a position to get married. Or maybe you didn't know about that either?

GREGERS. No, I certainly did not. [*Clapping him on the arm.*] But my dear Hjalmar, I can't tell you how delighted I am to hear all this—and remorseful too. I may have been unjust to my father after all—on a few points. Because this does reveal a kind heart, doesn't it. It's as if, in a way, he had a conscience ...

HJALMAR. A conscience ... ?

GREGERS. Well, well, whatever you want to call it, then. No, I really can't tell you how glad I am to hear this about my father. —So you're a married man, Hjalmar. That's more than I'm ever likely to be. Well, I trust you are happy in your marriage?

HJALMAR. Yes, indeed I am. She's as capable and fine a wife as any man could ask for. And she's by no means without culture.

GREGERS [*a little surprised*]. Why no, I don't suppose she is.

HJALMAR. Life itself is an education, you see. Her daily contact with me . . . besides which there's a couple of very intelligent fellows we see regularly. I assure you, you wouldn't know Gina again.

GREGERS. Gina?

HJALMAR. Why yes, don't you remember her name is Gina?

GREGERS. Whose name is Gina? I haven't the faintest idea what . . .

HJALMAR. But don't you remember she was employed here in this house for a time?

GREGERS [*looking at him*]. You mean Gina Hansen . . . ?

HJALMAR. Yes, of course I mean Gina Hansen.

GREGERS. . . . who kept house for us the last year of my mother's illness?

HJALMAR. Well of course. But my dear fellow, I know for a fact that your father wrote and told you I had got married.

GREGERS [*who has risen*]. Yes, he did that, all right. But not that . . . [*Pacing floor.*] Wait a minute—perhaps after all—now that I think about it. But my father always writes me such short letters. [*Sits on arm of chair.*] Listen, Hjalmar, tell me—this is interesting—how did you happen to meet Gina—your wife, that is?

HJALMAR. Oh, quite simply. Gina didn't stay very long here in this house. There was so much trouble here at the time, what with your mother's illness . . . Gina couldn't take all that, so she gave notice and left. That was the year before your mother died—or maybe it was the same year.

GREGERS. It was the same year. I was up at the works at the time. But afterwards?

HJALMAR. Well, Gina went to live with her mother, a Mrs. Hansen, a most capable and hard-working woman who ran a little eating place. She also had a room for rent, a really nice, comfortable room.

GREGERS. And you, I suppose, were lucky enough to find it?

HJALMAR. Yes, as a matter of fact it was your father who gave me the lead. And it was there—you see—that's where I really got to know Gina.

GREGERS. And so you got engaged?

HJALMAR. Yes. You know how easily young people get to care for each other—Hm . . .

GREGERS [*rises and walks around*]. Tell me—when you had got engaged—was it then that my father got you to . . . I mean—was it then that you started to take up photography?

HJALMAR. Yes, exactly. Because I did so want to get settled and have a home of my own, the sooner the better. And both your father and I felt that this photography business was the best idea. And Gina thought so too. Oh yes, there was another reason as well. It so happened that Gina had just taken up retouching.

GREGERS. *That* fitted in marvelously well.

HJALMAR [*pleased, rises*]. Yes, didn't it though? It *did* fit in marvelously well, don't you think?

GREGERS. Yes, I must say. Why, my father seems to have been a kind of Providence for you.

HJALMAR [*moved*]. He did not forsake his old friend's son in the hour of need. For he's a man with *heart*, you see.

MRS. SØRBY [*entering arm in arm with* HAKON WERLE]. Not another word, my dear Mr. Werle. You must not stay in there any longer staring at all those lights. It's not good for you.

WERLE [*letting go her arm and passing his hand over his eyes*]. I rather think you are right.

[PETTERSEN *and* JENSEN, *the hired waiter, enter with trays.*].

MRS. SØRBY [*to guests in other room*]. Punch is served, Gentlemen. If anybody wants some he'll have to come in here and get it.

THE FLABBY GENTLEMAN [walking over to Mrs. Sørby]. Good heavens, it is true you've annulled our precious right to smoke?

MRS. SØRBY. Yes, my dear Chamberlain, here in Mr. Werle's private domain it is forbidden.

THE THIN-HAIRED GENTLEMAN. And when did you introduce this harsh restriction into our cigar regulations, Mrs. Sørby?

MRS. SØRBY. After our last dinner, Chamberlain. I'm afraid certain persons allowed themselves to overstep the bounds.

THE THIN-HAIRED GENTLEMAN. And is one not allowed to overstep the bounds just a little, Madame Berta? Not even the least little bit?

MRS. SØRBY. Under no circumstances, Chamberlain Balle.

[*Most of the guests are now assembled in* WERLE's *study; the waiters hand around glasses of punch.*]

WERLE [*to* HJALMAR, *standing over by a table*]. What's that you're so engrossed in, Ekdal?

HJALMAR. It's just an album, Mr. Werle.

THE THIN-HAIRED GENTLEMAN [*drifting about*]. Ah yes, photographs! That's in your line, of course.

THE FLABBY GENTLEMAN [*in an armchair*]. Haven't you brought along any of your own?

HJALMAR. No, I haven't.

THE FLABBY GENTLEMAN. You should have. It's so good for the digestion, don't you know, to sit and look at pictures.

THE THIN-HAIRED GENTLEMAN. Besides contributing a mite to the general entertainment, you know.

A NEARSIGHTED GENTLEMAN. And all contributions are gratefully accepted.

MRS. SØRBY. The gentlemen mean, when you're invited out, you're expected to work a little for your dinner, Ekdal.

THE FLABBY GENTLEMAN. With a cuisine like this, *that* is an absolute pleasure.

THE THIN-HAIRED GENTLEMAN. Good Lord, if it's a question of the struggle for existence . . .

MRS. SØRBY. You're so right!

[*They continue the conversation, laughing and joking.*]

GREGERS [*quietly*]. You must join in, Hjalmar.

HJALMAR [*with a squirm*]. What am I to talk about?

THE FLABBY GENTLEMAN. Don't you agree, Mr. Werle, that Tokay may be regarded as a relatively healthy wine for the stomach?

WERLE [*by the fireplace*]. I can vouch for the Tokay you had today, at any rate; it is one of the very finest vintages. But of course you must have noticed that yourself.

THE FLABBY GENTLEMAN. Yes, it had a remarkably delicate bouquet.

HJALMAR [*uncertainly*]. Does the vintage make a difference?

THE FLABBY GENTLEMAN [*laughs*]. That's a good one!

WERLE [*smiling*]. There's certainly no point in putting a noble wine in front of *you*.

THE THIN-HAIRED GENTLEMAN. It's the same with Tokay as with photographs, Mr. Ekdal. Both must have sunlight. Or am I mistaken?

HJALMAR. Oh no. In photography, the sun is everything.

MRS. SØRBY. Why, it's exactly the same with chamberlains. They also depend on sunshine, as the saying goes—royal sunshine.

THE THIN-HAIRED GENTLEMAN. Ouch! That's a tired old joke.

THE NEARSIGHTED GENTLEMAN. The lady is in great form . . .

THE FLABBY GENTLEMAN. . . . and at our expense, too. [*Wagging his finger.*] Madame Berta! Madame Berta!

MRS. SØRBY. Well, but it *is* perfectly true that vintages can differ enormously. The old vintages are the best.

THE NEARSIGHTED GENTLEMAN. Do you count *me* among the old ones?

MRS. SØRBY. Oh, far from it.

THE THIN-HAIRED ONE. Listen to that! But what about *me*, dear Mrs. Sørby?

THE FLABBY GENTLEMAN. Yes, and me! Where do you put us?

MRS. SØRBY. You, among the sweet vintages, Gentlemen.

[*She sips a glass of punch; the chamberlains laugh and flirt with her.*]

WERLE. Mrs. Sørby always finds a way out—when she wants to. But Gentlemen, you aren't drinking! Pettersen, see to . . . ! Gregers, I think we might take a glass together. [*Gregers does not move.*] Won't you join us, Ekdal? I didn't get a chance to have a toast with you at table.

[GRABERG, *the bookkeeper, looks in at baize door*].

GRABERG. Excuse me, Mr. Werle, but I can't get out.

WERLE. What, have they locked you in again?

GRABERG. Yes, and Flakstad's gone home with the keys . . .

WERLE. Well, just come through here, then.

GRABERG. But there's somebody else . . .

WERLE. Come on, come on, both of you. Don't be shy.

[GRABERG *and* OLD EKDAL *enter from the office.*]

WERLE [involuntarily]. What the . . . !

[*Laughter and chatter of guests die down.* HJALMAR *gives a start at the sight of his father, puts down his glass, and turns away toward the fireplace.*]

EKDAL [*does not look up, but makes quick little bows to both sides as he crosses, mumbling*]. Beg pardon. Came the wrong way. Gate's locked . . . gate's locked. Beg pardon.

[*He and* GRABERG *go off, rear right.*]

WERLE [*between his teeth*]. Damn that Gråberg!

GREGERS [*staring open-mouthed, to* HJALMAR]. Don't tell me that was . . . !

THE FLABBY GENTLEMAN. What's going on? Who was that?

GREGERS. Oh, nobody. Just the bookkeeper and another man.

THE NEARSIGHTED GENTLEMAN [*to* HJALMAR]. Did you know the man?

HJALMAR. I don't know . . . I didn't notice . . .

THE FLABBY GENTLEMAN [*getting up*]. What the devil's the matter, anyway? [*He walks over to some of the others, who are talking in lowered voices.*]

MRS. SØRBY [*whispers to the servant*]. Slip him something outside, something real good.

PETTERSEN [*nods his head*]. I'll do that. [*Goes out.*]

GREGERS [*in a low, shocked voice, to* HJALMAR]. Then it really was he!

HJALMAR. Yes.

GREGERS. And you stood here and denied you knew him!

HJALMAR [*whispers vehemently*]. But how *could* I . . . ?

GREGERS. . . . acknowledge your own father?

HJALMAR [*bitterly*]. Oh, if you were in my place, maybe . . .

[*The conversation among the guests, which has been conducted in low voices, now changes to forced gaiety.*]

THE THIN-HAIRED GENTLEMAN [*approaching* HJALMAR *and* GREGERS *in a friendly manner*]. Ah, are we reminiscing about old student days, Gentlemen? Eh? Don't you smoke, Mr. Ekdal? Can I give you a light? Oh, no, that's right. We are not allowed . . .

HJALMAR. Thank you, I don't smoke.

THE FLABBY GENTLEMAN. Don't you have some nice bit of poetry you could recite for us, Mr. Ekdal? You used to do that so charmingly.

HJALMAR. I'm afraid I can't remember any.

THE FLABBY GENTLEMAN. Oh, what a pity. Well, Balle, what shall we do now?

[*Both men cross and go into the drawing room.*]

HJALMAR [*gloomily*]. Gregers—I'm going! You see, when once a man has felt the crushing blow of fate . . . Say good-bye to your father for me.

GREGERS. Sure, of course. Are you going straight home?

HJALMAR. Yes. Why?

GREGERS. I thought I might drop in later on.

HJALMAR. No don't do that. Not at my home. My house is a sad place, Gregers—especially after a brilliant banquet like this. We can always meet somewhere in town.

MRS. SØRBY [*has come up to them; in a low voice*]. Are you leaving, Mr. Ekdal?

HJALMAR. Yes.

MRS. SØRBY. Give my best to Gina.

HJALMAR. Thanks.

MRS. SØRBY. And tell her I'll be up to see her one of these days.

HJALMAR. Thanks, I'll do that. [*To* GREGERS.] Don't bother to see me out. I want to slip away unnoticed. [*He crosses room, then into drawing room, and goes off, right.*]

MRS. SØRBY [*softly to the servant, who has returned*]. Well, did you give the old man something?

PETTERSEN. Oh yes; I slipped him a bottle of brandy.

MRS. SØRBY. Oh, you might have thought of something better than that.

PETTERSEN. Not at all, Mrs. Sørby. There's nothing he likes better than brandy.

THE FLABBY GENTLEMAN [*in the doorway, with a sheet of music in his hand*]. What do you say we play something together, Mrs. Sørby?

MRS. SØRBY. Yes, let's do that.

GUESTS. Bravo! Bravo!

[*She and all the guests cross room and go off, right.* GREGERS *remains standing by fireplace.* WERLE *searches for something on the desk and seems to wish* GREGERS *to leave. As* GREGERS *does not move,* WERLE *starts toward the drawing room door.*]

GREGERS. Father, do you have a moment?

WERLE [*stops*]. What is it?

GREGERS. I'd like a word with you.

WERLE. Can't it wait till we're alone?

GREGERS. No, it can't. Because we might very well never be alone.

WERLE [*coming closer*]. And what is that supposed to mean?

[*During the following, the sound of a piano is distantly heard from the music room.*]

GREGERS. How could people here let that family go to the dogs like that?

WERLE. I suppose you mean the Ekdals?

GREGERS. Yes, I mean the Ekdals. After all, Lieutenant Ekdal was once your close friend.

WERLE. Alas, yes—all too close. Years and years I had to smart for it. He's the one I can thank for the fact that my good name and reputation were blemished in a way, mine too.

GREGER [*quietly*]. Was he in fact the only guilty one?

WERLE. Who else do you think!

GREGERS. After all, you and he were both in that big timber deal together . . .

WERLE. But was it not Ekdal who drew up the survey map of the area—that fraudulent map? He was the one who did all that illegal felling of timber on State property. In fact, he was in charge of the entire operation up there. I had no idea what Lieutenant Ekdal was up to.

GREGERS. I doubt Lieutenant Ekdal himself knew what he was doing.

WERLE. Maybe so. But the fact remains that he was found guilty and I acquitted.

GREGERS. Yes, I'm well aware there was no evidence.

WERLE. Acquittal is acquittal. Why do you have to rake up all that miserable old business that turned my hair gray before its time? Is this the sort of stuff you've gone and brooded over all those years up there? I can assure you, Gregers, here in town that whole story was forgotten ages ago—as far as it concerns me.

GREGERS. But what about the poor Ekdals!

WERLE. What exactly do you want me to do for those people? When Ekdal was released he was a broken man, altogether beyond help. There are people in this world who sink to the bottom the minute they get a couple of slugs in them, and they never come up again. You can take my word for it, Gregers, I've put myself out as far as I possibly could, short of encouraging all kinds of talk and suspicion . . .

GREGERS. Suspicion? Oh, I see.

WERLE. I have given Ekdal copying to do for the office, and I pay him far, far more for his work than it is worth . . .

GREGERS [*without looking at him*]. Hm; don't doubt *that*.

WERLE. What's the joke? Don't you think I'm telling you the truth? Naturally, you won't find anything about it in my books. I never enter expenses like that.

GREGERS [*with a cold smile*]. No, I daresay certain expenses are best not accounted for.

WERLE [*starts*]. What do you mean by *that*?

GREGERS [*with forced courage*]. Did you enter what it cost you to have Hjalmar Ekdal learn photography?

WERLE. I? What do you mean—enter?

GREGERS. I know now it was you who paid for it. And I also know it was you who set him up so cosily.

WERLE. There, and still I'm supposed to have done nothing for the Ekdals! I assure you, those people have certainly put me to enough expense.

GREGERS. Have you entered any of those expenses?

WERLE. Why do you keep asking that?

GREGERS. Oh, I have my reasons. Look, tell me—that time, when you took such a warm interest in your old friend's son—wasn't it exactly when he was about to get married?

WERLE. What the devil—how can I remember, after all these years . . . ?

GREGERS. You wrote me a letter at the time—a business letter, naturally—and in a postscript it said, nothing more, that Hjalmar Ekdal had married a Miss Hansen.

WERLE. That's right. That was her name.

GREGERS. But you neglected to mention that this Miss Hansen was Gina Hansen—our former maid.

WERLE [*with a scornful but forced laugh*]. No, because it certainly never occurred to me that you were particularly interested in our former maid.

GREGERS. I wasn't. But—[*lowers his voice*] there were others in this house who *were*.

WERLE. What do you mean by *that*? [*Flaring up.*] Don't tell me you're referring to *me!*

GREGERS [*quietly but firmly*]. Yes, I'm referring to you.

WERLE. And you dare . . .! You have the insolence to . . .! And that ingrate, that, that—photographer! How dare he come here with such accusations!

GREGERS. Hjalmar never said a word about this. I don't think he has the slightest suspicion of anything of the kind.

WERLE. Then where have you got it from? Whoever could have said a thing like that?

GREGERS. My poor, unhappy mother said it. The last time I saw her.

WERLE. Your mother! I might have guessed as much. You and she—you always stuck together. It was she that turned you against me from the start.

GREGERS. No, it was all the things she had to bear, till at last she gave way and went to pieces.

WERLE. Oh, she didn't have anything to bear! No more than plenty of others do, anyway. But there's no way of getting along with morbid, neurotic people—that's a lesson *I* learned, all right. And now here you are, nursing a suspicion like that—mixing up in all kinds of ancient rumors and slander against your own father. Listen here, Gregers, I honestly think that at your age you could find something more useful to do.

GREGERS. Yes, perhaps it is about time.

WERLE. Then maybe you wouldn't take things so seriously as you seem to do now. What's the point in your sitting up there at the works year in year out, slaving away like a common office clerk, refusing to draw a cent more than the standard wage? It's plain silly.

GREGERS. I wish I were so sure about that.

WERLE. Not that I don't understand you. You want to be independent, want to be under no obligation to me. Well, here is your chance to get your independence, to be your own master in everything.

GREGERS. Really? And in what way . . .?

WERLE. When I wrote you it was urgent that you come to town at once—hm . . .

GREGERS. Yes, what exactly is it you want me for? I have been waiting all day to hear.

WERLE. I propose that you become a partner in the firm.

GREGERS. I? In your firm? A partner?

WERLE. Yes. It need not mean we'd have to be together all the

time. You could take over the business here in town, and I
would move up to the works.

GREGERS. *You* would?

WERLE. Well, you see, I don't have the capacity for work that I
once had. I've got to go easy on my eyes, Gregers; they've started
to get a bit weak.

GREGERS. They've always been that way.

WERLE. Not like now. And besides . . . circumstances might perhaps
make it desirable for me to live up there—at any rate for a time.

GREGERS. I never dreamed of anything like that.

WERLE. Look, Gregers—I know we differ on a great many things.
But after all, we *are* father and son. Surely we ought to be able
to reach some sort of understanding.

GREGERS. To all outward appearances, I take it you mean?

WERLE. Well, even that would be something. Think it over, Gregers. Don't you think it could be done? Eh?

GREGERS [*looks at him coldly*]. There's something behind all this.

WERLE. How do you mean?

GREGERS. There must be something you want to use me for.

WERLE. In a relationship as close as ours surely one can always be
of use to the other.

GREGERS. Yes, so they say.

WERLE. I should like to have you home now for a while. I'm a
lonely man, Gregers; I've always felt lonely, all my life, but especially now that I'm getting along in years. I need somebody
around me.

GREGERS. You've got Mrs. Sørby.

WERLE. Yes, so I have. And she's become just about indispensable
to me. She's bright, she's easy-going, she livens up the house—
and that I need pretty badly.

GREGERS. Well, then. In that case you've got just what you want.

WERLE. Yes, but I'm afraid it can't last. A woman in this kind of
situation can easily have her position misconstrued. For that
matter, it doesn't do the man much good either.

GREGERS. Oh, when a man gives such dinner parties as you do, I
daresay he can take quite a few risks.

WERLE. Yes, but what about *her*, Gregers? I'm afraid she won't put
up with it much longer. And even if she did—even if, out of
devotion to me, she ignored the gossip and the aspersions and
such . . .? Do you really feel, Gregers, you with your strong sense
of justice . . .

GREGERS [*interrupts him*]. Get to the point. Are you thinking of
marrying her?

WERLE. Supposing I were? What then?

GREGERS. Yes, that's what I'm asking, too. What then?

WERLE. Would you be so dead set against it?

GREGERS. No, not at all. By no means.

WERLE. You see, I didn't know if perhaps, out of regard for the
memory of your mother . . .

GREGERS. I am not neurotic.

WERLE. Well, whatever you may or may not be, you've taken a

great load off my mind. I can't tell you how glad I am that I can count on your support in this matter.

GREGERS [*looks fixedly at him*]. Now I see what you want to use me for.

WERLE. Use you for? What an expression!

GREGERS. Oh, let's not be so particular in our choice of words—not when we are alone, at any rate. [*Short laugh*.] So that's it! That's why I had to make a personal appearance in town, come hell or high water. To put up a show of family life in this house for Mrs. Sørby's sake. Touching little tableau between father and son! *That* would be something new!

WERLE. How dare you talk like that!

GREGERS. When was there ever any family life around here? Never as long as I can remember! But now, all of a sudden, we could use a touch of home-sweet-home. Just think, the fine effect when it can be reported how the son hastened home—on wings of filial piety—to the aging father's wedding feast. *Then* what remains of all the rumors about what the poor dead wife had to put up with? Not a breath. Why, her own son snuffs them out.

WERLE. Gregers—I don't think there's a man on earth you hate as much as me.

GREGERS [*quietly*]. I've seen you too close up.

WERLE. You have seen me through your mother's eyes. [*Drops his voice a little*.] But don't forget that those eyes were—clouded, now and then.

GREGERS [*with trembling voice*]. I know what you're getting at. But who's to blame for Mother's tragic failing? *You*, and all those . . .! The last of them was that female you palmed off on Hjalmar Ekdal when you yourself no longer . . . ugh!

WERLE [*shrugs his shoulders*]. Word for word as though it were your mother talking.

GREGERS [*paying no attention*]. . . . And there he is now, that great trusting, childlike soul, engulfed in treachery—living under the same roof with such a creature. With no idea that what he calls his home is founded on a lie! [*Comes a step closer*.] When I look back upon your long career, it's as if I saw a battlefield strewn at every turn with shattered lives.

WERLE. I almost think the gulf between us is too wide.

GREGERS [*bows stiffly*]. So I have observed. Therefore I'll take my hat and go.

WERLE. Go? Leave the house?

GREGERS. Yes. For now at last I see an objective to live for.

WERLE. What objective is that?

GREGERS. You'd only laugh if I told you.

WERLE. Laughter doesn't come so easily to a lonely man, Gregers.

GREGERS [*pointing to the rear*]. Look, Father—your guests are playing Blind Man's Buff with Mrs. Sørby—Goodnight and good-bye.

[*He goes off, rear right. Laughter and banter are heard from the party, which comes into view in the drawing room*.]

WERLE [*mutters contemptuously after* GREGERS]. Huh! Poor devil. And *he* says he's not neurotic!

Act Two

HJALMAR EKDAL's *studio. The room, which is quite large, is apparently part of an attic. On the right is a pitched roof with a big skylight, half covered by a blue curtain. In the right corner at the rear is the entrance door; downstage on the same side, a door to the living room. On the left there are likewise two doors, with an iron stove between them. In the rear wall, wide double sliding doors. The studio is cheaply but comfortably furnished and arranged. Between the doors on the right and a little out from the wall stand a sofa and table and some chairs; on the table, a lighted lamp with shade; near the stove, an old armchair. Various pieces of photographic equipment here and there about the room. In the rear, left of the sliding doors, a bookcase containing a few books, some boxes and bottles of chemicals, various instruments, tools, and other objects. Photographs and small items such as brushes, paper, and the like are lying on the table.*

GINA EKDAL *is sitting at the table, sewing.* HEDVIG *is sitting on the sofa reading a book, her hands shading her eyes, her thumbs plugging her ears.*

GINA [*after glancing at her several times as if with suppressed anxiety*]. Hedvig! [HEDVIG *does not hear.*]

GINA [*louder*]. Hedvig!

HEDVIG [*takes away her hands and looks up*]. Yes, Mother?

GINA. Hedvig, darling, you mustn't sit and read so long.

HEDVIG. Oh, please, Mother, can't I read a little more? Just a little!

GINA. No, no. Now you put that book away. Your father doesn't like it; he never reads at night himself.

HEDVIG [*shuts the book*]. No, Father doesn't care much for reading.

GINA [*puts her sewing aside and picks up a pencil and a small notebook from the table*]. Can you remember how much we paid for the butter today?

HEDVIG. It was one crown sixty-five.

GINA. That's right. [*Writes it down.*] The amount of butter we go through in this house! Then there was the sausage and the cheese . . . let me see . . . [*Makes a note.*] . . . and then the ham . . . hm . . . [*Adding up.*] Yes, that already comes to . . .

HEDVIG. And the beer.

GINA. That's right, of course. [*Notes it down.*] It does mount up. But what can you do.

HEDVIG. But then you and I didn't need anything hot for dinner, since Father was going to be out.

GINA. Yes, that was a help. And besides I did take in eight crowns fifty for the pictures.

HEDVIG. My! As much as that?

GINA. Eight crowns fifty exactly.

[*Silence.* GINA *takes up her sewing again.* HEDVIG *takes paper and pencil and starts to draw, her left hand shading her eyes.*]

HEDVIG. Isn't it nice to think that Father's at a big dinner party at Mr. Werle's?

GINA. You can't say he's at Mr. Werle's, really. It was the son that invited him. [*Short pause.*] We've got nothing to do with old Mr. Werle.

HEDVIG. I can't wait till Father comes home. He promised to ask Mrs. Sørby for something good for me.

GINA. Oh yes, there's plenty of good things in *that* house, all right.

HEDVIG [*still drawing*]. Besides, I am just a bit hungry.

[OLD EKDAL *enters right rear, a bundle of papers under his arm and another parcel in his coat pocket.*]

GINA. How late you're home today, Grandpa.

EKDAL. They had locked up the office. Had to wait in Gråberg's room. Then I had to go through . . . hm.

HEDVIG. Did they give you any more copying to do, Grandfather?

EKDAL. This whole bundle. Just look.

GINA. Well, that's nice.

HEDVIG. And you've got another bundle in your pocket.

EKDAL. What? Nonsense, that isn't anything. [*Stands his walking stick away in the corner.*] This will keep me busy a long time, Gina. [*Draws one of the sliding doors in the rear wall a little to one side.*] Shhh! [*Peeks into the attic a while, then carefully slides the door to.*] Heh-heh! They're sound asleep, the whole lot of 'em. And she has settled in the basket by herself. Heh-heh!

HEDVIG. Are you sure she won't be cold in that basket, Grandfather?

EKDAL. Cold? What an idea! In all that straw? [*Walks toward rear door on left.*] Any matches in my room?

GINA. On the dresser.

[EKDAL *goes into his room.*]

HEDVIG. Isn't it nice Grandfather got all that copying to do.

GINA. Yes, poor old thing. Now he can make himself a little pocket money.

HEDVIG. Besides, he won't be able to sit all morning in that nasty café of Mrs. Eriksen's.

GINA. Yes, that's another thing.

[*A short silence.*]

HEDVIG. Do you think they're still sitting at the table?

GINA. Lord knows. I guess they could be, though.

HEDVIG. Just think, all the delicious things Father must be having! I'm sure he'll be in a good mood when he gets home. Don't you think so, Mother?

GINA. Oh yes. Now, if only we could tell him we got the room rented.

HEDVIG. But we don't need that tonight.

GINA. Oh, it would come in very handy, you know. It's no use to us just standing there empty.

HEDVIG. No, I mean it's not necessary because Father will be in a good mood tonight anyway. It's better to have the news about the room for another time.

GINA [*looks across at her*]. You like having something nice to tell your father when he gets home evenings?

HEDVIG. Sure, it makes things more cheerful.

GINA [*thinking this over*]. Why yes, I guess there's something in that.

[OLD EKDAL *enters from his room and makes for the door on front left.*]

GINA [*turning half around in her chair*]. Do you want something in the kitchen, Grandpa?

EKDAL. Yes. Don't get up. [*Goes out.*]

GINA. I hope he's not messing with the fire out there! [*Waits a moment.*] Hedvig, go see what he's up to.

[EKDAL *returns with a little mug of steaming water.*]

HEDVIG. Are you getting hot water, Grandfather?

EKDAL. Yes, I am. Need it for something. I've got writing to do, and the ink's gone as thick as mud—hm.

GINA. But you ought to eat your supper first, Grandpa. It's all set out for you.

EKDAL. Can't be bothered with supper, Gina. Terribly busy, I tell you. I don't want anybody coming into my room. Not anybody —hm.

[*He goes into his room.* GINA *and* HEDVIG *look at each other.*]

GINA [*in a low voice*]. Where on earth do you suppose he got the money?

HEDVIG. I guess from Gråberg.

GINA. No, impossible. Gråberg always sends the money to me.

HEDVIG. Then he must have got a bottle on credit somewhere.

GINA. Poor old soul. Who'd give *him* anything on credit?

[HJALMAR EKDAL, *in topcoat and gray felt hat, enters right.*]

GINA [*throws down her sewing and gets up*]. Why, Hjalmar, you're back already!

HEDVIG [*simultaneously jumping up*]. Father, what a surprise!

HJALMAR [*lays down his hat*]. Most of them seemed to be leaving now.

HEDVIG. So early?

HJALMAR. Well, it was a dinner party, you know. [*About to take off his topcoat.*]

GINA. Let me help you.

HEDVIG. Me too.

[*They help him off with his coat.* GINA *hangs it up on the rear wall.*]

HEDVIG. Were there many there, Father?

HJALMAR. Not too many. There were about twelve or fourteen of us at table.

GINA. Did you get to talk to everybody?

HJALMAR. Oh yes, a little. But actually Gregers monopolized me most of the evening.

GINA. Is Gregers as ugly as ever?

HJALMAR. Well, he isn't exactly a beauty.—Hasn't the old man come home?

HEDVIG. Yes, Grandfather's in his room writing.

HJALMAR. Did he say anything?

GINA. No, what about?

HJALMAR. He didn't mention anything about . . .? I thought I heard he'd been to see Gråberg. I think I'll go in and see him a moment.

GINA. No, no, I wouldn't do that . . .

HJALMAR. Why not? Did he say he didn't want to see me?

GINA. I guess he doesn't want *anybody* in there this evening . . .

HEDVIG [*making signs*]. Ahem—ahem!

GINA [*not noticing*]. . . . he's been out and got himself some hot water.

HJALMAR. Aha, is he sitting and . . .?

GINA. Yes, that's probably it.

HJALMAR. Dear me—my poor old white-haired father!—Well, let him be, let him get what pleasure he can out of life.

[OLD EKDAL, *in dressing gown and with lighted pipe, enters from his room.*]

EKDAL. You back? *Thought* I heard you talking.

HJALMAR. I just got in this minute.

EKDAL. Guess you didn't see me, did you?

HJALMAR. No. But they said you'd gone through—so I thought I'd catch up with you.

EKDAL. Hm, good of you, Hjalmar. —Who were they, all those people?

HJALMAR. Oh, different ones. There was Chamberlain Flor and Chamberlain Balle and Chamberlain Kaspersen and Chamberlain this-that-and-the-other; I don't know . . .

EKDAL [*nodding his head*]. Hear that, Gina? He's been hobnobbing with nothing but chamberlains.

GINA. Yes, I guess they're mighty high-toned in that house now.

HEDVIG. Did the chamberlains sing, Father? Or give recitations?

HJALMAR. No, they just talked nonsense. They did try to get me to recite something for them, but they couldn't make me.

EKDAL. They couldn't make you, eh?

GINA. Seems to me you could just as well have done it.

HJALMAR. No. One should not be at everybody's beck and call. [*Taking a turn about the room.*] I, at any rate, am not.

EKDAL. No, no. *Hjalmar*'s not that obliging.

HJALMAR. I don't see why *I* should be expected to provide the entertainment the one evening I'm out. Let the others exert themselves. Those fellows do nothing but go from one spread to the next, feasting and drinking day in and day out. Let *them* do something in return for all the good food they get.

GINA. I hope you didn't tell them that?

HJALMAR [*humming*]. Hm . . . hm . . . hm . . . Well, they were told a thing or two.

EKDAL. What, the chamberlains!

HJALMAR. And why not? [*Casually.*] Then we had a little controversy over Tokay.

EKDAL. Tokay, eh? Say, that's a grand wine.

HJALMAR [*pauses*]. It *can* be. But let me tell you, not all vintages are equally fine. It all depends on how much sunshine the grapes have had.

GINA. Why, Hjalmar, if you don't know just about everything!

EKDAL. They started arguing about that?

HJALMAR. They tried to. But then they were given to understand that it's exactly the same with chamberlains. Not all vintages are equally good in their case either—it was pointed out.

GINA. Honest, the things you come up with!

EKDAL. Heh-heh! So they had to put *that* in their pipes and smoke it!

HJALMAR. They got it straight in the face.

EKDAL. Hear that, Gina? He said it straight to the chamberlains' faces.

GINA. Imagine, straight in their face.

HJALMAR. Yes, but I don't want it talked about. You don't repeat this kind of thing. Besides, the whole thing went off in the friendliest possible manner, of course. They were all decent, warm-hearted people—why should I hurt their feelings? No!

EKDAL. Still, straight in the face . . .

HEDVIG [*ingratiatingly*]. How nice it is to see you all dressed up, Father. You do look nice in a tailcoat.

HJALMAR. Yes, don't you think so? And this one really doesn't fit too badly. It could almost have been made to order for me—a trifle tight in the armholes, maybe . . . Give me a hand, Hedvig. [*Takes the tailcoat off.*] I'll put on my jacket instead. Where'd you put my jacket, Gina?

GINA. Here it is. [*Brings the jacket and helps him on with it.*]

HJALMAR. There we are! Now don't forget to let Molvik have the tails back first thing in the morning.

GINA [*putting tailcoat aside*]. I'll take care of it.

HJALMAR [*stretching*]. Aaahh, that's more like it. And this type of loose-fitting casual house jacket really suits my style better. Don't you think so, Hedvig?

HEDVIG. Oh yes, Father!

HJALMAR. And if I pull out my tie like this into two flowing ends . . . look! Eh?

HEDVIG. Yes, it goes so well with your mustache and your thick curly hair.

HJALMAR. I wouldn't exactly call my hair curly. Wavy, rather.

HEDVIG. Yes, because the curls are so big.

HJALMAR. Waves, actually.

HEDVIG [*after a moment, tugs at his jacket*]. Father!

HJALMAR. Well, what is it?

HEDVIG. Oh, you know as well as I.

HJALMAR. Why no, I certainly don't.

HEDVIG [*half-laughing, half-whimpering*]. Oh yes you do, Daddy! Stop teasing!

HJALMAR. But what is it?

HEDVIG [*shaking him*]. Come on, give it to me, Daddy. You know, the good things you promised me.

HJALMAR. Oh, dear. Imagine, I completely forgot!

HEDVIG. Now you're just trying to fool me, Daddy! That's not very nice! Where did you hide it?

HJALMAR. No, honest, I really did forget. But wait a minute! I've got something else for you, Hedvig. [*Goes across and searches his coat pockets.*]

HEDVIG [*jumping and clapping her hands*]. Oh Mother, Mother!

GINA. See? If you just give him time . . .

HJALMAR [*with a sheet of paper*]. Look, here it is.

HEDVIG. That? It's just a piece of paper.

HJALMAR. It's the menu, Hedvig, the entire menu. Look, they had it specially printed.

HEDVIG. Haven't you got anything else?

HJALMAR. I forgot the rest, I tell you. But take my word for it, it's no great treat, all that fancy stuff. Now, why don't you sit down at the table and read the menu, and later on I'll tell you what the different courses taste like. Here you are, Hedvig.

HEDVIG [*swallowing her tears*]. Thanks.

[*She sits down but does not read.* GINA *makes signs to her, which* HJALMAR *notices.*]

HJALMAR [*pacing the floor*]. It's really incredible the things a family man is expected to keep in mind. And just let him forget the least little thing—right away he gets a lot of sour looks. Oh well, that's another thing you get used to. [*Stops by the stove, where* OLD EKDAL *is sitting.*] Have you looked in there this evening, Father?

EKDAL. You bet I have. She's gone in her basket.

HJALMAR. No, really? In her basket! She's beginning to get used to it, then.

EKDAL. Sure, I told you she would. But now, you know, there are still one or two other little things . . .

HJALMAR. Improvements, yes.

EKDAL. They've got to be done, you know.

HJALMAR. Yes, let's have a little chat about these improvements, Father. Come over here and we'll sit down on the sofa.

EKDAL. Right! Hm, think I'll just fill my pipe first . . . Got to clean it, too. Hm. [*Goes into his room.*]

GINA [*smiles to* HJALMAR]. Clean his pipe—I'll bet.

HJALMAR. Oh well, Gina, let him be—poor shipwrecked old man. —Yes, those improvements—we'd better get them out of the way tomorrow.

GINA. You won't have time tomorrow, Hjalmar.

HEDVIG [*interrupting*]. Yes he will, Mother!

GINA. Don't forget those prints that need to be retouched. They keep coming around for them.

HJALMAR. What! Those prints again? Don't worry, they'll be ready. Any new orders come in?

GINA. No, worse luck. Tomorrow I've got nothing but that double sitting I told you about.

HJALMAR. Is that all? Well, of course, if one doesn't make an effort . . .

GINA. But what more can I do? I'm advertising in the papers as much as we can afford, seems to me.

HJALMAR. Oh, the papers, the papers—you see for yourself what good *they* are. And I suppose there hasn't been anybody to look at the room, either?

GINA. No, not yet.

HJALMAR. That was only to be expected. If people don't show any initiative, well . . . ! One's got to make a determined effort, Gina!

HEDVIG [*going toward him*]. Couldn't I bring you your flute, Father?

HJALMAR. No, no flute for me. *I* need no pleasures in this world. [*Pacing about.*] All right, you'll see how I'll get down to work tomorrow, don't you worry. You can be sure I shall work as long as my strength holds out . . .

GINA. But, Hjalmar dear, I didn't mean it that way.

HEDVIG. Father, how about a bottle of beer?

HJALMAR. No, certainly not. I don't need anything . . . [*Stops.*] Beer? Was it beer you said?

HEDVIG [*gaily*]. Yes, Father, nice cold beer.

HJALMAR. Well—if you insist, you might bring in a bottle.

GINA. Yes, do that. That'll be nice and cozy.

> [HEDVIG *runs toward the kitchen door.* HJALMAR, *by the stove, stops her, looks at her, takes her face between his hands, and presses her to him.*]

HJALMAR. Hedvig! Hedvig!

HEDVIG [*happy and in tears*]. Daddy darling!

HJALMAR. No, don't call me that. There I sat indulging myself at the rich man's table—sat and gorged myself at the groaning board—and I couldn't even . . . !

GINA [*seated by the table*]. Oh, don't talk nonsense, Hjalmar.

HJALMAR. No, it's the truth. But you mustn't judge me too harshly. You know I love you, all the same.

HEDVIG [*throwing her arms around him*]. And we love you too, Daddy—so much!

HJALMAR. And if I *am* unreasonable once in a while, well—heavens above—remember I am a man beset by a host of cares. Ah, well! [*Drying his eyes.*] No beer, no, not at such a moment. Give me my flute.

> [HEDVIG *runs to the bookcase and fetches it.*]

HJALMAR. Thanks! That's right, yes. With flute in hand and you two at my side—ah!

> [HEDVIG *sits down at the table beside* GINA. HJALMAR *walks up and down and begins a Bohemian folk dance, playing it with vigor but in a slow elegiac tempo and with sentimental interpretation.*]

HJALMAR [*breaks off the tune, holds out his left hand to* GINA, *and says with strong emotion*]. What if this place *is* cramped and shoddy, Gina. It's still our home. And this I will say: here is my heart's abode.

[*He starts to play again. Soon after, there is a knock on the hall door.*]

GINA [*getting up*]. Shhh, Hjalmar—I think somebody's coming.

HJALMAR [*putting the flute on the shelf*]. Wouldn't you just know!

[GINA *walks over and opens the door.*]

GREGERS WERLE [*out in the hall*]. I beg your pardon . . .

GINA [*recoiling slightly*]. Oh!

GREGERS. . . . isn't this where Mr. Ekdal the photographer lives?

GINA. Yes, it is.

HJALMAR [*going toward the door*]. Gregers! You came after all? Well, come in then.

GREGERS [*entering*]. I told you I would drop in to see you.

HJALMAR. But tonight . . .? You left the party?

GREGERS. Both the party and my father's house. —Good evening, Mrs. Ekdal. I don't suppose you recognize me

GINA. Oh yes. You're not so hard to recognize, Mr. Werle.

GREGERS. No, I resemble my mother, of course. And no doubt you remember her.

HJALMAR. Did I hear you say you left the house?

GREGERS. Yes, I've taken a room at a hotel.

HJALMAR. Really? Well, as long as you're here, take off your coat and sit down.

GREGERS. Thanks. [*Removes his overcoat. He has changed into a plain gray suit of a countrified cut.*]

HJALMAR. Here, on the sofa. Make yourself comfortable.

[GREGERS *sits down on the sofa,* HJALMAR *on a chair by the table.*]

GREGERS. So this is where you keep yourself, Hjalmar. This is your place.

HJALMAR. This is the studio, as you can see . . .

GINA. But it's roomier in here, so this is mostly where we stay.

HJALMAR. We had a nicer place before, but this apartment has one great advantage—there's such a lot of splendid extra space.

GINA. And then we've got a room across the hall that we can rent out.

GREGERS [*to* HJALMAR]. Well, well—so you've got roomers besides.

HJALMAR. No, not yet. It's not so easily done as all that, you know; it calls for initiative. [*To* HEDVIG.] What about that beer?

[HEDVIG *nods and goes out to the kitchen.*]

GREGERS. Your daughter, I take it?

HJALMAR. Yes, that's Hedvig.

GREGERS. Your only child?

HJALMAR. Our only one, yes. She is our greatest joy in the world, and— [*lowers his voice*] she's also our deepest sorrow, Gregers.

GREGERS. What are you saying!

HJALMAR. Yes, Gregers. She's in grave danger of losing her eye-sight.

GREGERS. Going blind!

HJALMAR. Yes. So far, there are only the first signs, and things may still be all right for some time yet. But the doctor has warned us. It's inevitable.

GREGERS. But this is a terrible misfortune. How did she get like that?

HJALMAR [*sighs*]. Heredity, most likely.

GREGERS [*with a start*]. Heredity?

GINA. Yes, Hjalmar's mother also had bad eyesight.

HJALMAR. That's what Father says. I can't remember her myself.

GREGERS. Poor child. How does she take it?

HJALMAR. Oh, as you can imagine, we don't have the heart to tell her. She doesn't suspect a thing. Happy and carefree, chirping like a little bird, she is fluttering into life's eternal night. [*Overcome.*] Oh, Gregers, it's heartbreaking for me.

[HEDVIG *enters carrying a tray with beer and glasses, which she sets down on the table.*]

HJALMAR [*stroking her head*]. Thank you, thank you, Hedvig.

[HEDVIG *puts her arms around his neck and whispers in his ear.*]

HJALMAR. No, no sandwiches just now. [*Looks across.*] That is, unless Gregers would care for some?

GREGERS [*declining*]. No, no thanks.

HJALMAR [*with continued pathos*]. Oh well, perhaps you might bring in a few, after all. A crust would be nice, if you happen to have one. Just make sure there's plenty of butter on it.

[HEDVIG *nods delightedly and goes out again to the kitchen.*]

GREGERS [*who has followed her with his eyes*]. She looks strong and healthy enough to me in all other respects.

GINA. Yes, thank God. Otherwise there's nothing the matter with her.

GREGERS. She's going to look like you in time, Mrs. Ekdal. How old might she be now?

GINA. Hedvig's just fourteen; it's her birthday the day after tomorrow.

GREGERS. A big girl for her age.

GINA. Yes, she certainly shot up this last year.

GREGERS. The young ones growing up make us realize how old we ourselves are getting. —How long is it now you've been married?

GINA. We've been married already fifteen years—just about.

GREGERS. Imagine, is it that long!

GINA [*becomes attentive; looks at him*]. Yes, that's what it is, all right.

HJALMAR. Yes, it must be all of that. Fifteen years, give or take a couple of months. [*Changing the subject.*] They must have been long years for you, Gregers, up there at the works.

GREGERS. They seemed long while I was living through them—now, looking back, I hardly know where all that time went.

[OLD EKDAL *enters from his room, without his pipe, but with his old-fashioned lieutenant's cap on his head. His gait is a bit unsteady.*]

EKDAL. All right, Hjalmar, now we can sit down and talk about that . . . hm . . . What was it again?

HJALMAR [*going toward him*]. Father, there's somebody here. Gregers Werle . . . I don't know if you remember him.

EKDAL [*looks at* GREGERS, *who has risen*]. Werle? Is that the son? What does he want with me?

HJALMAR. Nothing. It's me he's come to see.

EKDAL. Oh. So there's nothing the matter?

HJALMAR. No, of course not.

EKDAL [*swinging his arm*]. Not that I care, you know. I'm not scared . . .

GREGERS [*goes up to him*]. I just wanted to bring you greetings from your old hunting grounds, Lieutenant Ekdal.

EKDAL. Hunting grounds?

GREGERS. Yes, up there around the Højdal works.

EKDAL. Oh, up there. Oh yes, I used to know my way around up there at one time.

GREGERS. You were a mighty hunter in those days.

EKDAL. So I was. True enough. You're looking at my officer's cap. I don't ask anybody's permission to wear it here in the house. Just as long as I don't go outside with it . . .

[HEDVIG *brings a plate of open-faced sandwiches, which she sets on the table.*]

HJALMAR. Come sit down now, Father, and have a glass of beer. Help yourself, Gregers.

[EKDAL *mutters and hobbles over to the sofa.* GREGERS *sits down on the chair nearest him.* HJALMAR *on the other side of* GREGERS. GINA *sits a little away from the table, sewing;* HEDVIG *stands beside her father.*]

GREGERS. Do you remember, Lieutenant Ekdal, how Hjalmar and I used to come up and visit you summers and at Christmas?

EKDAL. Did you? No, no, no, that I can't recollect. But I *was* a crack shot, if I do say so myself. Even used to shoot bears. Got nine of 'em, no less.

GREGERS [*looking sympathetically at him*]. And now your hunting days are over.

EKDAL. Oh, I wouldn't say *that*, old chap. Still manage a bit of shooting now and then. Of course, not in the old way. Because the forest, you know . . . the forest, the forest . . . ! [*Drinks.*] Is the forest in good shape up there now?

GREGERS. Not so fine as in your day. There's been a lot of felling.

EKDAL. Felling? [*Lowers his voice as if afraid.*] That's risky business, that. You don't get away with it. The forest takes revenge.

HJALMAR [*filling his glass*]. Here, Father, have a little more.

GREGERS. How can a man like you—such a lover of the great out-doors—how can you live in the middle of a stuffy city, shut in here by four walls?

EKDAL [*gives a little laugh and glances at* HJALMAR]. Oh, it's not so bad here. Not so bad at all.

GREGERS. But all those things that were once so much a part of you—the cool sweeping breeze, the free life in the forest and on the moors, among birds and beasts . . . ?

EKDAL [*smiling*]. Hjalmar, shall we show it to him?

HJALMAR [*quickly, a little embarrassed*]. No, no, Father. Not tonight.

GREGERS. What does he want to show me?

HJALMAR. Oh, it's only a kind of . . . You can see it another time.

GREGERS [*continues to the old man*]. Well, let me tell you what I had in mind, Lieutenant Ekdal. Why don't you come up to Højdal with me. I'll probably be going back soon. You could easily get some copying to do up there as well. While here you don't have a thing in the world to liven you up or amuse you.

EKDAL [*staring at him in astonishment*]. Me? Not a thing in the world to . . . !

GREGERS. Of course, you have Hjalmar. But then he has his own family. And a man like you, who has always been drawn to what is free and untamed . . .

EKDAL [*strikes the table*]. Hjalmar, he's got to see it now!

HJALMAR. But, Father, do you really think so? It's dark . . .

EKDAL. Nonsense! It's moonlight. [*Gets up.*] I tell you he's got to see it. Let me pass. Come on and help me, Hjalmar!

HEDVIG. Oh yes, go on, Father!

HJALMAR [*gets up*]. Well, all right.

GREGERS [*to* GINA]. What is it?

GINA. Oh, don't expect anything special.

[EKDAL *and* HJALMAR *have gone to the rear wall and each slides one of the double doors aside.* HEDVIG *helps the old man;* GREGERS *remains standing by the sofa;* GINA *sits unconcerned, sewing. Through the open doors can be seen a long, irregular-shaped attic with nooks and crannies and a couple of free-standing chimneys. Bright moonlight falls through skylights on some parts of the attic, while others are in deep shadow.*]

EKDAL [*to* GREGERS]. You're welcome to come right up close.

GREGERS [*goes up to them*]. But what *is* it?

EKDAL. Look and see. Hm.

HJALMAR [*somewhat embarrassed*]. All this belongs to Father, you understand.

GREGERS [*at the door, looking into the attic*]. Why, Lieutenant Ekdal, you keep poultry!

EKDAL. Should hope to say we keep poultry. They're roosting now. But you ought to see this poultry by daylight!

HEDVIG. And then there's . . .

EKDAL. Sh! Sh! Don't say anything yet.

GREGERS. And I see you've got pigeons, too.

EKDAL. Yes indeed, we've got pigeons all right! They have their nesting boxes up under the eaves, they do. Pigeons like to roost high, you see.

HJALMAR. They aren't all of them just ordinary pigeons.

EKDAL. Ordinary! Should say not! We've got tumblers, and a couple of pouters, too. But come over here! Do you see that hutch over there by the wall?

GREGERS. Yes. What do you use that for?

EKDAL. That's where the rabbits sleep at night, old chap.

GREGERS. Oh, so you have rabbits too?

EKDAL. You're damn right we have rabbits! He wants to know if we've got rabbits, Hjalmar! Hm! But now we come to the *real* thing! Now it comes! Move, Hedvig. Come and stand here; that's right! Now, look down there. —Can you see a basket with straw in it?

GREGERS. Why yes. And I see there's a bird sitting in the basket.

EKDAL. Hm—"a bird" . . .

GREGERS. Isn't it a duck?

EKDAL [*offended*]. Well, obviously it's a duck.

HJALMAR. But what *kind* of duck do you suppose it is?

HEDVIG. It's no common ordinary duck . . .

EKDAL. Hush!

GREGERS. And it's not a muscovy duck either.

EKDAL. No, Mr. —Werle, it's not a muscovy duck. It's a wild duck.

GREGERS. What, is it really? A wild duck?

EKDAL. Yessir, that's what it is. That "bird," as you called it—that's the wild duck. Our wild duck, old chap.

HEDVIG. My wild duck. It belongs to me.

GREGERS. And it can really live here in the attic? And thrive?

EKDAL. Of course, you understand, she's got a trough of water to splash around in.

HJALMAR. Fresh water every other day.

GINA [*turning to* HJALMAR]. Hjalmar, please, it's getting freezing cold in here.

EKDAL. Hm, let's shut the door then. Better not to disturb them when they're settled for the night, anyhow. Hedvig, lend a hand. [HJALMAR *and* HEDVIG *slide the attic door shut.*]

EDKAL. You can take a good look at her some other time. [*Sits down in the armchair by the stove.*] Oh, they're most remarkable, let me tell you, these wild ducks.

GREGERS. But how did you ever catch it, Lieutenant Ekdal?

EKDAL. Wasn't me that caught it. There's a certain man here in town we have to thank for her.

GREGERS [*struck by a thought*]. That man wouldn't happen to be my father, would he?

EKDAL. Oh yes indeed. Precisely your father. Hm.

HJALMAR. Funny you should guess that, Gregers.

GREGERS. Well, you told me before that you owed such a lot to my father, so it occurred to me that . . .

GINA. But we didn't get the duck from Mr. Werle personally ...

EKDAL. It's Håkon Werle we have to thank for her just the same, Gina. [*To* GREGERS.] He was out in a boat, you see, and took a shot at her. But it happens his sight isn't so good anymore, your father's. Hm. So she was only winged.

GREGERS. I see. She got some shot in her.

HJALMAR. Yes, a few.

HEDVIG. It was in the wing, so she couldn't fly.

GREGERS. So she dived to the bottom, I suppose?

EKDAL [*sleepily, his voice thick*]. Goes without saying. Always do that, wild ducks. Plunge to the bottom—as deep as they can get, old chap—bite themselves fast in the weeds and the tangle—and all the other damn mess down there. And they never come up again.

GREGERS. But, Lieutenant Ekdal, *your* wild duck did come up again.

EKDAL. He had such an absurdly clever dog, your father ... And that dog—it dived after and fetched the duck up again.

GREGERS [*turning to* HJALMAR]. And so you brought it here?

HJALMAR. Not right away. First it was taken to your father's house. But it didn't seem to thrive there, so Pettersen was told to do away with it ...

EKDAL [*half asleep*]. Hm ... yes, Pettersen ... Ass ...

HJALMAR [*lowering his voice*]. That was how we got it, you see. Father knows Pettersen slightly, and when he heard all this about the wild duck, he managed to get it turned over to him.

GREGERS. And now it's thriving perfectly well there in the attic.

HJALMAR. Yes, incredibly well. It's got quite plump. Of course, it's been in there so long now, it's forgotten what real wild life is like. That's the whole secret.

GREGERS. You're probably right, Hjalmar. Just don't ever let it catch sight of sea or sky ... But I mustn't stay any longer, I think your father's asleep.

HJALMAR. Oh, don't worry about that ...

GREGERS. But incidentally—didn't you say you had a room for rent—a vacant room?

HJALMAR. Yes, why? Do you happen to know somebody ... ?

GREGERS. May I have that room?

HJALMAR. You?

GINA. You, Mr. Werle?

GREGERS. May I have the room? I could move in first thing tomorrow morning.

HJALMAR. Sure, with the greatest pleasure ...

GINA. No, really, Mr. Werle, it's not in the least no room for you.

HJALMAR. Why Gina, how can you say that?

GINA. Well, that room's neither big enough or light enough, and ...

GREGERS. That doesn't matter too much, Mrs. Ekdal.

HJALMAR. I think it's quite a nice room, myself, and not so badly furnished, either.

GINA. But don't forget those two downstairs.

GREGERS. Who are they?

GINA. Oh, there's one that used to be a private tutor . . .

HJALMAR. That's Molvik. He studied to be a pastor, once.

GINA. . . . And then there's a doctor called Relling.

GREGERS. Relling? I know him slightly; he practiced for a while up at Højdal.

GINA. They're a couple of real characters, those two. Out on a binge as often as not, and then they come home all hours of the night, and they're not always what you'd call . . .

GREGERS. One soon gets accustomed to things like that. I hope I shall be like the wild duck . . .

GINA. Hm. I think you'd better sleep on it, all the same.

GREGERS. You certainly don't seem anxious to have me in the house, Mrs. Ekdal.

GINA. For crying out loud, whatever gives you *that* idea?

HJALMAR. Yes, Gina, you really are being strange. [*To* GREGERS.] But tell me, does this mean you'll be staying in town for a while?

GREGERS [*putting on his overcoat*]. Yes, now I think I'll stay.

HJALMAR. But not at your father's? What do you intend to do?

GREGERS. Ah, if only I knew that, Hjalmar—it wouldn't be so bad. But when you're cursed with a name like Gregers . . . ! "Gregers"—and then "Werle" on top of that! Have you ever heard anything so ghastly?

HJALMAR. Why, I don't think so at all.

GREGERS. Ugh! Phew! I could spit on a man with a name like that. But since it's my cross in life to be Gregers Werle—such as I am . . .

HJALMAR [*laughing*]. Ha-ha! Suppose you weren't Gregers Werle, what would you choose to be?

GREGERS. If I had the choice, I'd like most of all to be a clever dog.

GINA. A dog!

HEDVIG [*involuntarily*]. Oh no!

GREGERS. Yes, a really absurdly clever dog. The kind that goes in after ducks when they plunge and fasten themselves in the weeds and the tangle in the mud.

HJALMAR. Honestly now, Gregers—what *are* you talking about.

GREGERS. Oh well, it probably doesn't make much sense. Well then, first thing tomorrow morning—I'm moving in. [*To* GINA.] I won't be any trouble to you; I do everything for myself. [*To* HJALMAR.] The rest we'll talk about tomorrow. —Goodnight, Mrs. Ekdal. [*Nods to* HEDVIG.] Goodnight.

GINA. Goodnight, Mr. Werle.

HEDVIG. Goodnight.

HJALMAR [*who has lit a candle*]. Wait a minute, I'd better see you down, it's sure to be dark on the stairs.

[GREGERS *and* HJALMAR *leave by the hall door.*]

GINA [*gazing ahead, her sewing on her lap*]. Wasn't that crazy talk, wanting to be a dog?

HEDVIG. You know what, Mother—I think he meant something else.

GINA. What else could he mean?

HEDVIG. Oh, I don't know. But it was just as though he meant something different from what he was saying—the whole time.

GINA. You think so? Well, it sure was queer though.

HJALMAR [*returning*]. The light was still on. [*Blows out candle and puts it down.*] Ah, at last a man can get a bite to eat. [*Starts on the sandwiches.*] Well, there you see, Gina—if only you keep your eyes open . . .

GINA. What do you mean, keep your eyes open?

HJALMAR. Well, wasn't it lucky we finally got the room rented? And then imagine, to somebody like Gregers—a dear old friend.

GINA. Well, I don't know what to say, myself.

HEDVIG. Oh, Mother, it will be nice, you'll see.

HJALMAR. You *are* funny, you know. First you were so set on getting it rented, and now you don't like it.

GINA. Well, Hjalmar, if only it had been somebody else. . . . What do you think Mr. Werle's going to say?

HJALMAR. Old Werle? It's none of his business.

GINA. But can't you see there's something the matter between them again, since the young one is moving out? You know what those two are like with each other.

HJALMAR. Yes, that could be, but . . .

GINA. And now maybe Mr. Werle will think you were behind it . . .

HJALMAR. Let him think what he wants! Mr. Werle has done a great deal for me—God knows, I'm the first to admit it. But that doesn't mean I've got to be under his thumb all my life.

GINA. But Hjalmar, dear, he could take it out on Grandpa. Suppose he loses the little money he makes working for Gråberg.

HJALMAR. I almost wish he would! Isn't it rather humiliating for a man like me to see his poor old white-haired father treated like dirt? But now the fullness of time is at hand, I feel. [*Helps himself to another sandwich.*] As sure as I have a mission in life, I shall fulfill it!

HEDVIG. Oh yes, Father, do!

GINA. Shhh! Don't wake him up.

HJALMAR [*in a lower voice*]. I shall fulfill it, I tell you. The day will come, when . . . That's why it's such a good thing we got the room rented; it puts me in a more independent position. And independent is one thing a man with a mission in life has got to be. [*Over by the armchair, with feeling.*] My poor old white-haired Father . . . Trust in your Hjalmar! He has broad shoulders—strong shoulders, anyway. One fine day you'll wake up and . . . [*to* GINA.] Maybe you don't believe that?

GINA [*getting up*]. Sure, I believe it. But let's see about getting him to bed first.

HJALMAR. Yes, let's.

[*They carefully lift the old man.*]

Act Three

HJALMAR EKDAL'S *studio. It is morning; daylight is coming through the large window in the sloping roof; the curtain is drawn back.*

HJALMAR *is sitting at the table, busy retouching a photograph; several more pictures are lying in front of him. After a while,* GINA, *in coat and hat, enters by the hall door; she has a covered basket on her arm.*

HJALMAR. Back already, Gina?

GINA. Oh, yes. I've got no time to waste. [*Puts the basket on a chair and takes off her outdoor things.*]

HJALMAR. Did you look in on Gregers?

GINA. I sure did. And a fine sight it is in there. He certainly fixed the place up the minute he moved in.

HJALMAR. Oh?

GINA. Yes, he wanted to manage for himself, he said. So he decides to light the fire, and what does he do but turn down the damper so the whole room gets filled with smoke. Phew, there's a smell in there like . . .

HJALMAR. Oh dear.

GINA. And that's not the worst of it. Next he wants to put out the fire, so he goes and dumps all the water from the washbasin into the stove, so the whole floor's a stinking mess.

HJALMAR. What a nuisance.

GINA. I got the janitor's wife to clean up after him, the pig, but the place won't be fit to go into again till this afternoon.

HJALMAR. What's he doing with himself meanwhile?

GINA. He's going out for a while, he said.

HJALMAR. I also dropped in on him for a minute—while you were gone.

GINA. So I heard. You've gone and invited him to lunch.

HJALMAR. Just for a little snack, that's all. After all, it's his first day—we can hardly do less. You must have something in the house.

GINA. I'd better see what I can find.

HJALMAR. Make sure there's plenty, though. Because I think Relling and Molvik are also coming up. I happened to run into Relling on the stairs, you see, so of course I had to . . .

GINA. Well, so we've got to have those two besides?

HJALMAR. Good Lord—one more or less, what difference does that make?

OLD EKDAL [*opens his door and looks in*]. I say, Hjalmar . . . [*Notices* GINA.] Never mind.

GINA. Is there something you want, Grandpa?

EKDAL. No, no, it doesn't matter. Hm! [*Goes back inside his room.*]

GINA [*takes the basket*]. Make sure you keep an eye on him, so he don't go out.

HJALMAR. All right, all right, I will.—Say, Gina, a little herring salad would be very nice. Because I suspect Relling and Molvik were out on a binge last night.

GINA. If only they don't barge in before I can . . .

HJALMAR. No, of course they won't. Take your time.

GINA. Well, all right. Meantime you can get a little work done.

HJALMAR. I *am* working, can't you see? I'm working as hard as I can!

GINA. That way you'll get that off your hands, that's all I meant. [*She goes into the kitchen, with the basket.*]

[HJALMAR *sits a while, working on the photograph with a brush, laboring slowly and with distaste.*]

EKDAL [*peeps in, looks around the studio, and says in a low voice*]. You busy, Hjalmar?

HJALMAR. Yes, can't you see I'm sitting here struggling with these pictures?

EKDAL. All right, all right. Goodness' sake, if you're all that busy—hm! [*Goes back inside his room; the door remains open.*]

HJALMAR [*continues working in silence for a while, then puts down his brush and walks over to the door*]. Are *you* busy, Father?

EKDAL [*grumbling, inside his room*]. If you're so busy, then I'm busy too. Hm!

HJALMAR. Oh, all right. [*Returns to his work.*]

EKDAL [*after a while, appears again at his door.*] Hm, look, Hjalmar, I'm not really as busy as all *that.*

HJALMAR. I thought you were writing.

EKDAL. What the hell, that Gråberg can wait a day or two, can't he? I don't suppose it's a matter of life and death.

HJALMAR. Of course not. And besides, you're not a slave.

EKDAL. And then there was this other thing in there . . .

HJALMAR. That's just what I was thinking. Do you want to go in? Shall I open the door for you?

EKDAL. Wouldn't really be such a bad idea.

HJALMAR [*getting up*]. Then we'd have *that* off our hands.

EKDAL. Yes, exactly. It was supposed to be ready first thing tomorrow. It *is* tomorrow, isn't it? Hm?

HJALMAR. Oh, yes, it's tomorrow, all right.

[HJALMAR *and* EKDAL *each pull aside one of the double doors. The morning sun is shining in through the skylights. A few pigeons are flying back and forth; others are cooing on the rafters; from farther back in the attic, now and then, can be heard the clucking of hens.*]

HJALMAR. There, now you can go ahead with it, Father.

EKDAL [*going in*]. Aren't you coming along?

HJALMAR. Well, you know—I rather think . . . [*Sees* GINA *at the kitchen door.*] Who, me? No, I have no time, I've got work to do. —Now, how about this contraption of ours . . .

[*He pulls a cord, and inside the door a curtain comes down. Its lower part consists of a strip of old canvas, its upper part of a piece of fishing net stretched taut. The attic floor is thus no longer visible.*]

HJALMAR [*going across to the table*]. There. Maybe now I can have a few minutes' peace.

GINA. Does he have to go messing around in there again?

HJALMAR. I suppose you'd rather see him running down to Ma Eriksen's place? [*Sitting down.*] Do you want something? I thought you said . . .

GINA. I was only going to ask if you think we could set the table in here.

HJALMAR. Why not? I don't suppose there are any appointments this early?

GINA. No, I'm only expecting that engaged couple that want to be taken together.

HJALMAR. Damn! Couldn't they be taken together some other day!

GINA. But, Hjalmar, dear, I especially booked them for this afternoon, while you're taking your nap.

HJALMAR. Oh, that's all right then. Yes, let's eat in here.

GINA. All right. But there's no rush about setting the table, you can go on using it for a while yet.

HJALMAR. Well, can't you see I *am* using it for all I'm worth?

GINA. Then you'll be free later on, you see. [*Returns to the kitchen.*]

[*Short pause.*]

EKDAL [*in the attic door, behind the net*]. Hjalmar!

HJALMAR. What?

EKDAL. Afraid we'll have to move the water trough after all.

HJALMAR. Well, that's just what I've been saying all along.

EKDAL. Hm . . . hm . . . hm . . . [*Disappears inside again*].

. [HJALMAR *works a little while, glances toward the attic, and half gets up.* HEDVIG *enters from the kitchen.*]

HJALMAR [*sits down again quickly*]. What is it you want?

HEDVIG. I only wanted to be with you, Father.

HJALMAR [*after a while*]. I have a feeling you're kind of snooping around. Were you told to check up on me by any chance?

HEDVIG. No, of course not.

HJALMAR. What's your mother doing out there?

HEDVIG. Oh, she's busy making the herring salad. [*Walks over to the table.*] Isn't there some little thing I could help you with, Father?

HJALMAR. No, no. It's best I do it all myself—so long as my strength holds out. There's no need, Hedvig; so long as your father manages to preserve his health . . .

HEDVIG. Oh, come on, Daddy, you mustn't say such awful things. [*She wanders around a little, stops by the opening to the attic, and looks inside.*]

HJALMAR. What's he doing, Hedvig?

HEDVIG. Looks like he's making a new path up to the water trough.

HJALMAR. He'll never manage that by himself, never in the world! And here am I, condemned to sit here . . . !

HEDVIG [*going up to him*]. Let me have the brush, Father; I can do it.

HJALMAR. Nonsense; you'll only ruin your eyes.

HEDVIG. No I won't. Come on, give me the brush.

HJALMAR [*getting up*]. Well, it shouldn't take more than a minute or two.

HEDVIG. Pooh, take your time. [*Takes the brush.*] There. [*Sits down.*] And here's one I can copy from.

HJALMAR. But don't you dare strain your eyes! You hear? I'm not taking any responsibility; you'll have to take the responsibility yourself. I'm just telling you.

HEDVIG [*retouching*]. Yes, yes, of course I will.

HJALMAR. My, you're good at it, Hedvig. Just for a couple of minutes, you understand.

[*He sneaks past the edge of the curtain into the attic,* HEDVIG *sits at her work.* HJALMAR *and* EKDAL *are heard debating inside.*]

HJALMAR [*appears behind the netting*]. Oh, Hedvig, hand me those pliers on the shelf, will you? And the chisel, please. [*Turns to face into attic.*] Now you'll see, Father. Just give me a chance first to show you what I have in mind. [HEDVIG *fetches the tools he wanted from the shelf and reaches them in to him.*] That's it, thanks. Well, it certainly was a good thing I came.

[*He moves away from the opening. They can be heard carpentering and chatting within.* HEDVIG *stands watching them. Presently there is a knock on the hall door; she does not notice it.* GREGERS WERLE *enters and stands by the door a moment; he is bareheaded and without overcoat.*]

GREGERS. Ahem . . . !

HEDVIG [*turns and goes toward him*]. Good morning. Please, come right in.

GREGERS. Thank you. [*Looks toward the attic.*] Sounds like you've got workmen in the house.

HEDVIG. No, it's only Father and Grandfather. I'll tell them you're here.

GREGERS. No, no, don't do that; I'd rather wait a while. [*Sits down on the sofa.*]

HEDVIG. Everything is in such a mess . . . [*Starting to clear away the photographs.*]

GREGERS. Oh, just leave it. Are those photographs that have to be finished?

HEDVIG. Yes, a little job I'm helping Father with.

GREGERS. Please don't let me disturb you.

HEDVIG. Not a bit.

[*She moves the things back into her reach and settles down to work.* GREGERS *watches her in silence.*]

GREGERS. Did the wild duck sleep well last night?

HEDVIG. Yes, thank you, I think so.

GREGERS [*turning toward the attic*]. It looks quite different by day from what it did last night by moonlight.

HEDVIG. Yes, it can change such a lot. In the morning it looks different than in the afternoon, and when it's raining it looks different from when it's sunny.

GREGERS. Have you noticed that?

HEDVIG. Sure, anybody can see it.

GREGERS. Do you like to stay in there with the wild duck too?

HEDVIG. Yes, whenever I can.

GREGERS. I don't suppose you have much spare time, though. You go to school, of course?

HEDVIG. No, not any more. Father's afraid I'll hurt my eyes reading.

GREGERS. Oh, so he gives you lessons himself, then.

HEDVIG. He promised he would, but he hasn't had the time yet.

GREGERS. But isn't there anybody else to help you a little?

HEDVIG. Well, there's Mr. Molvik. But he isn't always, you know . . . er . . .

GREGERS. You mean he drinks?

HEDVIG. I guess so.

GREGERS. Well, in that case you've got time for all sorts of things. And in there, it must be like a world all its own—I imagine.

HEDVIG. Absolutely all of its own. And there are such a lot of strange things in there.

GREGERS. Really?

HEDVIG. Yes, big cases with books in them, and lots of the books have pictures.

GREGERS. Aha!

HEDVIG. Then there's an old writing desk with drawers and secret compartments, and a big clock with figures that are supposed to pop out on the hour. Only the clock doesn't go any more.

GREGERS. So time has stopped in there—in the wild duck's domain.

HEDVIG. Yes. And then there are old paint-boxes and things like that. And all those books.

GREGERS. And do you ever read the books?

HEDVIG. Oh yes, whenever I get the chance. But most of them are in English, and I can't read that. But then I look at the pictures. There's a great big book called *Harrison's History of London;* it must be a hundred years old, and there's an enormous lot of pictures in it. In front there's a picture of Death with an hourglass, and a girl. I think that's horrible. But then there's all the other pictures of churches and castles and streets and big ships sailing on the sea.

GREGERS. But tell me, where did all those wonderful things come from?

HEDVIG. Oh, an old sea captain used to live here once, and he brought them back with him. They called him "The Flying Dutchman." That's funny, because he wasn't a Dutchman at all.

GREGERS. He wasn't?

HEDVIG. No. But finally he didn't come back, and everything just stayed here.

GREGERS. Tell me something . . . When you sit in there looking at pictures, don't you wish you could go abroad and see the real wide world itself?

HEDVIG. Not at all! I want to stay here at home always and help my father and mother.

GREGERS. Retouching photographs?

HEDVIG. Well, not only that. Most of all I'd like to learn how to engrave pictures like the ones in the English books.

GREGERS. Hm. What does your father say to that?

HEDVIG. I don't think Father likes the idea. He's funny about things like that. Imagine, he talks about me learning basket-weaving and braiding straw! I certainly don't think much of that.

GREGERS. No, neither do I.

HEDVIG. Still, he's right when he says that if I'd learned basket-weaving I could have made the new basket for the wild duck.

GREGERS. You could have, true. And of course you'd have been just the right person for the job.

HEDVIG. Because it's *my* wild duck.

GREGERS. Of course it is.

HEDVIG. Oh yes. I own it. But Daddy and Grandfather can borrow it as often as they like.

GREGERS. I see. What do they do with it?

HEDVIG. Oh, they look after it and build things for it, and things like that.

GREGERS. I understand. Because the wild duck must be the most important creature in there.

HEDVIG. Of course, because she's a *real* wild bird. And besides, it's such a pity on her, poor thing. She's got nobody at all to keep her company.

GREGERS. No family, like the rabbits . . .

HEDVIG. No. The chickens also have plenty of others they grew up together with from the time they were baby chicks. But she's completely cut off from her own kind, poor thing. Everything's so strange about the wild duck, too. Nobody knows her and nobody knows where she comes from, either.

GREGERS. And then she has been down in the depths of the sea.

HEDVIG [*glances quickly at him, suppresses a smile, and asks*]. Why do you say "the depths of the sea"?

GREGERS. Why, what *should* I say?

HEDVIG. You could say "the bottom of the sea"—or "the sea bottom."

GREGERS. Can't I just as well say "the depths of the sea"?

HEDVIG. Yes. But it sounds so strange to hear other people say "the depths of the sea."

GREGERS. Why is that? Tell me.

HEDVIG. No, I won't. It's something silly.

GREGERS. Oh, I'm sure it isn't. Come on, tell me why you smiled.

HEDVIG. Well, it's because every time I happen to think about the way it is in there—when it kind of comes in a flash through my mind—it always seems to me that the whole room and every-thing in it is called "the depths of the sea."—But that's just silly.

GREGERS. I wouldn't say so at all.

HEDVIG. Well, it's only an attic.

GREGERS [*looking intently at her*]. Are you so sure of that?

HEDVIG [*astonished*]. That it's an attic?

GREGERS. Yes, do you know that for sure?

[HEDVIG *is silent, looking at him open-mouthed.* GINA *enters from the kitchen with a tablecloth and silverware.*]

GREGERS [*getting up*]. I'm afraid I've descended on you too early.

GINA. Oh well, you got to be someplace. Anyhow, everything's just about ready. Clear the table, Hedvig.

[HEDVIG *clears up; she and* GINA *lay the table during the following dialogue.* GREGERS *sits down in the armchair and starts leafing through an album of photographs.*]

GREGERS. I hear you know how to do retouching, Mrs. Ekdal.

GINA [*with a sidelong glance*]. Yes, I know how.

GREGERS. That was indeed most fortunate.

GINA. How do you mean—"fortunate"?

GREGERS. Seeing that Hjalmar became a photographer, I mean.

HEDVIG. Mother knows how to take pictures, too.

GINA. Oh yes, I managed to pick that up, all right.

GREGERS. So perhaps it is really you that carries on the business?

GINA. Well, when Hjalmar hasn't got the time himself . . .

GREGERS. He's very much taken up with his old father, I would imagine.

GINA. Yes. Besides it's no job for a man like Hjalmar, taking pictures of every Tom, Dick and Harry that comes along.

GREGERS. I quite agree. Still, once he's gone in for that line of work, shouldn't he . . .

GINA. Sure, Mr. Werle, you don't imagine Hjalmar is just a common ordinary photographer.

GREGERS. True enough. Nevertheless . . . [*A shot is fired inside the attic.*]

GREGERS [*jumps up*]. What was that!

GINA. Ugh, they're shooting again!

GREGERS. Do they *shoot* in there?

HEDVIG. They go hunting.

GREGERS. What on earth . . . ! [*Over by the door into the attic*]. Are you hunting, Hjalmar?

HJALMAR [*behind the netting*]. Oh, you're here? I had no idea, I was so busy . . . [*To* HEDVIG.] You might let a person know! [*Enters studio.*]

GREGERS. You go around shooting in the attic?

HJALMAR [*showing him a double-barreled pistol*]. Oh, only with this thing.

GINA. Yes, one of these days you and Grandpa's going to have an accident yet, with that pissle.

HJALMAR [*annoyed*]. I believe I have told you that a firearm such as this is called a pis*tol*.

GINA. Well, I can't see it makes it any safer, whatever you call it.

GREGERS. So you too have taken up hunting, Hjalmar?

HJALMAR. Only a bit of rabbit shooting now and then. Mostly for Father's sake, you understand.

GINA. Ain't men the limit—always got to have *some*thing to detract theirself with.

HJALMAR [*grimly*]. Yes, yes, we always have to distract ourselves with something.

GINA. That's just what I said.

HJALMAR. Hm. Oh well . . . [*To* GREGERS.] Yes, as I was about to say, by a lucky chance the attic is so situated that nobody can hear us shoot. [*Places the pistol on the top shelf.*] Don't touch the pistol, Hedvig! One of the barrels is loaded, remember that.

GREGERS [*looking in through the net*]. You have a hunting rifle too, I see.

HJALMAR. That's Father's old rifle. It's no good anymore, something's gone wrong with the lock. Still, it's fun to have around; we take it apart and clean it once in a while and grease it and put it together again. Of course, it's mostly Father that plays around with that sort of thing.

HEDVIG [*standing by* GREGERS]. Now you can really see the wild duck.

GREGERS. Yes, I was just looking at it. One of her wings droops a bit, it seems to me.

HJALMAR. Well, that's not so strange. After all, she was hit.

GREGERS. And she's dragging one foot slightly. Or am I mistaken?

HJALMAR. Perhaps, just a wee bit.

HEDVIG. Yes, that's the foot the dog got hold of.

HJALMAR. But aside from that there's not a thing the matter with her—which is really remarkable, considering she's got a charge of shot in her and that she's been between the teeth of a dog . . .

GREGERS [*with a glance at* HEDVIG]. . . . and has been in "the depths of the sea"—for so long.

HEDVIG [*smiles*]. Yes.

GINA [*busy at the table*]. My goodness, that blessed wild duck. You sure make a fuss over her.

HJALMAR. Hm. —Lunch ready soon?

GINA. Yes, right away. Hedvig, come give me a hand.

[GINA *and* HEDVIG *go out to the kitchen.*]

HJALMAR [*in an undertone*]. I don't think you'd better stand there watching Father. He doesn't like it.

[GREGERS *moves from attic door.*]

HJALMAR. Maybe I ought to close this door anyhow, before the others get here. [*Clapping his hand to scare the birds.*] Shoo, shoo—beat it! [*Lifting the curtain and pulling the doors together.*] This gadget here is my own invention. It's really quite amusing to have something like this to putter around with and fix up when it gets out of order. Besides which, of course, it's absolutely necessary; Gina doesn't want rabbits and chickens running around in the studio.

GREGERS. No, of course not. And I suppose it's your wife who's in charge here?

HJALMAR. As a rule I leave the routine business to her. That way I can retire to the living room and think about more important things.

GREGERS. What things actually, Hjalmar? Tell me.

HJALMAR. I wonder you didn't ask that sooner. Or maybe you haven't heard about the invention?

GREGERS. Invention? No.

HJALMAR. Really? You haven't? Well, of course, up there in the wilderness . . .

GREGERS. So you've made an invention!

HJALMAR. Not quite *made*, just yet—but I'm busy on it. As you can imagine, when I decided to devote myself to photography it was not merely in order to take pictures of a lot of nobodies . . .

GREGERS. Of course not. Your wife was just saying the same thing.

HJALMAR. I vowed that if I was going to dedicate my powers to this calling, I would raise it so high that it would become both a science and an art. And so I decided to work on this remarkable invention.

GREGERS. What does the invention consist of? What is it going to do?

HJALMAR. Come, come, my dear Gregers, you mustn't ask for details yet. It takes time, you know. Another thing—don't imagine it's vanity that spurs me on. I'm certainly not working for my own sake. Oh no, it is my life's mission that stands before me night and day.

GREGERS. What mission?

HJALMAR. Have you forgotten the silver-haired old man?

GREGERS. Your poor father, yes. But what can you actually do for him?

HJALMAR. I can restore his self-respect by raising the name of Ekdal once again to honor and dignity.

GREGERS. So that is your life's mission.

HJALMAR. Yes, I will rescue the shipwrecked old man. For shipwrecked he was, the moment the storm broke over him. By the time of that terrible investigation he was no longer himself. That pistol there, Gregers—the one we use to shoot rabbits—that has played a role in the tragedy of the House of Ekdal.

GREGERS. The pistol? Really?

HJALMAR. When sentence had been pronounced and he was to be imprisoned—he took that pistol in his hand . . .

GREGERS. He meant to . . . !

HJALMAR. Yes—but didn't dare. Lost his nerve. So broken, so demoralized was he already then. Oh, can you conceive it! He, an army officer, a man who had shot nine bears. He, who was descended from two lieutenant colonels—one after the other, naturally—. Can you conceive it, Gregers?

GREGERS. Yes, very well.

HJALMAR. Not I. Then, once again, the pistol figured in our family chronicle. When he had put on the gray prison uniform and sat behind bars . . . Oh, that was a terrible time for me, let me tell you. I kept the shades down on both my windows. When I peeped out, there was the sun, shining as usual. I couldn't grasp it. I saw people walking in the street, laughing and chatting about trivialities. I could not grasp it. It seemed to me that the whole of existence ought to come to a standstill, like an eclipse.

GREGERS. That's just how I felt, when my mother died.

HJALMAR. In such an hour did Hjalmar Ekdal point the pistol at his own breast.

GREGERS. You also thought of . . . !

HJALMAR. Yes.

GREGERS. But you did not fire.

HJALMAR. No. In the decisive moment I won the victory over myself. I chose to live. And believe me, it takes courage to choose life under those circumstances.

GREGERS. Well, that depends on how you look at it.

HJALMAR. No, my friend, no doubt about it. But it was all for the best. Because now I'll soon perfect my invention, and then Dr. Relling thinks, just as I do, that Father will be allowed to wear his uniform again. I will demand that as my sole reward.

GREGERS. So it's about wearing the uniform that he . . . ?

HJALMAR. Yes, that's what he yearns and pines for most of all. You have no idea how my heart bleeds for him. Every time we celebrate some little family occasion—like Gina's and my wedding anniversary, or whatever it may be—in trots the old man wearing his uniform of happier days. But just let him hear so much as a knock on the door—because he doesn't dare show himself like that in front of strangers, you see—back into his room he scurries as fast as his old legs will carry him. Think, Gregers, how heart-rending it is for a son to see such things!

GREGERS. About how soon do you think the invention will be perfected?

HJALMAR. Good lord, you mustn't ask me for details like dates. An invention is not a thing entirely under one's control. It's largely a matter of inspiration—of a sudden insight—and it's next to impossible to figure out in advance just when that may come.

GREGERS. But you *are* making progress?

HJALMAR. Sure, of course I'm making progress. I grapple every single day with the invention, I'm filled with it. Every afternoon, right after dinner, I shut myself in the living room, where I can concentrate in peace. But I simply must not be rushed; that doesn't do a bit of good. That's what Relling says, too.

GREGERS. And you don't think all this business in the attic there draws you away from your work, and distracts you too much?

HJALMAR. No, no, no. Quite the reverse. You mustn't say such things. After all, I can't go around day in day out everlastingly poring over the same exhausting problems. I must have something to occupy me during the waiting period. The inspiration, the intuition—look, when it's ready to come, it will come, and that's all.

GREGERS. My dear Hjalmar, I almost think there is something of the wild duck in you.

HJALMAR. The wild duck? How do you mean?

GREGERS. You have dived down and bitten yourself fast into the undergrowth.

HJALMAR. Are you by any chance alluding to the all but fatal shot that maimed my father—and me as well?

GREGERS. Not exactly. I wouldn't say that you are maimed. But you have landed in a poisonous swamp, Hjalmar; an insidious blight has got hold of you, and you have sunk down to the depths to die in darkness.

HJALMAR. I? Die in darkness! Now look here, Gregers, you'd really better quit talking such nonsense.

GREGERS. Don't worry, I'll get you up again. You see, I too have got a mission in life now. I found it yesterday.

HJALMAR. That's all very well, but just you leave me out of it. I can assure you that—apart from my understandable melancholy, of course—I am as content as any man could wish to be.

GREGERS. The fact that you are content is itself a result of the poison.

HJALMAR. Look, my dear Gregers, will you please cut out all this rot about blight and poison. I am not at all used to that sort of talk; in my house nobody ever talks to me about unpleasant things.

GREGERS. That I can well believe.

HJALMAR. No, because it's not good for me. And there are no swamp vapors here, as you put it. The roof may be low in the poor photographer's home, that I know—and my means are slender. But I am an inventor, man—and a bread-winner as well. That raises me above my humble circumstances ... Ah, here comes our lunch!

[GINA *and* HEDVIG *enter with bottles of beer, a decanter of schnapps, glasses, and other things for the lunch. At the same time,* RELLING *and* MOLVIK *enter from the hallway, both without hat or overcoat.* MOLVIK *is dressed in black.*]

GINA [*setting things on table*]. Well, here they come right on the dot.

RELLING. Once Molvik got the idea he could smell herring salad, there was no holding him. —Good morning again, Ekdal.

HJALMAR. Gregers, may I present Mr. Molvik; Dr. . . . that's right, you know Relling, don't you?

GREGERS. Slightly.

RELLING. Oh, it's Mr. Werle junior. Yes indeed, we once had a couple of skirmishes up at the Højdal works. You just moved in?

GREGERS. This morning.

RELLING. Molvik and I live on the floor below, so you're not far from doctor or parson, should you have need of either.

GREGERS. Thanks, it's not unlikely I may—yesterday we were thirteen at table.

HJALMAR. Oh, don't start on that creepy talk again!

RELLING. Relax, Ekdal. You can be damn sure it won't be you.

HJALMAR. I hope not, for my family's sake. Well, come sit down and let's eat, drink, and be merry.

GREGERS. Aren't we going to wait for your father?

HJALMAR. No, he'll have a bite later on in his room. Do sit down!
[*The men sit down at the table, and eat and drink.* GINA
and HEDVIG *go in and out, waiting on them.*]

RELLING. Molvik really tied one on last night, Mrs. Ekdal.

GINA. Yeah? Again?

RELLING. Didn't you hear him when I brought him home?

GINA. No, I can't say I did.

RELLING. That's good—because last night Molvik really was awful.

GINA. Is it true, Molvik?

MOLVIK. Let us draw a veil over last night's proceedings. Such episodes are totally foreign to my better self.

RELLING [*to* GREGERS]. It comes over him like a sort of possession,
so I am obliged to take him out on a binge. Because Mr. Molvik,
you see, is dæmonic.

GREGERS. Dæmonic?

RELLING. Molvik is dæmonic, yes.

GREGERS. Hm.

RELLING. And dæmonic natures are not made for the straight and
narrow; they've got to kick over the traces once in a while.
—Well, so you're still sticking it out up there at those ghastly
dark works?

GREGERS. I have till now.

RELLING. Say, did you ever collect on that claim you used to go
around with?

GREGERS. Claim? [*Grasps his meaning.*] Oh, that.

HJALMAR. Were you a bill collector, Gregers?

GREGERS. Oh, nonsense.

RELLING. He certainly was. He used to go around to all the workmen's shacks presenting something he called "the claim of the
ideal."

GREGERS. I was young in those days.

RELLING. You bet you were. Mighty young. And that claim of the
ideal—you never did get it honored as long as I was up there.

GREGERS. Nor afterwards, either.

RELLING. Well, then I imagine you've got the sense by now to
knock a little off the bill.

GREGERS. Never—not when I'm dealing with an authentic human
being.

HJALMAR. Well, that sounds reasonable enough. —Some butter,
Gina.

RELLING. And a slice of pork for Molvik.

MOLVIK. Ugh, not pork!
[*Knocking inside the attic door.*]

HJALMAR. Open up, Hedvig; Father wants to come out.
[HEDVIG *goes and opens the door a little;* OLD EKDAL *enters,
carrying a freshly flayed rabbit skin; she closes the door after
him.*]

EKDAL. Good morning, Gentlemen! Good hunting today. Bagged a
beauty.

HJALMAR. And you went and skinned it without waiting for me!

EKDAL. Salted it down, too. Good tender meat, rabbit. Sweet, too, tastes like sugar. Hearty appetite, Gentlemen! [*Goes into his room.*]

MOLVIK [*rising*]. Excuse me . . . I can't . . . I must get downstairs at once . . .

RELLING. Drink some soda water, man!

MOLVIK [*hurrying*]. Uh . . . uh! [*Exit through the hall door.*]

RELLING [*to* HJALMAR]. Let us drain a glass to the old Nimrod.

HJALMAR [*clinks glasses with him*]. Yes, to the sportsman on the brink of the grave.

RELLING. To the gray-headed . . . [*Drinks.*] By the way—is it gray hair he's got, or is it white?

HJALMAR. Sort of betwixt and between, I'd say. As a matter of fact, not much of either any more.

RELLING. Oh well, life can be good enough under a toupee. Yes, Ekdal, when you come right down to it, you are a lucky man. You have your beautiful goal to strive for . . .

HJALMAR. And I do strive, believe me.

RELLING. And then you've got your excellent wife, waddling so cosily in and out in her felt slippers, swaying her hips and making everything nice and comfortable for you.

HJALMAR. Yes, Gina . . . [*Nods to her*] you are a good companion to have on life's journey.

GINA. Oh, don't sit there bisecting me.

RELLING. And then your Hedvig, Ekdal, what?

HJALMAR [*moved*]. The child, yes! First and foremost, the child. Hedvig, come here to me. [*Stroking her hair.*] What day is it tomorrow, eh?

HEDVIG [*shaking him*]. Oh, don't say anything about that, Father.

HJALMAR. It pierces me to the heart to think how little we can do—only a little celebration in the attic . . .

HEDVIG. Oh, but that'll be just lovely!

RELLING. And wait till the marvelous invention comes out, Hedvig!

HJALMAR. Yes indeed—*then* you shall see! Hedvig, I am resolved to secure your future. You shall want for nothing as long as you live. For you, I shall demand . . . something or other. That will be the poor inventor's sole reward.

HEDVIG [*whispers, her arms around his neck*]. Oh you dear, dear Daddy!

RELLING [*to* GREGERS]. Well, now, don't you think it's nice, for a change, to sit at a well-laid table in a happy family circle?

HJALMAR. Yes, I really appreciate these meal-times.

GREGERS. I, for my part, do not thrive in swamp vapors.

RELLING. Swamp vapors?

HJALMAR. Oh, don't start on *that* again!

GINA. God knows there's no swamp vapors around here, Mr. Werle. I air the house out every blessed day.

GREGERS [*leaving the table*]. The stench I have in mind, you can hardly air out.

HJALMAR. Stench!

GINA. Yes, Hjalmar, how do you like that!

RELLING. Pardon me—I don't suppose it could be yourself that brought the stink with you from the pits up north?

GREGERS. It's just like you to call what I bring to this house a stink.

RELLING [*goes up to him*]. Listen here, Mr. Werle junior, I have a strong suspicion you are still carrying around that "claim of the ideal" unabridged in your back pocket.

GREGERS. I carry it in my heart.

RELLING. Well, wherever the hell you carry it, I advise you not to play bill collector here as long as I'm around.

GREGERS. And suppose I do?

RELLING. You'll be sent head first down the stairs. Now you know.

HJALMAR [*rising*]. No, Relling, really . . . !

GREGERS. Go ahead, throw me out . . .

GINA [*interposing*]. You can't do that, Relling. But I must say, Mr. Werle, you've got a nerve to talk to *me* about smells, after the mess you made with your stove.

[*There is a knock on the hall door.*]

HEDVIG. Mother, somebody's knocking.

HJALMAR. Darn! Now all we need is customers barging in.

GINA. I'll go . . . [*Goes and opens the door; gives a start; draws back.*] Oh! What the . . . !

[HAKON WERLE, *in a fur coat, takes a step into the room.*]

WERLE. I beg your pardon, but I believe my son is staying here.

GINA [*gulping*]. Yes.

HJALMAR [*coming forward*]. Sir, won't you do us the honor to . . . ?

WERLE. Thanks, I just want a word with my son.

GREGERS. Yes, what is it? Here I am.

WERLE. I wish to talk with you in your room.

GREGERS. In my room—all right . . . [*About to go.*]

GINA. God, no. It's not fit in there for . . .

WERLE. Very well, out in the hall, then. I want to talk to you in private.

HJALMAR. You can do it right here, Mr. Werle. Relling, come into the living room.

[HJALMAR *and* RELLING *exit right.* GINA *takes* HEDVIG *off with her to the kitchen.*]

GREGERS [*after a brief pause*]. Well, now we are alone.

WERLE. You let drop certain remarks last night . . . And in view of the fact that you've gone and moved in with the Ekdals, I can only assume that you have something or other in mind against me.

GREGERS. I intend to open Hjalmar Ekdal's eyes. He must see his position for what it is—that's all.

WERLE. Is that the objective in life you spoke of yesterday?

GREGERS. Yes. You have left me no other.

WERLE. Is it I, then, who twisted your mind, Gregers?

GREGERS. You've twisted my whole life. I'm not thinking of all that concerning Mother . . . But it's you I have to thank that I am forever driven and tormented by a guilty conscience.

WERLE. Aha, your conscience! So that's your trouble.

GREGERS. I should have stood up to you that time the trap was laid for Lieutenant Ekdal. I should have warned him—for I suspected well enough how it was all going to end.

WERLE. Yes, in that case you certainly ought to have spoken out.

GREGERS. I didn't dare. That's what a frightened coward I was. I was so unspeakably afraid of you—not only then but long after.

WERLE. You've got over that fear now, it appears.

GREGERS. Yes, fortunately. The crime committed against old Ekdal, both by myself and by—others—that can never be redeemed. But Hjalmar I can still rescue from all the lies and deceit that threaten to destroy him.

WERLE. Do you think you'll be doing him a favor?

GREGERS. I *know* it.

WERLE. I suppose you think our good photographer is the kind of man to thank you for such a friendly service?

GREGERS. Yes! He certainly is.

WERLE. Hm . . . we'll see.

GREGERS. And besides . . . if I am to go on living, I must find some cure for my sick conscience.

WERLE. It will never be well. Your conscience has been sickly right from childhood. It is a legacy from your mother, Gregers—the only thing she ever left you.

GREGERS [with a contemptuous half-smile]. So you still haven't swallowed your disappointment that she didn't bring you the dowry you counted on?

WERLE. Let us keep to the point. —Are you quite resolved to set young Ekdal on what you assume to be the right track?

GREGERS. Yes, quite resolved.

WERLE. Well, in that case I could have saved myself the trouble of coming up here. Then I suppose it's no use asking you to come back home?

GREGERS. No.

WERLE. And you won't join the firm, either?

GREGERS. No.

WERLE. Very well. But since I intend to marry again, your share of my estate will be turned over to you at once.

GREGERS [quickly]. No, I don't want that.

WERLE. You don't want it?

GREGERS. No, I don't dare. My conscience won't let me.

WERLE [after a pause]. Are you going up to the works again?

GREGERS. No, I consider myself released from your service.

WERLE. But what are you going to do?

GREGERS. Accomplish my mission. That's all.

WERLE. All right, but afterwards? What are you going to live on?

GREGERS. I've put aside a little of my salary.

WERLE. Yes, but how long will *that* last!

GREGERS. I think it will last out my time.

WERLE. What's that supposed to mean?

GREGERS. I'm answering no more questions.

WERLE. Good-bye, then, Gregers.

GREGERS. Good-bye.

[HAKON WERLE *goes.*]

HJALMAR [*peeping in*]. Has he gone?

GREGERS. Yes.

[HJALMAR *and* RELLING *enter; also* GINA *and* HEDVIG, *from the kitchen.*]

RELLING. Well, that fixed *that* lunch.

GREGERS. Put on your things, Hjalmar. You're coming with me for a long walk.

HJALMAR. Gladly. What did your father want? Anything to do with me?

GREGERS. Just come. We must have a little talk. I'll go get my coat. [*Goes out by the hall door.*]

GINA. You shouldn't go with him, Hjalmar.

RELLING. No, don't you do it, old man. Stay where you are.

HJALMAR [*getting his coat and hat*]. What! When an old friend feels the need to open his heart to me in private . . . !

RELLING. But damn it!—can't you see the fellow is mad, cracked, off his rocker!

GINA. There, what did I tell you? His mother used to get these here fits and conniptions too.

HJALMAR. All the more reason he needs a friend's watchful eye. [*To* GINA.] Be sure and have dinner ready on time. So long. [*Goes out by the hall door.*]

RELLING. What a calamity that fellow didn't go straight to hell down one of the Højdal pits.

GINA. Good God!—what makes you say that?

RELLING [*muttering*]. Oh, I have my reasons.

GINA. Do you think young Werle is really crazy?

RELLING. No, worse luck; he's no more crazy than most. But there's one bug he certainly has got in his system.

GINA. What's the matter with him, anyway?

RELLING. Well, I'll tell you, Mrs. Ekdal. He's got a severe case of inflamed integrity.

GINA. Inflamed integrity?

HEDVIG. Is that a kind of disease?

RELLING. Oh yes. It's a national disease. But it only breaks out sporadically. [*Nods to* GINA.] Thanks for lunch!

[*He goes out by the hall door.*]

GINA [*pacing the floor, disturbed*]. Ugh, that Gregers Werle—he always *was* a queer fish.

HEDVIG [*standing by the table and looking searchingly at her*]. I think this is all so strange.

Act Four

HJALMAR EKDAL'*s studio. Photographs have apparently just been taken; a camera covered with a cloth, a stand, two chairs, a console, and other portrait materials are set out in the middle of the room.*

Afternoon light; the sun is about to set; after a while it begins to get dark.

GINA *is standing at the open hall door with a dark slide and a wet photographic plate in her hand. She is speaking to somebody outside.*

GINA. Yes, positively. When I make a promise, I keep it. The first dozen will be ready on Monday. —Good-bye now, good-bye!

[*Footsteps can be heard going down the stairs.* GINA *shuts the door, puts the plate in the slide, and inserts the slide in the covered camera.*]

HEDVIG [*entering from the kitchen*]. Did they leave?

GINA [*tidying up*]. Yes, thank goodness. I finally got rid of them.

HEDVIG. Can you understand why Father isn't back yet?

GINA. You're sure he's not down at Relling's?

HEDVIG. No, he's not there. I just went down the back stairs and asked.

GINA. And his dinner standing there getting cold.

HEDVIG. Imagine! And Father's always so punctual about dinner.

GINA. Well, he'll be here soon, don't worry.

HEDVIG. Oh, I wish he'd come. Everything seems so strange.

GINA [*calls out*]. There he is!

[HJALMAR EKDAL *comes in through the hall door.*]

HEDVIG [*up to him*]. Father! We've been waiting and waiting for you!

GINA [*glancing across*]. You sure have been out a long time, Hjalmar.

HJALMAR [*without looking at her*]. I suppose I have, yes. [*He takes off his overcoat.* GINA *and* HEDVIG *try to help him; he waves them aside.*]

GINA. Maybe you ate someplace with Werle?

HJALMAR [*hanging up his coat*]. No.

GINA [*going toward the kitchen door*]. Then I'll go get your dinner.

HJALMAR. No, never mind. I don't want anything now.

HEDVIG [*coming closer*]. Aren't you feeling well, Father?

HJALMAR. Feeling well? Oh yes, tolerably. We had a tiring walk together, Gregers and I.

GINA. You shouldn't do that, Hjalmar, you're not used to it.

HJALMAR. Hm. There are lots of things a man must get used to in this world. [*Paces up and down.*] Did anybody come while I was out?

GINA. Only the engaged couple.

HJALMAR. No new orders?

GINA. No, not today.

HEDVIG. There'll be some tomorrow, Father, you'll see.

HJALMAR. I hope you're right, because tomorrow I mean to get down to work in real earnest.

HEDVIG. Tomorrow! Don't you remember what day it is tomorrow?

HJALMAR. Oh, that's right . . . Well, the day after tomorrow, then. From now on I intend to do everything myself; I want to do all the work entirely on my own.

GINA. What on earth for, Hjalmar? You'd only make your life a
misery. I can still manage the photography; you go on with the
invention.

HEDVIG. And what about the wild duck—and all the chickens and
rabbits . . .

HJALMAR. Don't talk to me about that junk! I'm never setting foot
in that attic again.

HEDVIG. But Father, you promised me there'd be a party
tomorrow . . .

HJALMAR. Hm, that's right. Well, starting the day after tomorrow,
then. That damn wild duck, I'd like to wring its neck!

HEDVIG [*cries out*]. The wild duck!

GINA. Well, I never!

HEDVIG [*shaking him*]. But Father, it's *my* wild duck!

HJALMAR. That's the only thing that stops me. I haven't the
heart—for your sake, Hedvig, I haven't got the heart. But deep
down I feel I ought to do it. I ought not tolerate under my roof
any creature that has been in that man's hands.

GINA. Goodness sake, just because Grandpa got it off that good-
for-nothing Petterson . . .

HJALMAR [*walking up and down*]: There are certain
demands . . . what shall I call them? Let us say—demands of the
ideal—certain claims that a man cannot disregard without peril
to his soul.

HEDVIG [*following him about*]. But think, the wild duck—that
poor wild duck!

HJALMAR [*halts*]. I *told* you I'll spare it—for your sake. Not a hair
of its head shall be . . . hm. As I said, I shall spare it. I have
more important things to think about now. But now you ought
to go for a little walk, Hedvig; the twilight is just right for you.

HEDVIG. I don't care to go out now.

HJALMAR. Yes, go on. Seems to me you're blinking your eyes a lot.
It's not good for you, all these fumes in here. The air is close
under this roof.

HEDVIG. Well, all right, I'll run down the kitchen way and walk
around a little. My hat and coat . . .? That's right, they're in my
room. Father—promise you won't do anything to the wild duck
while I'm gone.

HJALMAR. Not a feather of its head shall be touched. [*Presses her
to him.*] You and I, Hedvig—we two . . . ! Well, run along now.
[HEDVIG *nods to her parents and goes out through the
kitchen.*]

HJALMAR [*walks up and down without looking up*]. Gina.

GINA. Yes?

HJALMAR. As of tomorrow . . . or, let us say as of the day after
tomorrow—I wish to keep the household accounts myself.

GINA. You want to keep the accounts also?

HJALMAR. Yes, keep track of what we take in, at any rate.

GINA. Oh, God help us, *that's* soon done.

HJALMAR. I wonder. It seems to me you make the money go a

remarkably long way. [*Halts and looks at her.*] How do you do it?

GINA. That's because Hedvig and I need so little.

HJALMAR. Is it true that Father is highly paid for the copying he does for Mr. Werle?

GINA. I don't know if it's all that high. I don't know what the rates are for things like that.

HJALMAR. Well, roughly what *does* he get? I want to know.

GINA. It differs. I guess it comes to about what he costs us, and a little pocket money.

HJALMAR. What he *costs* us! You never told me that before!

GINA. No, how could I. It made you so happy to think he got everything from you.

HJALMAR. And in fact it comes from Mr. Werle!

GINA. Oh, don't worry. He can afford it.

HJALMAR. Light me the lamp!

GINA [*lighting the lamp*]. Besides, how can we tell if it actually comes from him; it could easily be Gråberg . . .

HJALMAR. Why do you suddenly drag Gråberg into this?

GINA. Well, I don't know, I just thought . . .

HJALMAR. Hm!

GINA. Anyway, it wasn't me that got Grandpa the copying to do. You know yourself it was Berta, the time she took service there.

HJALMAR. It seems to me your voice is trembling.

GINA [*putting the shade on the lamp*]. Is it?

HJALMAR. And your hands are shaking. Aren't they?

GINA [*firmly*]. Say it straight out, Hjalmar. What's he gone and told you about me?

HJALMAR. Is it true—*can* it be true—that there was something between you and Mr. Werle while you were working in his house?

GINA. It's not true. Not then, there wasn't. He was after me all right, that I will say. And the Missus thought there was something going on, and she made such a fuss and a hullaballoo about it and went for me tooth and nail. She sure did. —So I quit.

HJALMAR. But then, afterwards . . .!

GINA. Well, *you* know, I went home. And my mother . . . she wasn't exactly as straight as you thought she was, Hjalmar. Anyway, she got after me about this, that, and the other. Because by that time Werle was a widower.

HJALMAR. All right! And then?

GINA. Well, I guess you might as well know it. He wouldn't give up till he had his way.

HJALMAR [*striking his hands together*]. And this is the mother of my child! How could you keep a thing like that from me!

GINA. Yes, I know it was wrong. I should've told you long ago, I guess.

HJALMAR. Right at the *start* you should have told me—then I'd have known the sort of woman you were.

GINA. But would you have married me, just the same?

HJALMAR. What do *you* think?

GINA. There you are, that's why I didn't dare tell you at the time. You know how much I'd come to care for you. So how could I go and make my own life a misery?

HJALMAR [*pacing about*]. And this is my Hedvig's mother! And to realize that everything I lay my eyes on . . . [*Kicks a chair*] . . . my entire home . . . I owe to a favored predecessor! Oh, that old lecher!

GINA. Do you regret the fourteen-fifteen years we've had together?

HJALMAR [*fronting her*]. Tell me, have you not—every day, every hour—regretted this web of deceit you've spun around me, like a spider? Answer me! Have you really gone around here and not suffered agonies of remorse and shame?

GINA. Bless you, Hjalmar, I've had enough to think about just running the house and everything . . .

HJALMAR. You mean you never even give a thought to your past?

GINA. No, God knows I'd just about forgotten that old business.

HJALMAR. Oh, this dull, apathetic calm! That's what I find so outrageous. Imagine—not even a twinge of remorse!

GINA. But just tell me, Hjalmar—what would've become of you, if you hadn't had a wife like me?

HJALMAR. Like you!

GINA. Well, you've got to admit I've always been kind of more practical and with my feet on the ground than you. Well, of course I *am* a couple of years older.

HJALMAR. What would have become of me!

GINA. Because you weren't exactly living right when you first met me; you can't deny that.

HJALMAR. Is that what you call not living right? Oh, what would you know about a man's feelings when he falls into grief and despair—especially a man of my fiery temperament.

GINA. All right, all right, have it your way. Anyhow, I don't want to make no song and dance about it. Because you certainly turned out to be a real good man, once you got your own home and family. And now we'd got things so nice and comfortable here, and Hedvig and me was just thinking that soon we could spend a little on ourselves in the way of food and clothes.

HJALMAR. In this swamp of deceit, yes.

GINA. Oh, why did that nasty creature have to come poking his nose in here for!

HJALMAR. I, too, thought our home a happy one. What a delusion! And now where am I to find the inner force I need in order to bring forth my invention? Perhaps it will die with me. And then it will have been your past, Gina, that killed it.

GINA [*about to weep*]. Please, Hjalmar, you mustn't say a thing like that. When all my days I only tried to make everything the best for you!

HJALMAR. I ask you—what happens now to the breadwinner's dream? As I would lie in there on the sofa, pondering the invention, I suspected full well that it would drain the last drop of my strength. Well I knew that the day I held the patent in my hands, that day would mark my—final hour. And so it was my dream that you would be left the well-to-do widow of the late inventor.

GINA [*drying her tears*]. Hjalmar, don't talk like that. God forbid I should ever live to see the day I'm left a widow!

HJALMAR. Oh well, what's the difference. It's all over now, anyway. All over!

[GREGERS WERLE *cautiously opens the hall door and looks in.*]

GREGERS. May I come in?

HJALMAR. Yes, sure.

GREGERS [*advances, his face radiant with joy, and reaches out his hands to them*]. Well, you two dear people . . . ! [*Looks from the one to the other and whispers to* HJALMAR.] You haven't done it yet?

HJALMAR [*aloud*]. It is done.

GREGERS. It is?

HJALMAR. I have lived through the bitterest hour of my life.

GREGERS. But also, I trust, the most sublime.

HJALMAR. Anyway, for the time being it's done and over with.

GINA. God forgive you, Mr. Werle.

GREGERS [*in great amazement*]. But I don't understand this.

HJALMAR. What don't you understand?

GREGERS. So great an accounting—an accounting that a whole new way of life is to be founded on—a way of life, a partnership in truth, free of all deception . . .

HJALMAR. Yes, yes, I know. I know all that.

GREGERS. I was absolutely confident that when I came through that door I would be met by a radiance of transfiguration shining from the faces of both husband and wife. And all I see is this dull, heavy, gloomy . . .

GINA. Is that it. [*Takes the shade off the lamp.*]

GREGERS. You're not trying to understand me, Mrs. Ekdal. Well, well, I suppose you'll need time . . . But *you*, now, Hjalmar? Surely *you* must feel exalted by this great reckoning.

HJALMAR. Yes, naturally I do. That is—in a kind of way.

GREGERS. For surely nothing in the world can compare to finding forgiveness in one's heart for one who has erred, and raising her up to you with love.

HJALMAR. Do you think a man so easily gets over the bitter cup I just drained?

GREGERS. No, not an ordinary man, perhaps. But a man like *you* . . . !

HJALMAR. All right, I know, I know. But don't push me, Gregers. It takes time.

GREGERS. There is much of the wild duck in you, Hjalmar.

[RELLING *has entered by the hall door.*]

RELLING. What's this? Are we back to the wild duck again?

HJALMAR. Yes. The damaged trophy of Mr. Werle's sport.

RELLING. Werle senior? Is it him you're talking about?

HJALMAR. Him and . . . the rest of us.

RELLING [*to* GREGERS, *under his breath*]. Damn you to hell!

HJALMAR. What's that you're saying?

RELLING. I was expressing the fervent wish that this quack here would take himself off where he belongs. If he stays around here much longer, he's quite capable of messing you both up.

GREGERS. These two are not going to be "messed up," Mr. Relling. I need not speak for Hjalmar. Him we know. But she too must surely have, deep down inside, something worthy of trust, something of integrity . . .

GINA [*on the point of tears*]. Then why couldn't you leave me be like I was.

RELLING [*to* GREGERS]. Would it be impertinent to ask what it is exactly you want in this house?

GREGERS. I want to lay the foundation for a true marriage.

RELLING. So you don't think the Ekdals' marriage is good enough as it is?

GREGERS. It's probably as good a marriage as most, I regret to say. But a true marriage it has yet to become.

HJALMAR. You never did have an eye for the claim of the ideal, Relling.

RELLING. Nonsense, my boy! —Begging your pardon, Mr. Werle, but how many—at a rough guess—how many true marriages have you seen in your life?

GREGERS. Hardly a single one.

RELLING. Neither have I.

GREGERS. But I *have* seen innumerable marriages of the opposite sort. And I have had occasion to observe at close quarters the havoc such a marriage can wreak on both partners.

HJALMAR. A man's whole moral foundation can crumble under his feet; that's the terrible thing.

RELLING. Well, of course I've never been exactly married myself, so I can't judge about that. But this I do know, that the child is part of a marriage too. And you had better leave the child in peace.

HJALMAR. Oh—Hedvig! My poor Hedvig!

RELLING. Yes, see to it you keep Hedvig out of this. You two are grown people. In God's name, go ahead and muck up your own affairs to your heart's content. But I'm warning you—go easy with Hedvig, or you may end by doing her serious injury.

HJALMAR. Injury!

RELLING. Yes, or else she might do herself one—and maybe not only to herself.

GINA. How can you tell a thing like that, Relling?

HJALMAR. There's no immediate danger to her eyes, is there?

RELLING. This has nothing to do with her eyes. But Hedvig is at a difficult age. There's no telling *what* wild ideas she can get into her head.

GINA. Say, that's right! Lately she's started to fool around in such a peculiar way with the stove out in the kitchen. "Playing house on fire," she calls it. Sometimes I'm scared she *will* burn down the house.

RELLING. There you are; I knew it.

GREGERS [*to* RELLING]. But how do you explain a thing like that?

RELLING [*sullenly*]. Puberty, man.

HJALMAR. As long as the child has me! As long as I'm above the ground . . . !

[*There is a knock on the door.*]

GINA. Shhh, Hjalmar, there's somebody outside. [*Calls.*] Come in!

[*Enter* MRS. SØRBY, *in outdoor clothes.*]

MRS. SØRBY. Good evening!

GINA [*going toward her*]. Why, Berta, it's *you*!

MRS. SØRBY. It certainly is. Do I come at an inconvenient time?

HJALMAR. Gracious, no—a messenger from that house . . .

MRS. SØRBY [*to* GINA]. To tell the truth I hoped I wouldn't find your menfolk at home this time of day. So I dropped in to have a little chat with you and say good-bye.

GINA. Oh? Why? Are you going away?

MRS. SØRBY. Yes, tomorrow early—up to Højdal. Mr. Werle left this afternoon. [*Casually, to* GREGERS.] He sends his regards.

GINA. Imagine!

HJALMAR. So Mr. Werle has left? And you're following him?

MRS. SØRBY. Yes, Ekdal, what do you say to that?

HJALMAR. I say—beware!

GREGERS. Let me explain. My father is marrying Mrs. Sørby.

HJALMAR. Marrying her!

GINA. Oh, Berta—finally!

RELLING [*his voice trembling slightly*]. Surely this can't be true?

MRS. SØRBY. Yes, my dear Relling, it's quite true.

RELLING. You are going to get married again?

MRS. SØRBY. It looks like it. Werle has got a special license, and we're going to have a quiet wedding up at the works.

GREGERS. Then I suppose I must wish you joy, like a good stepson.

MRS. SØRBY. Thank you, if you really mean it. I do hope it will lead to happiness for both Werle and myself.

RELLING. You have every reason for hope. Mr. Werle never gets drunk—at least not to my knowledge. And I doubt he's in the habit of beating his wives, either, like the late lamented horse-doctor.

MRS. SØRBY. Oh, come now, let Sørby rest in peace. He had his good points too.

RELLING. Mr. Werle has better ones, I'm sure.

MRS. SØRBY. At any rate he didn't go and throw away the best that was in him. The man who does that must take the consequences.

RELLING. Tonight I will go out with Molvik.

MRS. SØRBY. Don't do that, Relling. Don't—for my sake.

RELLING. Can't be helped. [*To* HJALMAR.] Come along too, if you like.

GINA. No, thanks. Hjalmar don't go on such disserpations.

HJALMAR [*angrily, in an undertone*]. Oh, be still!

RELLING. Good-bye, Mrs. —Werle. [*Exit through hall door.*]

GREGERS [*to* MRS. SØRBY]. It appears that you and Dr. Relling are rather intimately acquainted.

MRS. SØRBY. Yes, we've known each other a good many years. As a matter of fact, at one time something or other might even have come of it.

GREGERS. It was certainly lucky for you it didn't.

MRS. SØRBY. You may well say that. But I have always been careful not to act on impulse. After all, a woman can't afford to throw herself away.

GREGERS. Aren't you the least bit afraid I might drop a hint to my father about this old friendship?

MRS. SØRBY. You may be quite sure I told him myself.

GREGERS. Oh?

MRS. SØRBY. Your father knows every last thing that anyone could possibly say about me with any truth. I've told him everything of that kind. It was the first thing I did when I realized what he had in mind.

GREGERS. Then I'd say you are exceptionally frank.

MRS. SØRBY. I have always been frank. For us women it's the best policy.

HJALMAR. What do you say to that, Gina?

GINA. Oh, us women can't all be the same. Some's made one way and some another.

MRS. SØRBY. Well, Gina, I do think it's best to go about things as I did. And Werle hasn't kept back anything about himself, either. You know, that's mainly what brought us together. With me he can sit and talk as openly as a child. He never got a chance to do that before. Imagine, a healthy, vigorous man like him, listening all his youth and the best years of his life to nothing but hell-fire sermons. And many a time sermons about completely imaginary offenses—to judge by what I've heard.

GINA. That's God's truth, all right.

GREGERS. If you ladies are going to embark on that topic, you'll have to excuse me.

MRS. SØRBY. There's no need to go on that account. I won't say another word. But I wanted you to know that I haven't hushed up a thing or done anything underhanded. People may say I'm making quite a catch—and so I am, in a way. But still, I don't think I'm getting any more than I'm giving. I will never let him down. And I can look after him and help him as nobody else can, now that he'll soon be helpless.

HJALMAR. Soon be helpless?

GREGERS [*to* MRS. SØRBY]. All right, all right, don't talk about it here.

MRS. SØRBY. It's no use trying to hide it any more, much as he'd like to. He's going blind.

HJALMAR [*struck*]. Going blind? But how extraordinary. He too?

GINA. Well, lots of people do.

MRS. SØRBY. And you can imagine what that means for a business-man. Well, I'll try to use my eyes for him as best I can. But now I really must be going, I've got a thousand things to do. —Oh yes, Ekdal, I was to tell you that if there's anything at all Mr. Werle can do for you, just get in touch with Gråberg.

GREGERS. That offer you may be sure Hjalmar Ekdal will decline with thanks.

MRS. SØRBY. Really? I didn't have the impression in the past . . .

GINA. No, Berta, Hjalmar don't need anything more from Mr. Werle.

HJALMAR [*slowly and with emphasis*]. Will you pay my respects to your intended husband and tell him that in the very near future I propose to call on Gråberg . . .

GREGERS. What! You want to do *that*!

HJALMAR. . . . to call on Gråberg, I repeat, and demand an account of what I owe his employer. I will pay that debt of honor . . . Ha-ha-ha, "debt of honor," that's a good joke! But enough of that. I will pay it all, with five per cent interest.

GINA. But Hjalmar, dear, God knows we haven't got the money for that.

HJALMAR. Will you inform your intended that I am working inde-fatigably on my invention. Tell him that what sustains me in that exhausting labor is the wish to free myself from a painful burden of debt. This is my motive for the invention. The entire proceeds shall be used to release me from my pecuniary obliga-tions to your future spouse.

MRS. SØRBY. Something has happened in this house.

HJALMAR. Yes, so it has.

MRS. SØRBY. Well, good-bye then. I still had something I wanted to talk to you about, Gina, but it will have to wait for another time. Good-bye.

[HJALMAR *and* GREGERS *bow silently;* GINA *follows* MRS. SØRBY *to the door.*]

HJALMAR. Not a step beyond the threshold, Gina!

[MRS. SØRBY *leaves;* GINA *shuts the door after her.*]

HJALMAR. There, Gregers; now I've got that load of debt off my mind.

GREGERS. Soon, anyway.

HJALMAR. I believe my attitude may be called correct.

GREGERS. You are the man I always took you for.

HJALMAR. In certain cases it is impossible to disregard the claim of the ideal. As provider for my family, naturally I'm bound to writhe and groan. Believe me, it's no joke for a man without pri-vate means to pay off a debt of many years' standing—a debt over which, so to speak, the dust of oblivion had already settled. But never mind. My human dignity also demands its rights.

GREGERS [*laying his hand on his shoulder*]. Dear Hjalmar—wasn't it a good thing that I came?

HJALMAR. Yes.

GREGERS. Getting your whole situation clarified—wasn't that a good thing?

HJALMAR [*a bit impatiently*]. Yes, of course it was. But there's one thing that outrages my sense of justice.

GREGERS. And what is that?

HJALMAR. It's this, that . . . Well, I don't know if I ought to speak so freely about your father.

GREGERS. Don't hesitate in the least on *my* account.

HJALMAR. Well, then. Can't you see . . . I think it's absolutely outrageous, to realize it turns out that it's not I but *he* who will achieve the true marriage.

GREGERS. How can you say such a thing!

HJALMAR. Because it's so. Aren't your father and Mrs. Sørby entering upon a marriage built on full confidence, built on complete and unconditional frankness on both sides? They sweep nothing under the carpet, nothing is hushed up between them. There has been declared between them, if I may so put it, mutual forgiveness of sin.

GREGERS. All right, what about it?

HJALMAR. Well—then it's all *there*. You said yourself this was the difficulty in founding the true marriage.

GREGERS. But Hjalmar, that's entirely different. Surely you're not going to compare either yourself or her with those two . . . ? Oh, *you* know what I mean.

HJALMAR. All the same, I can't get over the fact that there's something in all this that offends my sense of justice. Why, it looks exactly as if there were no divine Providence in the world.

GINA. For God's sake, Hjalmar, don't talk like that.

GREGERS. Hm; let's not get involved in those questions.

HJALMAR. Though on the other hand, I think I'm beginning to make out the hand of fate after all. He *is* going blind.

GINA. Oh, maybe it's not so certain.

HJALMAR. There's no doubt about it. At least we *ought* not to doubt it, because precisely in that fact lies the proof of just retribution. He blinded the eyes of a trusting fellow being once.

GREGERS. Alas, he has blinded many.

HJALMAR. And now comes Nemesis, mysterious and inexorable, and demands the man's own eyes.

GINA. Don't say such awful things! It scares me.

HJALMAR. It profits a man to immerse himself, once in a while, in the dark side of existence.

[HEDVIG, *in her hat and coat, comes in through the hall door, happy and breathless.*]

GINA. Are you back already?

HEDVIG. Yes, I didn't feel like walking any more. It was lucky, too, because I just met somebody outside the house.

HJALMAR. That Mrs. Sørby, I suppose.

HEDVIG. Yes.

HJALMAR [*pacing the floor*]. I hope you have seen her for the last time.

[*Silence.* HEDVIG *looks timidly from one to the other as though trying to gauge their mood.*]

HEDVIG [*approaching* HJALMAR, *ingratiatingly*]. Daddy . . . ?

HJALMAR. Well—what is it, Hedvig?

HEDVIG. Mrs. Sørby brought something for me.

HJALMAR [*halts*]. For you?

HEDVIG. Yes. It's something for tomorrow.

GINA. Berta always brings some little thing for your birthday.

HJALMAR. What is it?

HEDVIG. No, you're not supposed to find out yet. Mother is to bring it to me in bed first thing in the morning.

HJALMAR. All these intrigues; all these secrets . . . !

HEDVIG [*hastily*]. Oh, you can see it if you want. It's a big letter. [*Takes the letter out of her coat pocket.*]

HJALMAR. A letter too?

HEDVIG. The letter is all there is. The other thing is coming later on, I guess. But imagine—a letter! I never got a letter before. And it says "Miss" on the outside. [*Reads*] "Miss Hedvig Ekdal." Imagine—that's me!

HJALMAR. Let me see that letter.

HEDVIG [*handing it to him*]. There, you see?

HJALMAR. It's Mr. Werle's handwriting.

GINA. Are you sure, Hjalmar?

HJALMAR. See for yourself.

GINA. What would *I* know about it?

HJALMAR. Hedvig, may I open the letter—and read it?

HEDVIG. Yes, of course you may, if you want to.

GINA. Not tonight, Hjalmar. You know it's meant for tomorrow.

HEDVIG [*in a low voice*]. Oh, why not let him read it! It's bound to be something nice, then he'll be glad and everything will be all right again.

HJALMAR. I may open it, then?

HEDVIG. Yes, please do, Father. It will be fun to find out what it is.

HJALMAR. Very well. [*Opens the letter, reads it, and appears bewildered.*] What *is* this . . . ?

GINA. Why, what does it say?

HEDVIG. Please, Father—tell us!

HJALMAR. Be quiet. [*Reads it through again. He has turned pale, but speaks with control*]. It's a bequest, Hedvig, a deed of gift.

HEDVIG. Really? What do I get?

HJALMAR. Read it yourself.

[HEDVIG *goes over to the lamp and reads.*]

HJALMAR [*in an undertone, clenching his fists*]. The eyes! The eyes—and now this letter!

HEDVIG [*interrupts her reading*]. Yes, but it looks to me like it's Grandfather who's getting it.

HJALMAR [*takes the letter from her*]. You, Gina—can you understand this?

GINA. I don't know the first thing about it. Why don't you just *tell* me?

HJALMAR. Mr. Werle writes to Hedvig that her old grandfather need not trouble himself any more about the copying but that from now on he can draw a hundred crowns every month from the office . . .

GREGERS. Aha!

HEDVIG. A hundred crowns, Mother! I read that part.

GINA. That will be nice for Grandpa.

HJALMAR. . . . one hundred crowns, for as long as he needs it—naturally that means till he passes on.

GINA. Well, that's him provided for, poor old soul.

HJALMAR. But then it comes. You didn't read far enough, Hedvig. Afterwards, the gift passes to you.

HEDVIG. To me? All of it?

HJALMAR. You are assured the same amount for the rest of your life, he writes. Do you hear that, Gina?

GINA. Yes, I hear.

HEDVIG. Imagine—all the money I'm going to get! [*Shaking him.*] Father, Father, aren't you glad?

HJALMAR [*disengages himself from her*]. Glad! [*Walking about.*] Oh, what vistas, what perspectives open up before me! It's Hedvig—*she's* the one he's providing for so amply!

GINA. Naturally. She's the one with the birthday . . .

HEDVIG. Oh, but you'll get it anyway, Father! Don't you know I'll give it all to you and Mother?

HJALMAR. To your mother, yes! There we have it.

GREGERS. Hjalmar, this is a trap that's being set for you.

HJALMAR. Another trap, you think?

GREGERS. When he was here this morning, he said: "Hjalmar Ekdal is not the man you think he is."

HJALMAR. Not the man . . . !

GREGERS. "Just wait, you'll see," he said.

HJALMAR. See that I would let myself be bought off with a bribe . . . !

HEDVIG. Mother, what *is* this all about?

GINA. Go and take off your things.

[HEDVIG, *about to cry, goes out by the kitchen door.*]

GREGERS. Yes, Hjalmar, now we shall see who is right—he or I.

HJALMAR [*slowly tears the letter in two and lays the pieces on the table*]. Here is my answer.

GREGERS. Just as I thought.

HJALMAR [*goes over to* GINA, *who is standing by the stove, and speaks in a low voice*]. Now, I want the whole truth. If everything was over between you and him when you—"got to care" for me, as you call it—why did he arrange things so we could afford to get married?

GINA. I guess he thought he'd be able to come and go here as he liked.

HJALMAR. Only that? Wasn't he afraid of a certain possibility?

GINA. I don't know what you mean.

HJALMAR. I want to know if—your child has the right to live under my roof.

GINA [*drawing herself up, her eyes flashing*]. You ask me that!

HJALMAR. I want a straight answer. Is Hedvig mine—or . . . Well?

GINA [*looks at him with cold defiance*]. I don't know.

HJALMAR [*quavering*]. You don't know!

GINA. How should I know? A woman like me . . .

HJALMAR [*quietly, turning away from her*]. Then I have nothing more to do in this house.

GREGERS. Think well what you're doing, Hjalmar!

HJALMAR [*putting on his overcoat*]. There's nothing to think about, for a man like me.

GREGERS. On the contrary, there's everything in the world to think about. You three must stay together if you are to win through to the sublime spirit of sacrifice and forgiveness.

HJALMAR. I don't *want* to! Never! Never! My hat! [*Takes his hat*]. My house lies in ruins about me. [*Bursts into tears*]. Gregers, I have no child!

HEDVIG [*who has opened the kitchen door*]. What are you saying! [*Up to him.*] Father! Father!

GINA. Now look what you did!

HJALMAR. Don't come near me, Hedvig. Get away from me. I can't bear to look at you. Oh, those eyes . . . ! Good-bye. [*He makes for the door.*]

HEDVIG [*clinging to him, cries out*]. No! No! Don't leave me!

GINA [*shouts*]. Look at the child, Hjalmar! Look at the child!

HJALMAR. I won't! I can't! I must get out—away from all this. [*He tears himself loose from* HEDVIG *and goes.*]

HEDVIG [*despair in her eyes*]. He's leaving us, Mother! He's leaving us! He'll never come back any more!

GINA. Don't you cry, Hedvig. Your father's coming back, you'll see.

HEDVIG [*throws herself sobbing on the sofa*]. No, no, he's never coming back to us again.

GREGERS. You do believe I meant it all for the best, Mrs. Ekdal?

GINA. Yes, I imagine you did. But God forgive you all the same.

HEDVIG [*on the sofa*]. Oh, I just want to die! What did I do to him! Mother, you've got to get him home again!

GINA. Yes, yes, yes. Just calm down and I'll go out and look for him. [*Putting on her coat.*] Maybe he's gone down to Relling. But you mustn't lie there bawling like that. Promise?

HEDVIG [*sobbing convulsively*]. All right, I'll stop. If only Father comes back.

GREGERS [*to* GINA, *who is about to leave*]. Wouldn't it perhaps be better if you first let him go through his ordeal?

GINA. Oh, he can do that after. First of all we have to get the child quieted down. [*Goes out by hall door.*]

HEDVIG [*sitting up, drying her tears*]. Now you've got to tell me what's the matter. Why doesn't my father want me any more?

GREGERS. You're not to ask that till you're all grown up.

HEDVIG [*with little catches in her breath*]. But I çan't go on feeling so awful all the time till I'm grown up. —I know what it is. Maybe I'm not really Father's child.

GREGERS [*uneasily*]. How could that be?

HEDVIG. Mother could have found me somewhere. And now maybe Father got to know about it. I've read about things like that.

GREGERS. Well, even in that case . . .

HEDVIG. You'd think he could care for me just the same. Even more, almost. After all, we got the wild duck as a present too, and look how much I love her.

GREGERS [*glad to change the subject*]. Yes, that's right, the wild duck. Let's talk a little about the wild duck, Hedvig.

HEDVIG. That poor wild duck. He can't stand the sight of her either, any more. Imagine, he wanted to wring her neck!

GREGERS. Oh, he wouldn't do that.

HEDVIG. No, but he *said* it. And I think it's an awful thing to say, because I pray for the wild duck every night, that she should be safe from death and everything bad.

GREGERS [*looking at her*]. Do you say your prayers every night?

HEDVIG. Oh yes.

GREGERS. Who taught you that?

HEDVIG. Myself. One time when Father was terribly sick and had leeches on his neck, and he said he was lying at death's door.

GREGERS. Really?

HEDVIG. So I prayed for him when I went to bed. And I've kept it up ever since.

GREGERS. And now you pray for the wild duck too?

HEDVIG. I thought I'd better include her, because she was so sick in the beginning.

GREGERS. Do you also say your prayers in the morning?

HEDVIG. Of course not.

GREGERS. Why *not* in the morning, as well?

HEDVIG. Why, it's light in the morning, so what's there to be afraid of.

GREGERS. And that wild duck you love so much, your father wanted to wring its neck . . .

HEDVIG. No, he said he *ought* to do it, but that he would spare her for my sake. That was nice of him.

GREGERS [*drawing closer to her*]. But supposing now that you of your own free will sacrificed the wild duck for *his* sake?

HEDVIG [*rising*]. The wild duck!

GREGERS. Supposing you were ready to sacrifice for him the most precious thing you have in the world?

HEDVIG. Do you think that would help?

GREGERS. Try it, Hedvig.

HEDVIG [*softly, with eyes shining*]. Yes—I will.

GREGERS. Have you will power enough for that, do you think?

HEDVIG. I'll ask Grandfather to shoot her for me.

GREGERS. Yes, do that. But not a word about this to your mother!

HEDVIG. Why not?

GREGERS. She doesn't understand us.

HEDVIG. The wild duck . . . ? I'll do it in the morning!

[GINA *enters by the hall door.*]

HEDVIG [*up to her*]. Did you find him, Mother?

GINA. No, but I heard he'd been down to Relling and gone out with him.

GREGERS. Are you sure?

GINA. Yes, the janitor's wife said so. Molvik went with them too, she said.

GREGERS. At a time like this, when his soul so desperately needs to struggle in solitude . . . !

GINA [*taking off her coat*]. Yes, men sure are something. God only knows where Relling dragged him off to. I ran across to Ma Eriksen's, but they're not there.

HEDVIG [*fighting back her tears*]. What if he never comes back!

GREGERS. He'll come back. I shall get word to him in the morning, and then you'll *see* how he comes back. You can count on that. Sleep well, Hedvig. Goodnight. [*Goes out by hall door.*]

HEDVIG [*throws her arms around* GINA's *neck, sobbing*]. Mother! Mother!

GINA [*patting her back, sighing*]. Ah, yes. Relling knew what he was talking about, all right. This is what you get when these here maniacs get after you with their "claim of the ordeal."

Act Five

HJALMAR EKDAL's *studio in the cold gray light of morning. There is wet snow on the big panes of the skylight.*

GINA, *aproned and carrying a broom and dust cloth, enters from the kitchen and goes toward the living room door. At the same moment,* HEDVIG *rushes in from the hall.*

GINA [*stops*]. Well?

HEDVIG. Yes, Mother, I think he is down at Relling's . . .

GINA. What did I tell you!

HEDVIG. . . . because the janitor's wife said she heard Relling bring home two others when he came back last night.

GINA. I thought as much.

HEDVIG. But what good does it do, if he won't came up to us.

GINA. Well, at least I can go down and talk to him.

[OLD EKDAL, *in dressing gown and slippers and smoking his pipe, appears at the door of his room.*]

EKDAL. Say, Hjalmar . . . Isn't Hjalmar home?

GINA. No, he's gone out.

EKDAL. So early? In this blizzard? All right, suit yourself, I can do the morning tour without you.

[*He slides the attic door open.* HEDVIG *helps him. He goes in, and she closes the door after him.*]

HEDVIG [*in a low voice*]. Mother, just think, when poor Grandfather finds out that Father wants to leave us.

GINA. Silly! Grandpa mustn't hear anything about it. What a godsend he wasn't home yesterday in all that hullaballoo.

HEDVIG. Yes, but . . .

[GREGERS *enters through the hall door.*]

GREGERS. Well? Any trace of him?

GINA. He's downstairs at Relling's, from what I hear.

GREGERS. At Relling's! Has he really been out with those two?

GINA. Looks like it.

GREGERS. How *could* he—just when he desperately needed to be alone and really pull himself together . . . !

GINA. You can say *that* again.

[RELLING *enters from the hall.*]

HEDVIG [*up to him.*] Is Father with you?

GINA [*at the same time*]. Is he there?

RELLING. Yes, he's there all right.

HEDVIG. And you never told us!

RELLING. I know, I'm a bea-east. But first I had to look after that other bea-east, the dæmonic one, I mean. And then I dropped off into such a heavy sleep that . . .

GINA. What's Hjalmar got to say today?

RELLING. Not a thing.

HEDVIG. Isn't he talking at all?

RELLING. Not a blessed word.

GREGERS. Ah, no. I understand that so well.

GINA. What's he doing with himself then?

RELLING. He's lying on the sofa, snoring.

GINA. Oh? Yes, Hjalmar snores something terrific.

HEDVIG. He's asleep? Can he sleep now?

RELLING. Looks damn well like it.

GREGERS. It's understandable, after the spiritual upheaval he's been through . . .

GINA. And him not used to gallivantin' nights, either.

HEDVIG. Maybe it's a good thing he's getting some sleep, Mother.

GINA. That's what I'm thinking too. But in that case we'd better not wake him up too soon. Thanks a lot, Relling. Well, first I'll get the house cleaned and straightened up, and then . . . Come and help me, Hedvig.

[GINA *and* HEDVIG *go into the living room.*]

GREGERS [*turns to* RELLING]. How would you describe the spiritual turmoil going on in Hjalmar Ekdal?

RELLING. I'm damned if I've noticed any spiritual turmoil in him.

GREGERS. What! At such a turning point, when his whole life has acquired a new foundation . . . ! How can you imagine that with a character like Hjalmar's . . . ?

RELLING. Character! *Him?* If he ever had a tendency to anything as abnormal as you mean by "character," I assure you it was cleared out of him root and branch while he was still a boy.

GREGERS. That would indeed be strange—considering the tender upbringing he enjoyed.

RELLING. By those two crackpot, hysterical maiden aunts of his, you mean?

GREGERS. Let me tell you, *there* were women who never lost sight of the claim of the ideal . . . all right, now I suppose you'll start being funny again.

RELLING. No, I'm not in the mood. Besides, I know what I'm talking about, he has certainly spouted enough rhetoric about those "twin soul-mothers" of his. Personally, I don't think he has much to thank them for. Ekdal's misfortune is that in his own little circle he has always been taken for a shining light . . .

GREGERS. And you don't think he is? Deep down inside, I mean.

RELLING. I never noticed anything of the kind. That his father thought so—that doesn't mean a thing. The old Lieutenant always *was* a bit simple.

GREGERS. He's always been a man with the innocence of a child. That's what you don't understand.

RELLING. All right, all right. But then when our dear sweet Hjalmar managed to get into the University—after a fashion—right away he became the light of the future for his fellow students too. Of course, he was good-looking, the rascal—pink and white—just the type the girls fall for. And as he had that easy sentimentality and that appealing something in his voice, and a pretty knack for declaiming other people's poetry and other people's ideas . . .

GREGERS [*indignantly*]. Is it Hjalmar Ekdal you're talking about like this?

RELLING. Yes, with your permission. For that's what he looks like inside, this idol you are groveling to.

GREGERS. I hardly think I'm as blind as all that.

RELLING. Well, you're not far from it. You see, you are a sick man, too.

GREGERS. There you are right.

RELLING. Yes indeed. Yours is a complicated case. First there's this pesky fever of integrity you suffer from. And then, what's even worse, you're forever going around in a delirium of adoration—forever butting in where you don't belong, looking for something to admire.

GREGERS. Well, I certainly won't find anything of the sort where I do belong.

RELLING. The trouble is, you're so shockingly mistaken about those fabulous beings you dream up around you. Here you are at it again, coming to a tenement with your claim of the ideal. Nobody in this house is solvent.

GREGERS. If that's all you think of Hjalmar Ekdal, how can you take pleasure in being everlastingly in his company?

RELLING. Good Lord, I'm supposed to be a doctor of sorts, though I'm ashamed to say it. The least I can do is look after the sick I live in the same house with.

GREGERS. Really! Is Hjalmar Ekdal sick too?

RELLING. Pretty nearly everybody is sick, I'm afraid.

GREGERS. And what treatment are you giving Hjalmar?

RELLING. The usual. I see to it that his life-lie is kept going.

GREGERS. Life—lie? Did I hear you right . . . ?

RELLING. That's right, I said life-lie. You see, the life-lie is the stimulating principle.

GREGERS. May I ask what life-lie you're injecting into Hjalmar?

RELLING. Sorry, I don't betray professional secrets to quacks. You'd be in a position to mess him up for me even worse than you have. But the method is tried and true. I've used it on Molvik as well. Him I made "dæmonic"—that's *his* shot in the arm.

GREGERS. Then he's *not* dæmonic?

RELLING. What the devil does it mean, to be dæmonic? It's just some nonsense I hit on to keep life in him. If I hadn't done that, the poor harmless slob would have succumbed to self-contempt and despair years ago. Same with the old Lieutenant. Though he managed to find his treatment by himself.

GREGERS. Lieutenant Ekdal? What about him?

RELLING. Well, what do *you* think? He, the great bear-hunter, stalking rabbits in that dark attic. And there's not a happier sportsman alive than that old man when he's playing around in there with all that rubbish. The four or five dried-up Christmas trees he saved up, to him they're the same as the whole great living Højdal forest. The rooster and chickens, why, they're wild fowl in the treetops; and the rabbits bumping around underfoot, they are bears he grapples with, the lusty old Nimrod.

GREGERS. Poor, unfortunate old Lieutenant Ekdal—yes. He has certainly had to renounce the ideals of his youth.

RELLING. While I think of it, Mr. Werle junior—don't use this fancy word "ideals." We have a perfectly good plain one: lies.

GREGERS. Are you trying to say the two things are related?

RELLING. Yes, about like typhus and typhoid fever.

GREGERS. Dr. Relling, I won't give up till I have rescued Hjalmar from your clutches!

RELLING. So much the worse for him. Take away the life-lie from the average person, and you take his happiness along with it. [*To* HEDVIG, *who enters from the living room.*] Well, little duck-mother, I'll go down and see if Papa is still lying there pondering on that remarkable invention. [*Goes out by the hall door.*]

GREGERS [*approaching* HEDVIG]. I can see by your look that it's not yet accomplished.

HEDVIG. What? Oh, about the wild duck. No.

GREGERS. Your courage failed you, I suppose, when it came to the point.

HEDVIG. No, it's not that. But when I woke up this morning and remembered what we had talked about, it seemed so queer.

GREGERS. Queer?

HEDVIG. Yes, I don't know . . . Last night, right when you said it, I thought there was something so lovely about the idea; but after I slept and it all came back to me again, it didn't seem like anything much.

GREGERS. Ah no, you could hardly be expected to grow up in this house without being the worse for it in some way.

HEDVIG. I don't care anything about that. If only my father would come back . . .

GREGERS. Ah, had your eyes but been opened to what really makes life worthwhile—had you the true, joyful, courageous spirit of sacrifice, then you would see how fast he'd come back to you. —But I still have faith in you, Hedvig. [*He goes out through hall door.*]

> [HEDVIG *wanders about the room. She is about to go into the kitchen, when there is a knocking from within the attic.* HEDVIG *goes and opens the door a little way.* OLD EKDAL *comes out; she pushes the door to again.*]

EKDAL. Hm, not much fun going for your morning walk by yourself.

HEDVIG. Wouldn't you like to go hunting, Grandfather?

EKDAL. It's not hunting weather today. So *dark*. You can hardly see in front of you.

HEDVIG. Don't you ever feel like shooting something besides rabbits?

EKDAL. Why, aren't the rabbits good enough, maybe?

HEDVIG. Yes, but how about the wild duck?

EKDAL. Ho, ho, so you're scared I'll go and shoot your wild duck? Never in the world, child. Never.

HEDVIG. No, I guess you couldn't. It's supposed to be very hard to shoot wild ducks.

EKDAL. Couldn't I? Should hope to say I could.

HEDVIG. How would you go about it, Grandfather? —I don't mean with *my* wild duck, but with some other one.

EKDAL. Would aim to get the shot in just below the breast, you know. That's the surest. And then you've got to shoot *against* the lie of the feathers, see, not *with*.

HEDVIG. Do they die then, Grandfather?

EKDAL. Damn right they die—if you shoot 'em properly. Well, got to go and spruce up. Hm . . . you know why . . . hm. [*Goes into his room.*]

> [HEDVIG *waits a moment, glances toward the living room door, goes to the bookcase, and, standing on tiptoe, takes the double-barreled pistol down off the shelf and looks at it.* GINA, *with broom and dust cloth, enters from the living room.* HEDVIG *hastily puts back the pistol, without* GINA *noticing.*]

GINA. Don't go fooling with your father's things, Hedvig.

HEDVIG [*moving away from the bookcase*]. I only wanted to straighten up a little.

GINA. Why don't you go in the kitchen and see if the coffee is still hot, I'm taking a tray down to him when I go.

> [HEDVIG *goes out.* GINA *begins to clear the studio. Presently the hall door is hesitantly opened, and* HJALMAR EKDAL *looks in. He has his overcoat on, but no hat. He looks unwashed and unkempt; his eyes are sleepy and dull.*]

GINA [*stops in the midst of sweeping and looks at him*]. Bless me, Hjalmar—are you back after all?

HJALMAR [*enters, answers in a dull voice*]. I come—only to depart at once.

GINA. Yes, yes, I imagine. But, gosh sakes! Don't you look a sight!

HJALMAR. A sight?

GINA. And just look at your good wintercoat! Well, that's had it.

HEDVIG [*at the kitchen door*]. Mother, do you want me . . . [*Sees* HJALMAR, *gives a shout of joy and runs toward him.*] Father! Father!

HJALMAR [*turns aside and waves her away*]. Go away! Go away! [*To* GINA.] Get her away from me, I tell you!

GINA [*in a low voice*]. Go in the living room, Hedvig.
[HEDVIG *goes in silently.*]

HJALMAR [*busy, pulling out the table drawer*]. I must have my books with me. Where are my books?

GINA. What books?

HJALMAR. My scientific works, naturally—the technical journals I use for my invention.

GINA [*looking in the bookcase*]. Is it these here that there's no covers on?

HJALMAR. Yes, of course.

GINA [*puts a pile of unbound volumes on the table*]. Shouldn't I get Hedvig to cut the pages for you?

HJALMAR. Nobody needs to cut pages for me.
[*Short silence.*]

GINA. So you've made up your mind to leave us, Hjalmar?

HJALMAR [*rummaging among the books*]. That goes without saying, I should think.

GINA. All right.

HJALMAR [*vehemently*]. You expect me to stay around here and have a knife twisted in my heart every minute of the day?

GINA. God forgive you for thinking I could be that bad.

HJALMAR. Prove to me . . . !

GINA. Seems to me *you're* the one that's got something to prove.

HJALMAR. With a past like yours? There are certain claims . . . I am tempted to call them claims of the ideal . . .

GINA. And what about Grandpa? What's to become of *him*, poor old thing?

HJALMAR. I know my duty. The helpless old man comes with me. I must go into town and make the necessary arrangements . . . Hm . . . [*Hesitantly.*] Has anybody found my hat on the stairs?

GINA. No. Did you lose your hat?

HJALMAR. Of course I had it on when I came back last night, there's no doubt about that. But now I can't find it.

GINA. Gosh sakes, wherever did you go with them two rowdies?

HJALMAR. Oh, don't bother me with trivialities. Do you think I'm in a mood to remember details?

GINA. I only hope you didn't catch a cold, Hjalmar. [*Goes into kitchen.*]

HJALMAR [*talking angrily to himself in a low voice as he empties the drawer*]. You're a scoundrel, Relling!—A villain is what you are! You rotten traitor! —If I could just get somebody to murder you!
[*He puts some old letters to one side, finds the torn gift*

document of the day before, picks it up and looks at the pieces. As GINA *enters, he quickly puts them down again.*]

GINA [*setting a laden coffee tray on the table*]. Here's a drop of something hot, in case you'd like it. And some cold cuts.

HJALMAR [*glances at the tray*]. Cold cuts? Never again, under this roof! True, I've taken no solid nourishment for nearly twenty-four hours, but never mind. —My notes! The beginning of my memoirs! Where have you put my diary and all my important papers? [*Opens the door to the living room, but draws back.*] There she is again!

GINA. For God's sake, Hjalmar, the child's got to be *some*place.

HJALMAR. Get out.

[*He stands back.* HEDVIG, *terrified, comes into the studio.*]

HJALMAR [*his hand on the door knob, to* GINA]. As I spend these last moments in what was once my home, I wish to be spared the presence of intruders . . . [*Goes into the living room.*]

HEDVIG [*darting towards her mother, asks in a low and trembling voice*]. Does he mean me?

GINA. Stay in the kitchen, Hedvig. Or no—better go to your own room. [*To* HJALMAR, *as she goes in to him.*] Wait a minute, Hjalmar, don't mess up the whole bureau. I know where everything is.

HEDVIG [*stands motionless for a moment, in terror and confusion, biting her lips to keep from crying. Then she clenches her hands convulsively and says softly*]. The wild duck!

[*She steals across and takes the pistol from the shelf, opens the attic door a little, slips in and pulls it shut after her.* HJALMAR *and* GINA *begin arguing in the living room.*]

HJALMAR [*appears with some notebooks and a pile of old sheets of paper, which he puts on the table*]. Oh, what good will the valise do! There are a thousand things I've got to drag along with me.

GINA [*follows with the valise*]. Well, leave the rest for the time being, just take a clean shirt and some underwear.

HJALMAR. Phew! All these exhausting preparations! [*Takes off his overcoat and throws it on the sofa.*]

GINA. Meantime your coffee's standing there getting cold.

HJALMAR. Hm. [*Without thinking, he takes a mouthful, and then another.*]

GINA [*dusting the backs of the chairs*]. Your worst job will be finding another attic big enough for the rabbits.

HJALMAR. What! Am I expected to drag along all those rabbits too?

GINA. Well, Grandpa can't do without his rabbits, you know that.

HJALMAR. He'll darn well have to get used to it. There are more important things in life than rabbits that I have to give up.

GINA [*dusting the bookcase*]. Should I put your flute in the bag for you?

HJALMAR. No. No flute for me. But give me the pistol.

GINA. You want to take that old gun with you?

HJALMAR. Yes. My loaded pistol.

GINA [*looking for it*]. It's gone. He must have taken it in with him.

HJALMAR. Is he in the attic?

GINA. Sure he's in the attic.

HJALMAR. Hm. Poor lonely old man. [*He eats an open-face sandwich, finishes his cup of coffee.*]

GINA. If only we hadn't rented out the room, you could've moved in there.

HJALMAR. And stay under the same roof as . . . ! Never! Never!

GINA. But couldn't you move into the living room for a day or two? There you could have everything all to yourself.

HJALMAR. Never, within these walls!

GINA. Well, how about moving in with Relling and Molvik, then?

HJALMAR. Don't mention their names to me! I get sick just thinking about them. Oh no, I must out into the storm and the snowdrifts—go from house to house seeking shelter for my father and myself.

GINA. But Hjalmar, you haven't got a hat! You lost your hat, remember?

HJALMAR. Oh, that despicable pair, those depraved villains! A hat must be procured. [*Takes another sandwich.*] Arrangements must be made. After all, I don't propose to catch my death of cold. [*Looks for something on the tray.*]

GINA. What are you looking for?

HJALMAR. Butter.

GINA. In a minute. [*Goes into the kitchen.*]

HJALMAR [*calls after her*]. Oh, don't bother. Dry bread is good enough for me.

GINA [*bringing a butter dish*]. Here you are. It's fresh churned, they told me.

[*She pours him another cup of coffee. He sits down on the sofa, spreads more butter on his bread, eats and drinks in silence for a while.*]

HJALMAR. Could I, without being interfered with by anyone—and I mean *anyone*—stay in the living room a day or two, do you suppose?

GINA. Sure you could, if you wanted.

HJALMAR. Because I don't see much likelihood of moving all of Father's things in such a rush.

GINA. And another thing, too. First you'll have to tell him you're not going to live with us others no more.

HJALMAR [*pushes his cup away*]. That too, yes. To have to go into all these complicated matters all over again . . . I must consider ways and means. I must have breathing space. I can't take on all these burdens in a single day.

GINA. No, and in such rotten weather, too.

HJALMAR [*moving Werle's letter*]. I see this paper is still lying around.

GINA. Yes, I didn't touch it.

HJALMAR. Not that that scrap of paper concerns me . . .

GINA. Well, *I* certainly don't intend to use it.

HJALMAR. . . . still, I don't suppose we should just let it get destroyed. In all the confusion while I'm moving out it could easily . . .

GINA. I'll take care of it, Hjalmar.

HJALMAR. After all, the letter belongs to Father in the first place; it's his business whether he wants to make use of it or not.

GINA [*sighing*]. Yes, poor old Father . . .

HJALMAR. Just to be on the safe side . . . Where will I find some paste?

GINA [*goes to the bookshelf*]. Here's the paste.

HJALMAR. And a brush?

GINA. The brush is here too. [*Brings him the things.*]

HJALMAR [*picks up a pair of scissors*]. Just a strip of paper along the back . . . [*Cutting and pasting.*] Far be it from me to lay hands on somebody else's property—least of all a penniless old man's. —Well, or on—the other person's, either . . . There we are. Let it stay there a while. And when it's dry—remove it. I don't wish to lay eyes on that document again. Ever!

[GREGERS WERLE *enters from the hall.*]

GREGERS [*a little surprised*]. What—you sitting here, Hjalmar?

HJALMAR [*gets up quickly*]. I sank down from sheer exhaustion.

GREGERS. I see you've had breakfast, though.

HJALMAR. The body, too, makes claims on us occasionally.

GREGERS. What have you decided to do?

HJALMAR. For a man like myself there is but one way open. I am in the process of gathering together my most important possessions. But you realize it takes time.

GINA [*a bit impatient*]. Well, do I get the room ready for you, or do I pack the bag?

HJALMAR [*after an irritated glance at* GREGERS]. Pack—and get the room ready.

GINA [*takes the valise*]. All right. I'll put in the shirt and the other things, then. [*Goes into the living room and shuts the door behind her.*]

GREGERS [*after a short pause*]. I never dreamed it would end like this. Is it really necessary for you to leave house and home?

HJALMAR [*paces restlessly up and down*]. What do you expect me to do?—I'm not made for unhappiness, Gregers. I must have things nice and secure and peaceful around me.

GREGERS. But *can't* you stay? Just try. To my mind you now have a firm foundation to build on—so start all over again. And remember, you have your invention to live for, besides.

HJALMAR. Oh, don't talk about the invention. It may be a long way off yet.

GREGERS. Really?

HJALMAR. For God's sake, what do you expect me to invent, anyway? They've already invented just about everything. It gets to be more difficult every day . . .

GREGERS. After all the work you've put into it . . . !

HJALMAR. It was that dissolute Relling who got me into it.

GREGERS. Relling?

HJALMAR. Yes, he was the one who first called attention to my talent for making some marvelous invention or other in photography.

GREGERS. Aha! . . . It was Relling!

HJALMAR. Oh, what deep satisfaction I got out of that thing. Not so much the invention itself, but because Hedvig believed in it—believed with all the faith and fervor of a child . . . that is, like a fool I went around imagining she believed in it.

GREGERS. Can you really think that Hedvig deceived you!

HJALMAR. I'm ready to think anything now. It's Hedvig that stands in the way. She'll end up shutting the sun out of my life forever.

GREGERS. Hedvig! You mean Hedvig? How could *she* do anything like that?

HJALMAR [*without answering*]. It's beyond words, how I loved that child. Beyond words, how happy I was every time I came home to my humble rooms and she would run to greet me, with her sweet blinking eyes. Oh, credulous fool that I was! I loved her so unutterably—and so I persuaded myself of the fiction that she loved me the same.

GREGERS. Are you saying it wasn't true?

HJALMAR. How can I tell? Gina I can't get a word out of. And anyway she has absolutely no conception of the principles involved in the situation. But I do feel the need to unburden myself to you, Gregers. It's this terrible doubt . . . Maybe Hedvig never really loved me at all.

GREGERS. You may yet have proof that she did. [*Listening.*] What's that? The wild duck's cry?

HJALMAR. She's quacking. Father's in there.

GREGERS. Is he! [*Joy lights up his face.*] I tell you, you may yet have proof that your poor misunderstood Hedvig loves you!

HJALMAR. Oh, what proof can she give me! I don't dare believe in any assurance from *that* quarter.

GREGERS. Surely Hedvig is incapable of deception.

HJALMAR. Oh, Gregers, that's just what isn't so certain. Who knows what Gina and that Mrs. Sørby have sat here whispering and tittle-tattling about? And nothing escapes Hedvig, believe me. It could even be that the birthday gift wasn't such a surprise. As a matter of fact, I thought I noticed something of the kind.

GREGERS. What on earth has got into you!

HJALMAR. My eyes have been opened. Just you watch—you'll see, the gift is only a beginning. Mrs. Sørby always did have a great liking for Hedvig, and now of course she's in a position to do whatever she wants for the child. They can take her away from me any time they like.

GREGERS. Hedvig would never leave you. Never.

HJALMAR. Don't be too sure. With them standing and beckoning to her with full hands? And I who have loved her so unutterably . . . ! I, whose greatest joy it would have been to take her gently by the hand and lead her, as one leads a child that's afraid of the dark through a great empty room! —I feel it now with painful certainty—the poor photographer in his attic apartment never really meant anything to her. She was just shrewd enough to play along with him till the time was ripe.

GREGERS. Hjalmar, you don't believe that yourself.

HJALMAR. The terrible thing is just that I don't know what to believe—that I can *never* know. But do you really doubt that I'm right? Hoho, my dear Gregers, you count too much on the claim of the ideal! Just let the others come with overflowing hands and call to the child: Leave him; life awaits you here with us . . .

GREGERS [*quickly*]. Yes, what then, do you think?

HJALMAR. If I asked her then: Hedvig, are you willing to turn your back on life for me? [*Laughs scornfully.*] Thanks a lot—you'd soon hear the answer I'd get!

[*A pistol shot is heard from within the attic.*]

GREGERS [*shouts with joy*]. Hjalmar!

HJALMAR. Damn! Now he has to go hunting into the bargain.

GINA [*entering*]. Ugh, Hjalmar, it sounds like the old man's banging away in there by himself.

HJALMAR. I'll go have a look . . .

GREGERS [*quickly, excitedly*]. Wait! Do you know what that was?

HJALMAR. Of course I know.

GREGERS. No, you don't. But *I* know. That was the proof!

HJALMAR. What proof?

GREGERS. It was a child's act of sacrifice. She's got your father to shoot the wild duck.

HJALMAR. Shoot the wild duck!

GINA. Imagine . . . !

HJALMAR. Whatever for?

GREGERS. She wanted to sacrifice to you the most precious thing she had in the world. Because then, she thought, you would be sure to love her again.

HJALMAR [*softly, with emotion*]. Oh, that child!

GINA. The things she'll think of!

GREGERS. All she wanted was to have your love again, Hjalmar. She felt she couldn't live without it.

GINA [*fighting back her tears*]. There you see, Hjalmar.

HJALMAR. Gina, where is she?

GINA [*sniffling*]. Poor little thing, sitting out in the kitchen, I guess.

HJALMAR [*crosses, and throws open the kitchen door*]. Hedvig— come! Come to me! [*Looks around.*] No, she's not in here.

GINA. Then she must be in her little room. (*Hjalmar walks out.*)

HJALMAR [*offstage*]. No, she's not here either. [*Re-enters the studio.*] She must have gone out.

GINA. Well, you wouldn't let her stay anyplace in the house.

HJALMAR. Oh, if only she'd come home soon—so I can tell her . . . Everything will be all right now, Gregers. Now I really believe we can start life over again.

GREGERS [*quietly*]. I knew it. Redemption would come through the child.

[OLD EKDAL *appears at the door of his room. He is in full uniform, and is busy trying to buckle on his saber.*]

HJALMAR [*astonished*]. Father! You *there*?

GINA. You were shooting in your *room*?

EKDAL [*approaches indignantly*]. So, now you go hunting without me, do you, Hjalmar?

HJALMAR [*tense, bewildered*]. You mean it wasn't you that fired the shot in the attic?

EKDAL. Me? Hm!

GREGERS [*calls out to* HJALMAR]. She has shot the wild duck herself!

HJALMAR. What *is* all this? [*Rushes to the attic door, tears it open, looks in, and screams.*] Hedvig!

GINA [*running to the door*]. My God, what is it?

HJALMAR [*going inside*]. She's lying on the floor!

GREGERS. Hedvig? On the floor? [*Follows* HJALMAR *in.*]

GINA. [*At the same time.*] Hedvig! [*Enters the attic.*] No! No! No!

EKDAL. Ho-ho, so *she's* taken to hunting too, now.

[HJALMAR, GINA, *and* GREGERS *carry* HEDVIG *into the studio. Her right hand hangs down, the fingers still gripping the pistol.*]

HJALMAR [*dazed*]. The pistol went off. She's been hit. Call for help! Help!

GINA [*runs out into the hall and shouts down*]. Relling! Relling! Dr. Relling, come up here quick!

[HJALMAR *and* GREGERS *lay* HEDVIG *down on the sofa.*]

EKDAL [*quietly*]. The forest's revenge.

HJALMAR [*on his knees beside* HEDVIG]. She'll come to, right away. She's coming to—yes, yes, yes.

GINA [*having returned*]. Where is she hit? I can't see a thing . . .

[RELLING *hurries in, followed closely by* MOLVIK. *The latter is without vest or collar, and his jacket is unbuttoned.*]

RELLING. What's going on here?

GINA. They say Hedvig shot herself.

HJALMAR. Come here and help!

RELLING. Shot herself! [*He pushes the table aside and starts to examine her.*]

HJALMAR [*still kneeling, looking anxiously up at him*]. Surely it can't be serious? What, Relling? She's hardly bleeding at all. Surely it can't be serious?

RELLING. How did this happen?

HJALMAR. Oh, how do I know . . .

GINA. She wanted to shoot the wild duck.

RELLING. The wild duck?

HJALMAR. The pistol must have gone off by itself.

RELLING. Hm. Indeed.

EKDAL. The forest's revenge. Still, I'm not afraid. [*Goes into the attic and shuts himself in.*]

HJALMAR. Well, Relling . . . why don't you *say* something?

RELLING. The bullet entered the chest.

HJALMAR. Yes, but she's coming to!

RELLING. Can't you see? Hedvig is dead.

GINA [*burst into tears*]. Oh, my baby! My baby!

GREGERS [*huskily*]. In the depths of the sea . . .

HJALMAR [*springing up*]. No, no, she's *got* to live! Oh dear God, Relling—just for a moment—just long enough so I can tell her how unutterably I loved her the whole time!

RELLING. The heart's been hit. Internal hemorrhage. She died instantly.

HJALMAR. And I drove her away from me like an animal! And in terror she crept into the attic and died for love of me. [*Sobbing.*] Never to be able to make up for it! Never to be able to tell her. . . ! [*Clenches his hands and cries to heaven.*] Oh, Thou above . . . ! If Thou *art* there! Why hast Thou done this thing to me . . .

GINA. Hush, hush, you mustn't carry on like this. I guess maybe we didn't have the right to keep her.

MOLVIK. The child is not dead. She but sleeps.

RELLING. Nonsense.

HJALMAR [*quiets down, goes over to the sofa, folds his arms, and looks at* HEDVIG]. There she lies, so stiff and still.

RELLING [*trying to free the pistol*]. It's so tight, so tight.

GINA. No, no, Relling, don't hurt her fingers. Leave the gun be.

HJALMAR. She shall take it with her.

GINA. Yes, let her. But the child's not going to lie out here for a show. She'll go into her own little room, that's what. Give me a hand, Hjalmar.

[HJALMAR *and* GINA *take* HEDVIG *between them.*]

HJALMAR [*as they carry her out*]. Oh, Gina, Gina, can you bear this!

GINA. We'll have to help each other. Now she's as much yours as mine.

MOLVIK [*stretching forth his arms and mumbling*]. Praised be the name of the Lord. Dust unto dust . . . dust unto dust . . .

RELLING [*whispers*]. Shut up, man! You're drunk.

[HJALMAR *and* GINA *carry the body out by the kitchen door.* RELLING *shuts it after them.* MOLVIK *slinks out into the hall.*]

RELLING [*crosses to* GREGERS]. No one will ever persuade me that this was an accident.

GREGERS [*who has stood horror-stricken, twitching convulsively*]. Who can say how this terrible thing happened.

RELLING. There were powder burns on her dress. She must have pressed the muzzle right against her chest and fired.

GREGERS. Hedvig has not died in vain. Did you see how this sorrow brought out all the nobility in him?

RELLING. Most people become noble when they stand in the presence of death. But how long do you think this glory of his will last?

GREGERS. Surely it will last and flourish for the rest of his life!

RELLING. Before the year is out little Hedvig will be nothing more to him than a theme for pretty declamations.

GREGERS. You dare say that about Hjalmar Ekdal!

RELLING. We'll talk about it again when the first grass has withered on her grave. *Then* listen to the vomit about "the child untimely torn from its father's breast," *then* watch him wallow in sentimentality and self-admiration and self-pity. Just you wait!

GREGERS. If *you* are right, and *I* am wrong, then life's not worth living.

RELLING. Oh, life wouldn't be too bad if it weren't for these blessed bill collectors who come pestering us poor folk with their claims of the ideal.

GREGERS [*staring into space*]. In that case, I'm glad my destiny is what it is.

RELLING. And may I ask—what *is* your destiny?

GREGERS [*on the point of leaving*]. To be the thirteenth man at table.

RELLING. The devil it is.

A Note on the Translation

To capture the cadence and nuances of the dialogue, the translator of a play naturally listens only to the original, avoiding the distraction of other voices. But when I had done my work, I looked over some of the many fine translations which have appeared since I first read *The Wild Duck* in English, to discover that the great need to supplant the Archer translation had already been met. Yet I hope that this new version will serve the American reader and particularly the actor, for I have aimed not only to preserve the living speech rhythms of the dialogue but have ordered the phrasing so as to set important points where they will strike the ear without deliberate stressing. Later in this volume (pp. 208–215) I shall consider the dialogue in relation to various characters in the play; here I shall account for specific minor deviations from Ibsen's text.

The boldest of these was to alter Hjalmar's well-known line to Hedvig about the menu card which he brings home from Werle's dinner party (Act II); but the information that "menu" means bill of fare is not only gratuitous, it side-steps a question that *is* apt to occur to us today. I myself wondered whether Ibsen was not overdoing the ostentatiousness of the Werle party—at least three extra waiters, a printed menu for a dinner originally planned for twelve—before confirming the historical accuracy of such display in Norway during the 1880's, and so I have Hjalmar comment on the fact that the menu was especially printed for the occasion.

"By a lucky chance the attic is so situated that nobody can hear us shoot," Ibsen has Hjalmar explain to Gregers, to account for such goings-on in a city dwelling. The size of the unfinished attic and the many chimneys in it, as well as the janitor's wife referred to on three occasions, establish the fact that the Ekdal home is on the top floor of an apartment building, not a private home. Relling and Molvik, who live on the floor below, are not the Ekdals' lodgers, as they are repeatedly called in summaries of the play. When Gina mentions the extra room across the hall that they can let and Gregers says, "Well, well—so you've got roomers besides," Hjalmar replies, "No, not yet." And if the room were one of several, Hjalmar would hardly say, later in Act II, "That's why it's such a good thing we got the room rented; it puts me in a more independent position. And independent is one thing a man with a mission in life has got to be." I have therefore translated Relling's line to Gregers about coming again to a poor man's house with the claim of the ideal (Act V) as "coming to a tenement with your claim of the ideal"; I have also taken the liberty of calling the workmen's cottages at Højdal "shacks," since to Americans the word "cottage," far from conveying the idea of poverty, might suggest quaintness and charm.

To distinguish Gina's old position in the Werle home from Mrs.

Sørby's, I have Gregers refer to her as "our former maid," although *hus-jomfru* (literally "housemaid") is given in dictionaries as "housekeeper." But Mrs. Sørby is listed in the dramatis personæ as *husbestyrerinde*, "house manager," which means something quite different in English.

The anachronism "neurotic" (according to NED, the term first appeared in two medical texts in 1887) I admitted after much hesitation, but to translate *overspændt* literally as "overstrained" would sacrifice not only clarity to authenticity but force as well. Werle uses the term about his dead wife (Act I), so that Gregers' line later in the scene, "I am not neurotic," is a retort to a rankling accusation: whatever his mother may have been, *he* is not neurotic. And it would hardly do justice to the curtain line of Act I to have Werle fling anything less than "neurotic" as an insult after him.

It may interest the reader to know that when Hjalmar says to Gregers in Act III, "And there are no swamp vapors here, as you put it," Gregers has not "put it" this way in the original *(sumpluft)* either. This is the sort of slip that could happen in conversation, and I have let it stand. But it must be admitted that Ibsen does occasionally anticipate himself, or contrive, or insist, to such a degree that one is tempted to edit as one translates.

In view of Relling's derision of Gregers' idealism, and especially after his hilarious report of Hjalmar sleeping off the night's dissipation (Act V), it seems so forced to introduce the life-lie theme by making Gregers ask Rell-ing, "Can you explain to me the spiritual turmoil that is now going on in Hjalmar Ekdal?" that I have toned this down to, "How would you describe the spiritual turmoil going on in Hjalmar Ekdal?" A more radical change concerns Relling's metaphor for the life-lie, (the injection of) a vital stimulant. Gregers' view that it is, rather, a poison or infection may account for his line, "May I ask what sort of life-lie Hjalmar is infected with?" But surely Ibsen is confusing the image when, in Relling's reply, he has him say about his treatment of Molvik, "Him I've made 'dæmonic.' That's the fontanelle I've had to apply to *his* neck." This "fontanelle" (an artificial ulcer for the discharge of pus) on the neck I have, in conformity with Relling's "stimulating principle," rendered "shot in the arm"; and to specify Relling's active role in the treatment I have altered Gregers' question to, "May I ask what life-lie you're injecting into Hjalmar?"

Curiously, Ibsen nodded when, in the final version of the play, he forgot that he had eliminated the lines in the first draft of Act I about Hedvig being Hjalmar's only child. When Gregers arrives at the Ekdals' he under-standably assumes that Hedvig is the daughter of the house, but his first questions about her presuppose facts he cannot possibly know: "So *that's* your daughter?" (underline in fair copy, page 66; no italics in print), "And of course she is an only child?" As it is, only the break between the two acts preserves the illusion of probability, for whereas in the first draft of Act II Gregers merely proposes to spend the night at a hotel, in the finished play, during the time consumed by the domestic scene on Hjalmar's return from the dinner party, Gregers breaks with his father, changes his clothes, and actually moves to a hotel. It would have been out of character under any circumstances for him to inquire of Petter-sen or Mrs. Sørby about Hjalmar's family; in this rush, it is out of the question. I have therefore changed his lines about Hedvig to "Your daughter, I take it?" and "Your only child?"

Apparently other translators felt no more qualms than I about correcting such curious failures in taste as these: when the dead Hedvig is carried in from the attic (Act V), the stage directions actually call for Gina and Gregers to drag her on stage; and when Gina stops Relling from trying to free the pistol from Hedvig's hand she says, "No, no, Relling, don't break her fingers."

Finally, the credit for the one gem in this translation belongs to Professor Reinert, whose ingenuity in finding equivalents for Gina's verbal blunders is truly phenomenal. In one instance he improves on Ibsen. At the close of Act IV, summing up the dangers of the claim of the ideal, Gina says in the original: "This is what happens when crazy people come and present the intricate demand." According to Shaw's report on a London performance of the play, "this quintessence of the whole comedy—'that's what comes when crazy people go about making the claims of the what-d'yer-call-it'—went home right up to the hilt in our midriffs," which seems to mean, in the context of the right laughs in the right places, that it brought the house down. Since the Reinert version of the line made me roar with laughter without benefit of performance or audience response, I have borrowed "the claim of the ordeal," planting the word "ordeal" for Gina in Gregers' earlier speech to her about Hjalmar fighting his bitter fight by making it, "Wouldn't it perhaps be better if you first let him go through his ordeal?"

The introduction of current colloquialisms and slang into the translation undoubtedly reduces its life-span, but surely that is a lesser evil than to attenuate the life of the play itself. I have tried to reproduce not only the varying degrees of formality in the characters' dialogue but also the difference in tone of each one's address to every other character—one of the delights of *The Wild Duck*.

The Writing of the Play

The Manuscript†

Dates of Composition

Work on The Wild Duck fell into three clearly defined stages: fifteen months or so of desultory, preliminary planning from the winter of 1882–3 onwards until April 1884; eight weeks of active drafting in dialogue form in the period mid-April to 13 June; and eleven weeks of revision in the period 15 June to 30 August 1884.

The first probable reference to the play was in a letter of 11 Jan. 1883 to his publisher Frederik Hegel, in which Ibsen mentioned work on a new play to be in four acts and dealing with contemporary life; in another letter two days later, he made reference to a possible visit to Sweden in the summer if he managed to complete the new drama he was busy working on; on 21 February, in another letter to Hegel, he referred again to the 'new work' he was pondering. The likelihood is that the first set of rough notes (A1 below) having clear reference to The Wild Duck dates from about this time.

Throughout the summer of 1883 and the following winter there were occasional references to the new drama. On 4 June 1883 he wrote to Hegel that he hoped to find the peace and quiet necessary for his new play in Gossensass in the Tyrol; he stayed there from 25 June to late October 1883, reporting on 5 September to Hegel that his new play would not be ready before winter; he returned to Rome, after a short stay on the way at Bolzano, on about 1 November 1883. The next five months were unproductive: on 22 January he confessed in a letter to Laura Grundtvig that it caused him extreme displeasure to have to sit and work at his desk; and on 30 March 1884 he complained that his attention had recently been taken up, more than he wished, by what was happening in Norway; nevertheless he was occupied 'in thinking about a new dramatic work'. The rest of the preliminary notes (A2–9 below) belong no doubt in part to this time, but also overlap on to the time when he was drafting Act I in dialogue form.

One of the preliminary notes (A5) and also the beginning of Act I of the first draft (B1) are dated 20 April 1884; and on 21 April he

† From The Oxford Ibsen, Volume VI, translated and edited by James Walter McFarlane (New York: Oxford University Press, 1960), pp. 428–29, 430–36, 243–88. Copyright © by Oxford University Press, 1960. Reprinted by permission of the publishers.

wrote to Hegel that, although the political events in Norway during the winter had upset him and prevented him from working on his new play, he was now hard at it; he estimated that the draft of the play would be complete and ready for its final revision about mid-June. The first draft has Act I dated 20–28 April and the beginning of Act II 2 May. This version was abruptly broken off and a new draft begun, the manuscript of which is dated: end of Act II 24 May, Act III 25–30 May, Act IV 2–8 June, Act V 9–13 June. On 14 June he reported to Hegel that the play was complete in draft form; he promised to begin the final revision the following day in the hope of having it ready for the printer about mid-September.

The final revision was begun in Rome; then on 30 June he left for Gossensass, where the rest of the revision was undertaken. His letters from Gossensass to his wife and son, who were holidaying in Norway, allow the progress of the revision to be dated with considerable accuracy: Act II was finished 12 July, Act III written 14–30 July, Act IV finished 17 August and the play finally completed on 30 August 1884. This final stage entailed a complete overhauling of the dialogue, what Ibsen in a letter to Georg Brandes on 25 June 1884 defined as 'the finer formulation of the language and the more energetic individualization of the characters and dialogue'. He was happily occupied; to his son Sigurd he wrote on 9 August that he found the work extremely congenial, and that the play occupied his thoughts all the time even when he was not at his desk; and on 27 August he confessed: 'It is a great joy for me to be working on this play which keeps on growing in its detail: I will feel the miss of it when I have to let it go: but at the same time I shall of course be glad.' On 2 September the manuscript was sent off to Copenhagen; it was published on 11 November 1884 in an edition of 8,000, and it had a new printing on 1 December 1884.

Notes and Jottings

Nine separate sets of notes relevant to The Wild Duck have survived, of varying length, and dating from probably early 1883, before the drama had begun to take proper shape, to about April 1884, when Ibsen was actively working on the first draft of Act I. Of these A1–5 are on the same kind of paper watermarked 'Imperial Treasury de la Rue'; but it is not at all certain that all the sides of any one folded sheet were always written on one and the same occasion; A6 and 7 also share the same kind of paper, the former being a folded sheet octavo, the latter a single leaf, being the torn half of such a folded sheet; they are also both in pencil, and the character of the rapid handwriting is the same on each. A8 and 9 also share the same kind of paper, the former being written in a pencilled hand similar to that of A6 and 7; A9 is more carefully written in ink.

In addition there is one fragmentary and one fuller draft of the play, the latter containing many interleaved emendations.

A1. Written on four sides of a folded sheet octavo, probably in early 1883, possibly as early as December 1882. Some of the ideas mentioned here are echoed in Ibsen's correspondence: e.g. sheep in a community of wolves, letter of 23 March 1884; Holger Drachmann's volte-face, letters of 27 Dec. 1883 and 17 Jan. 1884; an echo also of his views on the 'new nobility' in his Trondheim speech of 1885 and in Rosmersholm. For a note on 'E.L.' and 'A.K.' see A4 below; 'A. the printer' is no doubt a reference to the figure of Aslaksen, who appears in The League of Youth and An Enemy of the People.

'Free-born men' is cant. They do not exist. Marriage, the relationship between man and woman, has ruined the human race, set the brand of slavery on everybody.

E.L. has come to the conclusion that no improvement is possible by emancipation. The work of creation has been a failure from the start. He is a half-baked pessimist, without any initiative, a futile dreamer.

Patriotism and such things are but passing phases.

Scientists should not be allowed to torture animals to death; let doctors experiment on journalists and politicians.

Modern society is not a society of people; it is merely a society of males.

When liberal-minded men want to bring about some improvement in the position of women in society, they first inquire whether public opinion—men—will approve. It is the same as asking wolves whether they favour new measures for the protection of sheep.

Many a doctrinaire agitator has gradually gone over to become his own grandfather (Drachmann, for example).

E.L.'s marrying beneath him has in one way become a 'true marriage' in that during his married life he has sunk down or in any case has not grown. Now he cannot dispense with his wife—With her, things have gone likewise.

He has to spend the evening with some distinguished people; but he finds it tiring and a strain. He returns to his narrow home surroundings.

Rather like A. the printer, he has had a glimpse of a higher world; that is his misfortune.

In becoming civilized, man undergoes the same change as when a child grows up. Instinct weakens, but powers of logical thought are developed. Adults have lost the ability to play with dolls.

'The sixth sense.' E.L.'s favourite thought is of hypnotic influence.

We make fun of Germany's 34 fatherlands; but having just as many in Europe is equally ludicrous. North America manages with one or—for the moment—with two.

His refined nature will not allow him to confess openly that he does not believe in patriotism and things like that.

The pity is that our best thoughts are thought by our worst scoundrels.

E.L., the photographer, the unsuccessful poet, dreams of a socialist revolution, the revolution of the future, of science. Poison in the breakfast. . . .

A.K., the sybarite, enjoys an aesthetic indignation at poverty and misery. He enjoys his visits to his one-time school friend, now starving, without being conscious of the real reason.

To wish and to will. Our worst faults are the consequences of confusing the two things.

What drivel! They maintain the right of the majority, and yet those with the vote represent only a small arbitrarily limited minority.

All existing things, art, poetry, etc., break down into new categories as does the mind of the child in the spirit of the adult.

Liberty consists of giving the individual the right to liberate himself, each according to his personal needs.

Introduce the episode of the mortally sick person. Use Deininger as a model.

Women artists and business women try to conceal their sex. On their pictures, their nameplates, etc., they put only the initial of their first name so that people will think they are men—e.g. M.Sm., E.Zogb., etc.

E.L. is socialist-minded; but he dare not confess it; he has a family, and is therefore not independent.

Those among us having the vote are in a minority. Is then the minority right?

Conscience is not a stable thing. It varies in different individuals and with time. That of the country folk is old-fashioned, obsolescent. It is between obsolescent and developing consciences that party battles are fought.

A new nobility will take shape. It will not be one of birth or of money, nor of ability or knowledge. The nobility of the future will be a nobility of mind and will.

Christianity in various ways demoralizes and hinders both men and women.

They say suicide is immoral. But what of a life of slow suicide—out of regard for one's surroundings?

A.K.-d: to be well-fed, tucked up in a soft bed, and listening to the pouring rain and thinking about difficult journeys in bad weather and cold—that is a great delight.

A2. *Written on four sides of a folded sheet, octavo:*

Characters

(a) *first side*
The old dismissed official.
> White haired, broken in spirit by his prison sentence. Earns a little by clerical work.

His vain wife.
> Half crazy as a result of the family's misfortunes. Herself partly to blame without realizing it. Stupid idolatry of son. Moaning and complaining.

The son with the wasted talents.
> Feeling of piety towards his parents holds him, the family shame oppresses him.

The son's wife.
> Slightly older than him; practical gifts, prosaic, from simple home.

The rich old ship-owner and merchant.
> An old roué in secret.

His son, the rich social writer.
> Widower; fights for the rights of the poor; regards it as a sport.

(b) *second and third sides*
The host: Yes, my dear Chamberlain, what have you to say about the Liebfraumilch? Chamb. Yes indeed, I must say it was faultless. 2nd Chamb. Huh, I suppose it cost you a pretty penny? Eh? The host: You can take your oath on that. It's one of the very very best vintages, I can tell you. Gregers. Is there any sort of difference among the vintages. The host: Well, you are a fine one! It's not much good putting good wine in front of you. 2nd Cham. It's the same with hock as it is with . . . with photographs, Mr. . . . , it's a matter of sunlight. Or am I wrong? Gregers. No indeed, the light certainly has something to do with it. . . . H.L. The past few years haven't been particularly good for the production of chamberlains. 1st Chamb. No, the weather's been a bit cloudy as you might say; not enough sunshine.—Gregers. So it is a bit with chamberlains as it is with different sorts of wine. 2nd Chamb. How do you mean, my dear sir? Gregers. Not all the vintages are equally good. The

host: Just listen to *him*, gentlemen! Graaberg (from the office) I beg your pardon, but there's somebody here who wants to be out. The host: Don't worry. (Here comes the episode with the old man. Hired servant. Don't forget the cognac, Pettersen. Embarrassed pause. 2nd Chamb. makes sarcastic remarks. Gregers is offended⟨ ⟩⟩ Al.K. That isn't very nice of you. Chamb. But I ⟨'but' *crossed out*⟩ assure you; I didn't mean the slightest thing by that. Mrs. M (with cigarette) No, the chamberlain is very good at heart. But, heavens, all of us have to work for a living. (N.B. this topic has been mentioned before by the host to Gregers.)

H.L. 'the capon' goes and 'enjoys' all the 'little girls' he is on familiar terms with.

In Act I, the merchant finishes by abusing the photographer after they have drunk too much. Halfdan leaves. At home he gives nothing away, he gives a different account of the events at the party, has been the centre of attraction, etc.—The next day the more noble-minded ones visit him—His mother is in the asylum. She went mad as a result of the family misfortunes. Possibility that the son also, etc.

Old Ekdahl keeps pigeons and other birds. Passion for hunting. . . . He has an old gun. . . . Hedvig—decision. . . .

Mrs. S. Slip him something outside, something good. P. Certainly (goes).

Mrs. S. Well, did he get anything? P. Yes, I slipped him a bottle of cognac. Mrs. S. Oh, you might have found something a bit better than that. P. No, Mrs. S., cognac is the best thing he knows.

(c) *fourth page discusses the character of A.K.* (eventually Gregers Werle, see note A4 below)

Al.K. has no objection to his father marrying Mrs. M. First because that would be better than possible scandals with the servant girls, and also because when his father marries, he must make a settlement on his son.

A.K. would not mind marrying Mrs. M. himself, but in that case his father would presumably not marry, and not make any settlement either, and 'it is not good for capital to stay too long in the hands of old people. 400,000 kroner in the hands of a man of 34 is more productive than a million in the hands of a man in his sixties⟨'⟩.

Nor would the chamberlain have any objection to marrying Mrs. M. But his income is not adequate, so—

A3. One folded sheet, octavo; the first side has a list of characters, with an indication of the age of some; on the fourth side, some notes and draft dialogue, probably written down on some later occasion, perhaps whilst drafting Act I.

(a) *first side*

The Characters

63   Walle, merchant, factory owner, etc.

35   ⟨*originally* 37⟩ Halfdan Walle, his son

67   Ekdahl, former bailiff
     ⟨'Mrs. Ekdahl' *crossed out*⟩, his wife

37   ⟨*originally* 35⟩ Gregers Ekdahl, their son, photographer
     ⟨'Hedvig, his wife' *crossed out*⟩

39   Gina, his wife

14   Hedvig, their eldest daughter, 14-15 years
     ⟨'Their three' *crossed out*⟩ younger children

35   Mrs. Berta ⟨*originally* Lövstad⟩ Sörby, the merchant's house-
     keeper
     Nanne, a teacher
     Flor, a chamberlain (the one with the anecdotes)
     Rasmussen, a chamberlain (satirical)
     Sæther, a chamberlain (gallant, stupid)
     Graaberg, the merchant's chief clerk
     Pettersen, the merchant's personal servant
     Flasrud, his driver
     Guests, hired servants, etc.
     (The action takes place in Kristiania)

(b) *fourth side*

Comparison with wild ducks: when they are wounded——, they go to the bottom, the stubborn devils, and bite on fast——; but if you have a good dog, and it is in shallow water⟨?⟩, then——Hedvig like the wild duck.——Gregers's knowledge of children's first and deepest sorrows. They are not cares about love; no, they are family sorrows—painful home circumstances—

Gregers: But is Molvik's religious preaching any good? 'The Doctor' Well, it isn't up to much, you know. But it can always serve quite well for the poor and people like that.

Hedvig's description of what it was like the first time she saw a big expanse of water looking down from a height.

People are sea-creatures—like the wild duck—not land creatures— Gregers was made for the sea. All people will in time live on it when the dry land is inundated. Then family life will stop.

A4. *One folded sheet, octavo, written on the first side only:*

Models

Edvard Larsen/Alexander Kjelland/Mrs. Colban/Rektor Steen/ Miss Riis/Hartvig Lassen/Chamberlain Gran/Chamberlain Christenssen / Assessor Saxlund / Professor Lochmann / Udvig / Midling / Ross, the painter.

⟨Edvard Larsen, (i.e. Edward Larssen), a poetaster and photographer who took the first known photograph of Ibsen. Alexander Kielland (1849-1906), Norwegian novelist, with a highly articulate (but, perhaps in Ibsen's view, not altogether genuinely felt) sense of social indignation; Ibsen was never personally acquainted with him. Rector Steen (1827-1906), leading left-wing politician, was later Prime Minister 1898-1902. Hartvig Lassen (1824-97) literary critic and historian, was attached to Kristiania Theatre from 1873. Miss Riis, Mrs. Colban and C. M. Ross belong to Ibsen's circle of acquaintances in Rome. F. Lochmann was a professor of medicine whom Ibsen met in Uppsala in 1877 when both received honorary degrees. Udvig had probably been a fellow student of Ibsen's.⟩

A5. *Written on the first and part of the second side of a folded sheet, octavo; dated 20 April 1884:*
In the house of the rich old factory owner. Elegant and comfortable smoking-room; upholstered sofas and easy chairs; lighted lamps and candelabra. At the rear, a large open door with curtains drawn back. Within can be seen the billiard-room, similarly lit up. Right, front, in the smoking-room is the door leading into the office; left beyond the fireplace is a double door leading to the dining-room. Loud conversation of many guests is heard within; somebody taps a knife on a glass; silence follows; a toast is proposed; shouts of 'hurrah' and 'bravo'; again the noise and buzz of conversation.

A couple of liveried servants and two or three hired servants in black are putting the smoking-room and billiard-room in order.

A hired servant comes with the old 'former' . . . from the right in the billiard-room.—Hired servant (to house servant): Pettersen, there's a man here, who——P. Lord, are you here at this time? The fmr. I have to get into the office. P. Oh, but it was shut over an hour ago. The fmr. Yes, I saw that, but——(looks towards the door on the right) P. Yes, you can come through here; because Graaberg is still sitting in there. The fmr. Thanks (moves to go in). The other servant. Here, you, give me a hand with this table. The fmr. Who, me? Oh, yes, the table (helps). The servant. Thanks. The fmr. Perhaps I can go in now. P. Yes, just go in. (He goes in to the right.)

A6. *Written in pencil on four sides of a folded sheet, octavo; same kind of paper as A7. Ink entry at head of first side:* 'Act I/In the house of Walle, the merchant' *crossed out.*

(a) *first side*
The danger of undermining the ideals. The irony of fate in belong-

ing to another generation. Hedvig's drawings are not her own creations; the moment she realizes this, she does not draw any more. All happiness is past once she discovers that her father's suspicions of her admiration are roused, fights, evasions, observations, etc.

———

There is always one ideal left remaining——Gregers, who denies all the others, believes in 'friendship'——Hjalmar sees through the egoistic reasons.

———

Hjalmar is also admired in the family because he supports his father; but this he doesn't do!

(b) second side
Every family runs 'to the end of the line' in one generation, and in it in a certain individual. The Werle family has reached its peak: the old merchant. The son represents something new. ⟨'The same is the case' *crossed out.*⟩ The case is different with Hedvig—

———

Hjalmar was regarded by his parents as being very handsome; believes it himself; is not.

———

Act I finishes with Gregers reproaching the members present concerning Hjalmar, whereupon he breaks with his father.

———

Act II finishes like this: It is the family that has ruined him!

(c) third side
GREGERS. Do you think I have invented all this? Oh no, I have given up inventing things. But it exists out there, concealed—— Patriotism is dead——etc.——

(d) fourth side
The doctor is lying. (Dahl), it is a lie—well, then let us let this bird go—Theologian (Schibsted) I—Sch—Mr. Sch—Mr. Sch the graduate——etc.

———

In Gregers there remains one element of superstition. At dinner there are 13 at table.

———

In Act I Hjalmar tells a highly romantic story of how his mother went mad with grief because his future had been ruined, and that his father committed his crimes out of love for his son. Gregers becomes attentive;—later another explanation, prosaic but true.

A7. *Written rapidly in pencil on one side of a loose sheet, the torn half of a folded sheet similar to A6.*

E.L.
    Yes, but let us just look at all this business about ideals. Do
    you believe in religion?
    No
E.L. In morals—no( ) Science (no)——
E.L. Well—but you believe in patriotism, don't you? In good old
    Norway?
    Yes, of course.

A8. *Written on the first side of a folded sheet, small octavo, in
rapid pencilled handwriting similar in character to that in A6 and
7.*

The complication of what is inherited and what is habitual

——

Hedvig's attraction to the sea

——

her shyness

——

the need to keep her in on account of her weak eyes

A9. *Carefully written in ink on the first side of a folded sheet,
small octavo, same sort of paper as A8.*

Act I

Introduction by means of the servants; Old Ekdal. The merchant
Werle and Mrs. Sörby; the merchant and Gregers (?). Gregers
and Hjalmar. The guests; Old Ekdal. Gregers and Werle.

Act II

Gina and Hedvig: Old Ekdal. The former and Hjalmar. Old Ekdal
and the former. Gina, Hedvig, Hjalmar and Gregers; conversation
about how things are at Werle's house. The former and Old Ekdal;
conversation about the old days up at the works, then about the
wild duck. Gregers rents the room.

Selections from the Drafts

First Draft of *The Wild Duck*

Act I is dated *20.4.84–28.4.84. The setting is a smoking-room
(i.e. not a study) beyond which can be glimpsed a billiard room (i.e.
not a sitting-room); otherwise the disposition of the room and its
furniture is not greatly dissimilar from the final text.*
    *The opening moments of the Act, until the point where the guests
emerge from the dining-room, differ slightly from the final text*

at a few points: (a) there is no reference to the party as being given in Gregers's honour; (b) Pettersen abruptly asks Ekdahl [sic] to give a hand with moving a table; (c) Ekdahl is described here as 'white-haired' and is reported to have earlier been 'an attorney' (i.e. not a lieutenant); and (d) there is no reference to the dirty trick he is supposed to have played on Werle. The draft continues:

> [*A couple of servants open the dining-room doors from within. The whole party comes out gradually.* WALLE *Senior first, with* MRS. SÖRBY ⟨*originally 'an elderly lady'*⟩ *on his arm. He takes her through the billiard room to the adjoining room on the right; groups of gentlemen, both young and old, follow and stand about the billiard room and smoking-room.* Chamberlains FLOR, KASPERSEN *and* SÆTHER *come out conversing with* GREGERS WALLE. HALFDAN EKDAHL *comes last.*]

FLOR. Whew! What a dinner! Took a bit of getting through!

KASPERSEN. Oh, if you put your mind to it, it's incredible what you can manage in three hours. What do you say, Mr. Sæther?

SÆTHER. Where there's a will there's a way, he-he!

FLOR. That's all right if you've got a stomach like yours, Mr. Kaspersen.

KASPERSEN [*stroking* FLOR'*s waistcoat*]. I fancy your own should take a fair amount.

FLOR. Ah, if it could only digest all it can take, then . . .

GREGERS WALLE. There are remedies for everything, Mr. Flor; why else do you suppose a wise Providence made mineral waters?

KASPERSEN. Tut, tut, now you're being all Parisian again.

GREGERS WALLE. It's difficult to get out of the habit, I'm afraid. I have just returned from Paris.

WALLE [*returns* ⟨'*with* MRS. SÖRBY' *added later*⟩]. What is that you are so engrossed in, Ekdahl?

HALFDAN. It is just an album, Mr. Walle.

WALLE. Well now, photographs. That's right up your street.

KASPERSEN. Have you brought any of your own with you? Any you've done yourself? Eh?

HALFDAN. No, I haven't.

WALLE. You should have done, then you could have contributed to the entertainment, you see.

MRS. SÖRBY. Everybody has to work for his supper in this house, Mr. Ekdahl.

EKDAHL ⟨*error for* WALLE⟩. Ha, ha, ha! That's very true.

FLOR. And *that*, where the food is good, is sheer pleasure.

MRS. SÖRBY. Mr. Flor does his work for the ladies until the sweat pours off him.

FLOR. For the lady, Mrs. Sörby; the lady of the house.

MRS. SÖRBY. Well that's easy today. And Mr. Kaspersen . . . now what does he do?

FLOR. He produces jokes . . .

MRS. SÖRBY. Did you say *re*-produces. . . .

KASPERSEN [*laughs*]. Now you're getting rather naughty.

FLOR. I did say produces right enough, but . . .

KASPERSEN. Good heavens, you can only use the talents you've got.

MRS. SÖRBY. But of course! That's why Mr. Sæther is always willing to turn over the music.

SÆTHER. Ha, ha!

GREGERS [*quietly*]. You must join in, Hjalmar.

HJALMAR EKDAHL [*shrugs his shoulders*]. What do you expect me to say?

WALBERG ⟨*i.e.* WALLE/WERLE⟩. Throw your cigarette-end away and help yourself to a proper cigar.

KASPERSEN. Well now, has Mrs. Sörby been properly smoked-in?

MRS. SÖRBY [*lighting a cigarette*]. I'll attend to that myself.

SÆTHER. Well, just look at that.

FLOR. Remarkably fine Tokay.

VALBERG ⟨*i.e.* WALLE/WERLE⟩. You're right there. But it's cost a pretty penny; it's one of the finest vintages, don't you know.

HJALMAR EKDAL ⟨*sic*⟩. Does the vintage make any difference?

VALBERG. By heavens, that's good. There's obviously not much point in putting good wine in front of *you*.

KASPERSEN. It's the same with Tokay as with photographs, Mr. Ekdahl. There has to be sunlight, or am I wrong?

HJALMAR EKDAHL. No, indeed. Light certainly plays a part.

MRS. SÖRBY. Well then it's exactly the same with you court officials. You have to have a place in the sun as well.

KASPERSEN. Come, come, that joke's a bit ancient.

FLOR. Mrs. Sörby is reproducing.

MRS. SÖRBY. That's as may be. But it's a fact that vintages vary tremendously.

KASPERSEN. But you surely rank me with the fine vintages, Mrs. Sörby?

MRS. SÖRBY. I'm sure you're the same vintage, all three of you.

VALBERG. Ha, ha, ha! There's one in the eye for you. Drink up and have another, gentlemen. In such swinishly cold weather ⟨*originally the speech ended here*⟩. A good drink, a warm comfortable home . . . or so I believe it to be, at least. Look no further than your own four walls for true well-being.

[*The guests touch glasses and drink.*]

GRAABERG [*at the baize door*]. Excuse me, sir, but I can't get out.

WALLE. What, you locked in again?

GRAABERG. Yes, and Flaksrud's gone off with the keys.

WALLE. Well, you had better come through this way.

GRAABERG. But there's somebody else as well. . . .

WALLE. Come on, come on, both of you. Don't be shy.

[GRAABERG *and* OLD EKDAHL *come out through the baize door.*]

WERLE [*involuntarily*]. Ah!

[*The laughter and chatter of the guests stop abruptly.* HJALMAR *starts up at the sight of his father and turns away.* GRAABERG *and* OLD EKDAHL *go out through the billiard room.* ⟨'*Off to the right*' *added later.*⟩]

WERLE [*mumbling*]. Damn that Graaberg!

GREGERS. Surely that was never . . .

SÆTHER. What was that? Who was it?

GREGERS. Oh, nobody.

SÆTHER [*to* HJALMAR]. Did *you* know the man?

HJALMAR. I don't know . . . I didn't notice. . . .

SÆTHER. Coming in past locked doors? I must find out about this.
[*Goes over to the others.*]

MRS. SÖRBY [*whispers to the servant*]. Slip him something outside,
something really good.

PETTERSEN. Certainly.
[*Goes out*]

GREGERS [*softly*]. Then it really *was* him!

HJALMAR. Yes it was.

GREGERS. And you denied him!

HJALMAR. How could I . . . ?

GREGERS. I'm very much afraid you've grown up a coward,
Hjalmar.

HJALMAR. Oh, if you were in my shoes, then . . .
[*The conversation among the guests which has been conducted in low voices, now changes over to forced
conviviality.*]

KASPERSEN [*approaching* HJALMAR *and* GREGERS *in friendly
fashion*]. Ah! Here you are standing reviving old memories.
Won't you have a light for your cigar, Mr. Ekdahl? [*Reaching
him a candle.*] Here.

HJALMAR. Thank you, but I won't smoke now.

FLOR. Haven't you some poem or other to read to us, Mr. Ekdahl?
There was a time once when you wrote such charming poems.

HJALMAR. No, I have none here.

FLOR. All well at home? Your children—you have children . . . ?

HJALMAR. I have a daughter.

FLOR. And what does she do?

HJALMAR. Hedvig draws.

FLOR. Indeed. She has inherited the artistic temperament, then.

SÆTHER [*joining them*]. No, it wasn't past locked doors. He came
on legitimate business.

KASPERSEN [*amiably turns him round*]. My dear Sæther, you're
talking nonsense.
[*Leads him away.*]

FLOR. God knows what *he's* chattering about.
[*Goes away.*]

HJALMAR [*whispers*]. I'll go now, Gregers. Say goodbye to your
father for me.

GREGERS. Yes, of course. Are you going straight home?

HJALMAR. Yes, why?

GREGERS. Nothing . . . just that I'll look in and see you later.

HJALMAR. No, don't do that. Not my home. We can always meet
somewhere in town.

MRS. SÖRBY. Are you leaving, Ekdahl?

HJALMAR. Yes.

MRS. SÖRBY. Give my regards to Gina.

HJALMAR. Thank you.

[*He tries to steal out as unobtrusively as possible, to the right.*]

MRS. SÖRBY [*softly, to* PETTERSEN]. Well, did the old fellow get anything?

PETTERSEN. Yes, I slipped him a bottle of brandy.

MRS. SÖRBY. Oh, you might have found him something a bit better than that.

PETTERSEN. Not at all Mrs. Sörby. Brandy is the best thing he knows.

FLOR [*in the doorway of the billiard room, with a sheet of music in his hand*]. Shall we play something for you, Mrs. Sörby?

MRS. SÖRBY. Yes indeed, let's do that.

GUESTS. Bravo! Bravo!

[*They all go out right, through the billiard room. During what follows, a piano can be faintly heard.*]

GREGERS. Just a moment, Father.

WERLE. What is it?

GREGERS. I want a word with you.

WERLE. Can't it wait until the others have gone?

GREGERS. No, it can't. It may turn out that I shall leave before the others.

WERLE. Leave? You want to leave? What do you mean by *that*?

GREGERS. How could people here let that family go to the dogs like that?

WERLE. Do you mean the Ekdahls?

GREGERS. Yes, I mean the Ekdahls. Old Ekdahl was such a close friend of yours once. And in any case there was one occasion in his life when he was very useful to you.

WERLE. Oh, you're thinking of that old business of the court case. That account was settled long ago. You can rest assured he got proper recompense.

GREGERS. Let that pass. But since then, Father. Everything else. . . .

WERLE. I don't know what you mean by 'else.' There isn't anything else! Not one word did he address to me while there was still time. He didn't know himself what a mess he was in until it all came to light, and then of course it was too late.

GREGERS. It's not that either I was talking about. It's since, afterwards. . . .

WERLE. Yes afterwards. When he came out, he was a broken man. You can take my word for it, Gregers, I have done everything in my power to help him. I've put him on doing copying for the office and I've paid him far, far more for his work than it's worth. You smile at that? Perhaps you think I'm not telling you the truth? I admit there's nothing in my books to account for it, I never enter expenses of that kind. . . .

GREGERS [*smiles*]. No, there are some expenses better not accounted for.

⟨Then not greatly dissimilar from the final version—except that

⟨instead of Werle being unable to remember the details of Hjalmar's wedding 'after all these years', he says here: 'It must be about eighteen or nineteen years ago,' to which Gregers replies: 'It is now about seventeen years ago'—until:⟩

WERLE. You surely never intend to go raking up old rumours and gossip. I honestly think that at your age, you might find something a bit more useful to do.

GREGERS. We two have always had divided opinions on what was useful.

WERLE. Both on what was useful and on everything else. Gregers, I don't think there's any man in this world you hate as much as me.

GREGERS [*whispering*]. I've seen you at far too close quarters.

WERLE. The truth is, you've seen me with your mother's eyes.

GREGERS. And you have never been able to forgive me for taking after my mother . . . and for feeling sorry for her.

WERLE. Listen now, Gregers. There are a lot of things where we don't exactly hit it off, but all the same, we are father and son. I think we should be able to reach some sort of understanding between us. On the surface at any rate.

GREGERS. In the eyes of the world, as they say. Is that what you mean?

WERLE. Yes, if you like to put it that way. Think it over, Gregers. Don't you think something like that might be done? Eh?

GREGERS [*looking at him coldly*]. Now you obviously want to make use of me for something.

WERLE. When two people are as closely connected as we are, one always has some use for the other, Gregers.

GREGERS. Yes. That's what they say.

WERLE. When I wrote to you to come home, I'll not deny I had something extra in mind.

GREGERS. Hm!

WERLE. Yes, because our affairs generally, the settlement of your mother's legacy and all the rest, could have been dealt with by letter, of course. But now that—unfortunately—it is no longer necessary for you to live down there . . .

GREGERS. Well?

WERLE. I should like to have you home for a while. I am a lonely man, Gregers. I've always felt lonely, all my life, but especially now I'm getting on a bit in years. I need somebody near me.

⟨Then not greatly dissimilar from the final version until:⟩

GREGERS. When has there ever been any family life here? But now there's a sudden need for something of that kind. Yes, indeed that's quite clear. Think of the good impression it must create when it is rumoured how the son hurried home—on wings of devotion—to his aged father's wedding feast. So there is a perfectly happy relationship between the two of them then, after

all! Yes of course. Father and son—in heaven's name, could it be
otherwise! It's the natural order.

WERLE. Yes, it ought to be the natural order, Gregers.

GREGERS. I don't care a jot for either nature or her order.

WERLE. Listen here. I admit there's a great deal to find fault with
in my way of life—[*With raised voice.*] but there are some
things I insist on having respected in my house.

GREGERS [*bows slightly*]. So I have observed. And so I take my hat
and go.

WERLE. Go . . .? Leave the house?

GREGERS. Yes. There is only one thing in this world for which I
have any respect.

WERLE. And what may that be?

GREGERS. You would laugh if you knew.

WERLE. Laughter doesn't come so easily to a lonely man, Gregers.

GREGERS [*points towards the billiard room*]. Look, Father, your
guests are playing Blind Man's Buff with Mrs. Sörby. Good night
and goodbye.

　　　　　　　　　　[*He goes out to the right*]

WERLE [*smiling scornfully after him*]. Huh . . . ! And he says he's
not neurotic.

⟨*The beginning of Act I is dated 2.5.84. The setting is largely as
in the final version, except that there is only one door on the right
wall (the main entrance) instead of two as ultimately; otherwise
the arrangement of fixtures and furniture is roughly the same. Mrs.
Ekdahl sits sewing at the table, Hedvig sits on the sofa, drawing.
The scene opens:*⟩

MRS. EKDAHL. How much did you pay for the butter today?

HEDVIG. It was 45 öre.

MRS. EKDAHL. And then there's the beer as well. You see . . .
straight off there's more than one crown.

HEDVIG. Yes, but Father got four crowns fifty for the photographs.

MRS. EKDAHL. Was it all that much?

HEDVIG. Yes, it was exactly four crowns fifty.

　　　　　　　　　　　[*Silence.*]

MRS. EKDAHL. Hm . . . wouldn't I like to know how your father's
getting on at the party.

HEDVIG. Yes, wouldn't it be fun if we could see him?

　　　　[OLD EKDAHL *comes in through the door right* ⟨*originally
left*⟩ *with a paper parcel under his arm.*]

HEDVIG. You're very late home today, Grandfather.

EKDAHL. Graaberg held me up, he always makes such a fuss about
things, that man.

MRS. EKDAHL. Did you get any more copying to bring home,
Father?

EKDAHL. Yes, all this lot.

MRS. EKDAHL. That was nice.

EKDAHL [*sets his umbrella down*]. There's enough to keep me going for a long time here, Gina. [*Draws one of the sliding doors in the rear wall, a little to one side*]. Hush! [*Peeps into the dark room; closes the door*]. He! He! They're all sitting sleeping nicely together. [*Goes towards the furthest door on the left.*] Will I find some matches in here?

MRS. EKDAHL. The matches are on the chest of drawers.

[EKDAHL *goes in.*]

HEDVIG. It was jolly good, Grandfather getting all that copying to do.

MRS. EKDAHL. Yes, poor old soul; he can earn himself a few coppers.

HEDVIG. And besides, he'll not be able to sit all morning down at that horrid Ma Eriksen's place.

MRS. EKDAHL. Yes, that's another thing. I wonder though—I don't really know—but I sometimes wonder if men aren't nicer when they've had a drink. . . .

HEDVIG. Ugh, no! They may be nicer; but it's so uncertain. . . .

MRS. EKDAHL. How do you mean, uncertain?

HEDVIG. I mean it's uncertain for other people. You're never quite sure how you have them.

MRS. EKDAHL [*looks at her*]. When have you noticed *that*?

HEDVIG. Oh, you can always see it. Molstad and Riser are often tipsy, both of them.

MRS. EKDAHL. It was those two you meant then?

[OLD EKDAL ⟨*sic*⟩ *comes in again and makes for the door front, left.*]

MRS. EKDAHL [*half turning on her chair*]. Do you want something in the kitchen, Father?

EKDAHL. Yes, I do. But don't get up.

[*Goes out.*]

MRS. EKDAHL. I hope he isn't messing about with the fire in there! Just go and see what he's up to, Hedvig.

[EKDAHL *comes in again with a little jug of steaming water.*]

HEDVIG. Have you been getting some hot water, Grandfather?

EKDAHL. Yes, I have. I want it for something. I've got some writing to do and the ink's gone all thick like porridge.

MRS. EKDAHL. But you mustn't sit up late and ruin your eyes, Father.

EKDAHL. I haven't time to worry about eyes, Gina. I'm busy I tell you. I don't want anybody coming into my room.

[*Goes into his room.*]

⟨*Then not greatly dissimilar from the final version—except that there is no reference by Hjalmar to the fact of Gregers having monopolized him at the dinner, nor Gina's question as to whether Gregers was still as nasty as ever—until:*⟩

EKDAHL. No, no! You don't catch Hjalmar as easily as that, not him!

HJALMAR. I don't see why *I* should be expected to be the one to provide the entertainment when I happen to have an evening out. I gave them to understand that, too. Yes, I even found myself having to put a couple of the gentlemen firmly in their places.

MRS. EKDAHL. No . . . did you really!

EKDAHL. Some of the Court officials?

HJALMAR. Yes, it was indeed. We were having an argument about Tokay. . . .

EKDAHL. To be sure, it's a good wine.

HJALMAR. But, you know the different vintages are not equally good; it all depends on how much sunshine the grapes have had. . . .

MRS. EKDAHL. Why, Hjalmar, the things you know!

EKDAHL. And that's what they started arguing with you about?

HJALMAR. They tried it on, but they were given to understand ⟨originally 'I *let them know*'⟩ that it was exactly the same with Court officials. Not all *their* vintages were equally good either, I said.

MRS. EKDAHL. Really, the things you think of!

EKDAHL. And you said that to them. . . .

HJALMAR. Straight to their faces.

EKDAHL. There you are, Gina, he let them have it straight to their faces.

MRS. EKDAHL. Well, fancy! Straight to their faces.

HJALMAR [posing by the pedestal]. Yes, I stood so, you see— leaning against the fireplace and I played with my right glove, and then I told them.

EKDAHL. Straight to their faces.

HEDVIG. What fun it is to see Daddy in evening dress. You look so nice in evening dress, Daddy.

HJALMAR. Yes, I do don't I? And it's almost as if it had been made for me. A little tight under the arms perhaps—[*Takes the coat off.*] But I'll have my jacket on now—[*Does so.*] it feels more homely. [*To* GINA.] Don't forget to let Molvik have the coat back first thing in the morning.

MRS. EKDAHL. We'll see to that all right.

HJALMAR [*sits down on the sofa*]. Ah, there's nothing as comfortable as a corner of your own sofa, with your feet under your own table. . . .

MRS. EKDAHL. And with a glass of beer to have with your pipe. . . .

HJALMAR. Have we some beer in?

MRS. EKDAHL. Yes, we haven't forgotten it.
[*Goes out into the kitchen.*]

HEDVIG. Here's your pipe and tobacco. . . .

HJALMAR. Thanks. I've really been longing for my pipe. Werle's cigars are all right, but there's nothing to beat a good pipe in the long run.

MRS. EKDAHL [*comes in from the kitchen with beer bottles and glasses*]. Here, now you can quench your thirst.

HJALMAR. Splendid. Come along now, Father, we'll have a glass of beer together.

EKDAHL. Hm, I think I'll just fill my pipe first.
[*Goes into his room.*]
MRS. EKDAHL [*smiles*]. He wants to fill his pipe.
HJALMAR. I know, I know, leave him alone, poor old Father.
[*There is a knock on the door to the right.*]
MRS. EKDAHL. Hush, wasn't that a knock at the door? Who can it be?
[*Goes and opens the door.*]
GREGERS [*in the passage*]. Excuse me, doesn't Ekdahl the photographer live here?
MRS. EKDAHL. Yes, he does.
HJALMAR [*gets up*]. Gregers! Is that you after all? Come along in.
GREGERS [*comes in*]. I told you I'd be looking in, didn't I?
HJALMAR. But tonight . . . ? Have you left the party?
GREGERS. Both the party and the house. Good evening, Mrs. Ekdahl. Do you remember me from the old days? Do you recognize me again?
MRS. EKDAHL. Oh yes, of course.
HJALMAR. You say you've left the house . . .?
GREGERS. Yes, I'll stay in a hotel tonight and tomorrow I'll find myself some lodgings. You have a couple of rooms to rent, haven't you, Hjalmar?
HJALMAR. Yes, we have, but . . .
MRS. EKDAHL. But it really wouldn't be suitable for you, Mr. Werle.
GREGERS. Don't worry about that, I'm sure I'll like it and I think we should be able to agree about the rent.
HJALMAR. Well, that was a stroke of luck for us. . . . Now that you're here, won't you sit down?
GREGERS. Thanks. You live like real artists here.
HJALMAR. As you see, it's the studio. . . .
MRS. EKDAHL. But there's more room here, so we prefer to be in here.
⟨*This draft breaks off abruptly at this point, undated.*⟩

Second Draft of *The Wild Duck*

Act I is undated; the 'fat,' 'balding' and 'near-sighted' guests of the final version are here variously Chamberlains Flor and Kaspersen; there is no exchange of remarks between Werle père and Gregers about there having been thirteen at table and the opening of the immediately following conversation between Gregers and Hjalmar is rather less circumstantial; otherwise Act I in this draft is not greatly dissimilar from the final version.

Act II, the end of which is dated 24.5.84, still has a setting which lacks the second (i.e. living-room) door in the right wall. From the beginning of this Act until the conversation given below the development is not greatly dissimilar from the final version, except that the following details and exchanges are different or lacking: (a) the 'eye-strain' motif is still attached to Old Ekdal [sic] (see

p. 97 in the first draft) and not yet to Hedvig; (b) the whole of the conversation between Hedvig and Hjalmar about the latter's wavy hair and the menu is lacking; (c) Hjalmar's flute-playing with the attendant sentimental conversation from his 'Hedvig! Hedvig!' to Gregers's entrance is lacking; and (d) there is no reference to Hedvig's approaching hereditary blindness. Then:

GREGERS. You were a great sportsman then, Lieutenant Ekdal.

EKDAL. I was, yes, I was. Went shooting every day. ⟨'The uniform' inserted later.⟩

GREGERS. But you don't go shooting any more?

EKDAL. I don't go shooting any more, no. That is to say, not in that way.

HJALMAR. Sit down now, Father, and get yourself a glass of beer. Won't you sit down, Gregers?

[EKDAL *and* GREGERS *take the seats on the sofa, the others sit at the table.*]

GREGERS. Do you remember that Christmas I came up to visit you with Hjalmar, Lieutenant?

EKDAL. At the works? That must be a long time ago.

GREGERS. That must surely be more than twenty years ago. It was the winter there were so many wolves up there.

EKDAL. Ah, was it that winter! Then perhaps you were with us the nights we lay in the stables on the look-out for them?

GREGERS. To be sure, I was. Hjalmar was also with us the first night, but he got fed-up with it. But I stuck it out. Don't you remember you'd put a dead horse outside the stable door?

EKDAL. Yes, indeed. It was lying just beside a big hawthorn bush.

GREGERS. That's quite true.

EKDAL. And then there was a pile of stones alongside that cast a shadow in the moonlight—

GREGERS. Yes, the moon *was* shining those nights as bright as it is tonight.

EKDAL. But wolves don't like moonlight. But do you remember that morning in the half-light, after the moon had gone down . . . ?

GREGERS. When thirteen of them came in a pack . . . ?

EKDAL. No, do you remember that! I shot one of them beside the carcase, and another as they ran away.

GREGERS. Yes, there's no doubt about it, you were a great sportsman, Lieutenant Ekdal.

EKDAL. Ah yes, ah yes. Not so bad. I've shot bears; shot all kinds of things, both animals and birds. For the forest you see . . . the forest, the forest . . . ! What are the forests like up there now?

⟨Then not greatly dissimilar from the final version, until:⟩

HJALMAR. How could you guess that?

GREGERS. You told me before you owed such a lot of different things to my father and so I thought . . .

GINA. We didn't get the duck straight from Mr. Werle himself. . . .

EKDAL. But it's him we have to thank for it just the same. He was out shooting, you see, and he shot at her, but she was only winged. . . .

GREGERS. Aha! she got a slug or two in her, did she?

HJALMAR. Yes, she got a couple from behind.

GREGERS. Aha! From behind?

EKDAL. Wild duck must always be shot from behind.

GREGERS. Naturally. There's a better chance of hitting from behind.

EKDAL. It's quite understandable; if you shoot at the breast, it glances off.

HEDVIG. It was in the wing, so she couldn't fly.

GREGERS. And then she dived right down to the bottom, eh?

EKDAL [*sleepily*]. Yes, that's the way with wild ducks. They go plunging right to the bottom . . . as deep as they can get, hold on with their beaks to the weeds at the bottom and then they never come up again.

GREGERS. But Lieutenant Ekdal, *your* wild duck came up again.

EKDAL. Yes, because your father had such an absurdly good dog, you see. One of those dogs that are all the latest fashion, long-haired and web-footed. It dived down and brought the wild duck up again.

GREGERS. And then you got it?

HJALMAR. We didn't get it straight away. First it was taken to your father's, but it didn't really thrive there.

GREGERS. No, it isn't the right sort of place for wild ducks.

HJALMAR. No, you can imagine, amongst all the tame ones. They were always at her and stole her food so she didn't get a chance to recover. So Pettersen was told to put it down.

EKDAL [*half asleep*]. Hmm . . . yes . . . Pettersen . . . yes.

HJALMAR [*softly*]. That was the way we got it, you see, through Father knowing Pettersen; and when he heard all the business about the wild duck, he got it turned over to him.

GREGERS. And now it's thriving perfectly well there in the loft.

HJALMAR. Excellently. It's been so long in there now, it's forgotten what real wild life is like. And that's the only thing that counts.

GREGERS. I'm sure you are right, Hjalmar. If you want to keep wild ducks . . . and have them thrive and grow big and fat . . . I think you have to keep them locked up in a loft so that they never catch sight of the clouds or the sea.

HJALMAR. Yes, yes, that way they forget, you see. And, heavens, what they have forgotten they don't miss either.

GREGERS. No, and in time they grow fat. But, I say Hjalmar, you said you had some rooms to let—vacant rooms.

⟨Then, apart from Gregers's disgust at the sound of his own name, not greatly dissimilar from the final version, to the end of the Act.⟩

⟨*Act III is dated 25.5.84–30.5.84. The opening exchanges lack any reference to the mess in Gregers's room, thus:*⟩

HJALMAR. Are you back again already, Gina? Did you look in on Gregers?

GINA. Yes. He's arranged everything the way he wants. He says he'll look after himself.

HJALMAR. I've been in to see him too.

GINA. So I heard. And you've asked him in to lunch.

⟨*Then not greatly dissimilar from the final version, until:*⟩

HJALMAR [*getting up*]. And then we'd have *that* off our hands.

EKDAL. Exactly, yes, exactly.

[HJALMAR *and* EKDAL *open the upper half of the door to the loft; the morning sun is shining in through the skylights; pigeons are flying about in all directions and some sit cooing on the rafters; the cocks and hens crow and cackle occasionally.*]

HJALMAR [*opens one of the lower half-doors a little*]. Make yourself thin, Father.

EKDAL [*crawls through the opening*]. Aren't you coming?

HJALMAR. Yes, I rather think... [*Sees* GINA *at the kitchen door.*] No, I haven't time. I must work. And what about the net. . . . [*He pulls a string; a piece of fishing net, stretched taut, falls down in front of the door opening.*]. There now. [*Goes over to the table.*]

GINA. Is he in there again?

HJALMAR. Would you rather he'd gone running off to Ma Eriksen's? Is there anything you want? You said . . .

GINA. I just wanted to ask if you thought we could lay the table in here?

HJALMAR. Yes. I take it we haven't got anybody booked for today?

GINA. No.

HJALMAR. Well, it's to be hoped there won't be any callers either, and then we can eat in here.

GINA. All right, but there's no hurry now. There's nothing to stop you using it a while yet.

HJALMAR [*sits down again*]. Oh, Lord, I'll be using the table right enough.

[GINA *goes out into the kitchen.*]

EKDAL [*appears behind the net*]. I'm afraid we'll have to move the water trough after all, Hjalmar.

HJALMAR. Yes, that's just what I've been saying all along.

EKDAL. Hm, hm, hm!

[*Can no longer be seen.* HJALMAR *does a little work, glances over at the loft and half gets up.* HEDVIG *comes in from the kitchen.*]

HJALMAR [*sits down again quickly*]. What do you want? Are you supposed to be keeping an eye on me, or something?

HEDVIG. No, of course not. Isn't there something I could help you with?

HJALMAR. No, no. I'd best see to it myself . . . as long as my strength lasts.

[HEDVIG *goes over to the opening and looks into the loft a while.*]

HJALMAR. What's he doing, Hedvig?

HEDVIG. Looks like a new way up to the water trough.

HJALMAR [*gets up*]. He'll never manage *that* alone, never in this world. Look Hedvig, there's a clever girl, you take the brush. . . .

HEDVIG. Yes of course, Daddy.

HJALMAR. It'll only take a minute. It's this retouching . . . here's one to copy from.

HEDVIG. Yes, I know how to do it. I've done some of the others, you know.

HJALMAR. Only a minute and I'll have *this* off my hands.

[*He pushes one of the lower half-doors open a little way, crawls into the loft and pulls the door to after him.* HEDVIG *sits retouching.* HJALMAR *and* EKDAL *can be heard arguing within.*]

⟨Then not greatly dissimilar from the final version, but with some omissions—no reference to Hedvig's weak eyes and that she has left school supposedly to be coached by Hjalmar and Molvik; nor to the 'Flying Dutchman'; nor to Hjalmar's insistence on Hedvig's going to learn basketwork; lacking also are a number of Gina's malapropisms—until the moment when Gina and Hedvig go into the kitchen leaving Hjalmar and Gregers together alone:⟩

HJALMAR [*crawls through the lower half-door and comes into the studio*]. I won't ask you to go in to see Father, he doesn't like it. I'd better shut it up before the others arrive. [*He draws the netting and shuts the upper half-doors.*] All these gadgets are very necessary, you see, because Gina doesn't like having the rabbits and the hens in the studio.

GREGERS. Naturally. A good housewife like her . . .

HJALMAR. This thing with the fishing net is my own invention. Really it's great fun having something like this to look after, and mending it when it gets broken now and again.

GREGERS. We have certainly got on in the world, we two, Hjalmar.

HJALMAR. What do you mean by that?

GREGERS. I have got on most, because I'll soon have reached the point where I'm no damned use for anything.

HJALMAR. You don't have to be of use for anything. You can live perfectly well without that.

GREGERS. Do you believe that?

HJALMAR. Yes, I shouldn't think you need have any worries.

GREGERS. But what about yourself?

HJALMAR [*more quietly*]. Can I help it that things turned out as they did . . . that I was thrown off my course . . . ?

GREGERS. It's not that I mean. . . .

HJALMAR. Perhaps you mean I don't work hard enough to better myself. Perhaps you think I don't put my back into things enough.

GREGERS. I haven't the faintest idea how hard you put your back into things.

HJALMAR. Yes, of course you are thinking there's too much time wasted on useless things.

GREGERS. Not time, but will.

HJALMAR. But can I leave my poor old father absolutely on his own? Isn't it understandable that I should spare a bit of thought for the little things that keep *him* happy.

GREGERS. Is it entirely for your father's sake?

HJALMAR. Oh no, it is perhaps for my own as well. I need something to distract me from reality.

GREGERS. Then you are not happy, after all?

HJALMAR. Happy, happy? Yes, in a way I am. I'm all right—up to a point. But you must realize that for a man like me, a photographer's job is just a passing phase.

GREGERS. Indeed.

HJALMAR. Naturally. And therefore . . . to put it plainly, Gregers, I need something that can fill in the interval. . . .

GREGERS. Can work not do that?

HJALMAR. No, no, no! Not work alone. I need to dream the intervening time away . . . leap across it.

GREGERS. And when that time is passed, what then?

HJALMAR. Ah, then comes the big moment, I hope.

GREGERS. What big moment?

HJALMAR. Well, I have a mission.

GREGERS. What kind?

HJALMAR. A mission—an aim in life. I am the one who will raise the family name to honour again. Who else could do it?

GREGERS. Is that your mission, then?

HJALMAR. Yes, of course.

GREGERS. And what line do you intend to take?

HJALMAR. But my dear fellow, how can I tell you that beforehand. It depends so enormously on how things stand when the moment comes.

GREGERS. And you have no doubt the moment will come?

HJALMAR. That would be to doubt my whole destiny in life.

GREGERS. Are you so certain you *have* a destiny?

HJALMAR. Are you mad?

GREGERS. You know, Hjalmar, there's a bit of the wild duck about you. You were once wounded and you have plunged down and bit fast to the weeds.

HJALMAR. That's ludicrous.

GREGERS. But now I'm going to see if I can't get you up again. For I think I too have a sort of mission, you know. Not in the way you think of it . . . not because I feel it is a destiny or an obligation to others, but because I feel it is necessary for *me*.

HJALMAR. No, my dear Gregers, I don't understand a word of all this. . . . Ah, we'll soon be having lunch now.

[GINA *and* HEDVIG *carry in bottles of beer, a decanter of brandy, glasses and other things for the table; at the same time* RELLING *and* MOLVIK *enter from the right.*]

⟨Then, except that there is no mention of Relling and Gregers having known each other before, not greatly dissimilar from the final version until:⟩

RELLING. Molvik has a demonic nature.

GREGERS. Hm.

MOLVIK. Yes, people will insist on saying that about me.

RELLING. And demonic natures can't keep on the straight and narrow, you see. Such people have to kick over the traces now and then. You must have lived a very long time up there at the works, Mr. Werle.

GREGERS. I've lived there a good many years.

RELLING. How the devil did you stick it out?

GREGERS. Oh, when one has books, then . . .

RELLING. Books! You just drive yourself silly, reading them.

GREGERS. But there are people up there as well.

RELLING. Yes, the workpeople. You know, my dear sir, I dare bet you have a mission in life.

GREGERS. I believe I have.

HJALMAR. And it is a belief that gives strength, Relling.

RELLING. Yes, that's something you could tell him a thing or two about.

HJALMAR. Ah, yes.

[*There is a knock on the loft door.*]

GINA. Hedvig, open up for Grandfather.

[HEDVIG *opens the door a little.* OLD EKDAL *crawls out.*]

EKDAL [*mumbles*]. Good morning, gentlemen. Enjoy your lunch. Hm.

[*He goes into his room.*]

RELLING. Let us drink to him, Ekdal, and may he soon wear his uniform again.

HJALMAR. Thank you.

GREGERS. Uniform?

RELLING. His lieutenant's uniform, of course.

GREGERS [*looks at* HJALMAR]. Is that the only thing you think about?

HJALMAR. Well, his restitution goes with it. But it's the uniform that's important to Father. An old soldier . . .

GREGERS. Yes, but what about you? You yourself, Hjalmar, surely you have no patience with the likes of that.

RELLING. What more should he want, damn it?

GREGERS. Then it is only the stigma you want to get rid of?

RELLING. I don't see anything wrong with that myself.

GREGERS. And here was I thinking it was the guilt you wanted to clear him of.

RELLING. Now we're for it.

HJALMAR. What's done can't be undone.

GREGERS. Do you think he was as guilty as it appeared?

HJALMAR. I don't think he had any idea what he'd done.

GREGERS [*gets up*]. And yet you have lived here all these years, gone numbly through life, waiting and waiting . . . or perhaps not even that.

RELLING. You've been brooding too long up there in the forests, Mr. Werle.

GREGERS. If I'd had the good fortune to have a father like yours . . .

HJALMAR. The good fortune. . . .

GREGERS. . . . then I'd have been a different son to him. . . . But it's your environment that has dragged you down in the mud.

RELLING. Well, what do you know!

MOLVIK. Are you referring to me?

HJALMAR. What have you to say about my environment?

GINA. Hush, hush, Hjalmar. Don't say any more about it.

GREGERS. I have this to say, that anybody who lives his life, his most intimate domestic life, in a swamp of lies and deceit and secrecy . . .

HJALMAR. Have you gone mad!

RELLING [*jumps up*]. Shut up, Mr. Werle.

HJALMAR. His most intimate domestic life . . .

[*There is a knock at the door, right.*]

GINA. Hush, be quiet, there's someone there.

[*She goes to the door.*]

HJALMAR. Have you gone completely mad, Gregers?

GINA [*opens the door and draws back*]. Oh, what on earth!

[HAAKON WERLE, *wearing a fur coat, takes a step into the room.*]

WERLE. I beg your pardon, but I believe my son is supposed to be living here.

GINA [*gulping*]. Yes.

HJALMAR [*who has got up*]. Won't you . . .?

WERLE. Thanks. I wish to speak to my son.

GREGERS. Yes, what is it? Here I am.

WERLE. I wish to speak with you in your room.

GREGERS. And I, for my part, prefer to have witnesses.

WERLE. What I want to speak to you about is not the sort of thing that . . .

GREGERS. To begin with, I am not interested in discussing anything but the Ekdals' affairs.

WERLE. The Ekdals' affairs?

GREGERS. And these two gentlemen are almost a part of the household.

WERLE. What I have to discuss with you, concerns only you and me.

GREGERS. Since Mother died, I think there is only one thing in the world that concerns me, and that is the affairs of the Ekdals.

HJALMAR. I don't know what else there is to discuss about our affairs.

WERLE. Nor I.

GREGERS. But I do, and I intend to shout it at every street corner. Every manjack in the country will know that Lieutenant Ekdal was not the guilty one, but somebody who has gone scot free from that day to this.

WERLE. You dare, you crazy fool . . .! I suppose it's me you are referring to.

GREGERS. No, I refer more particularly to myself.

WERLE. What are you thinking about? You knew nothing about it. . . .

GREGERS. I had my doubts at the time it was all going on up there. If I had spoken to Ekdal then, while there was still time . . .

WERLE. Then why didn't you speak?

GREGERS. I didn't dare because of you.

WERLE. Excuses, stories, sheer fantasy. You gave evidence in court yourself. . . .

GREGERS. Ah, what a coward I was. I was afraid to take my share of the blame.

WERLE. Oh, it's this desperate sick conscience of yours.

GREGERS. You are the one who made my conscience sick.

WERLE. You are mistaken, it's a heritage from your mother, Gregers. The one thing she did leave you.

GREGERS. You still haven't been able to forget that you <'made a mistake when you' *inserted later*> thought she would bring you a fortune.

WERLE. Let's not talk about that. I have come to ask if you will come home with me again.

GREGERS. No.

WERLE. And you won't come into the firm, either?

GREGERS. No.

⟨Then, except for the reappearance of Molvik in addition to the other characters at the end of the Act, not greatly dissimilar from the final version.⟩

⟨Act IV is dated 2.6.84–8.6.84. It is given below in full.⟩

> HJALMAR EKDAL's *studio. Afternoon. It is growing dusk.* HEDVIG *is moving about the studio.* GINA *comes in from the kitchen.*

GINA. Still no sign?

HEDVIG. No.

GINA. Are you sure he's not in with Werle?

HEDVIG. No, it's locked.

GINA. And not with Relling either?

HEDVIG. No, I've been down twice to ask.

GINA. And his dinner's standing there getting cold.

HEDVIG. Yes. Can you think what's become of him, Mother? Daddy's generally on the dot for dinner.

GINA. Oh, don't fret, he'll be here soon.

HEDVIG [*after a pause*]. Do you think it's a good thing Werle's come to live with us?

GINA. Why shouldn't it be?

HEDVIG. Well, I don't know, but it was nice when we were on our own. And I think Relling is better for Daddy than Werle.— Dear, what has become of him?

GINA [*shouts*]. There he is.

[HJALMAR EKDAL *comes in from the right.*]

HEDVIG [*going to meet him*]. Daddy, you've come at last!

GINA. We've waited ages for you, Hjalmar.

HJALMAR. Yes, I have been rather a long time.

GINA. Have you had something to eat with Gregers Werle?

HJALMAR. No.

GINA. Then I'll bring your dinner in for you.

HJALMAR. No, don't bother. I won't eat anything now.

HEDVIG. Are you all right, Daddy?

HJALMAR. Oh yes, not so bad. We went for a very long walk. . . .

GINA. You shouldn't have, Hjalmar; you're not used to it.

HJALMAR. One can get used to a great many things. Have there been any bookings today?

GINA. No, not today.

HEDVIG. There's sure to be some tomorrow, Daddy, you'll see.

HJALMAR. That would be very nice. For tomorrow I'm going to get down to things. I want to do everything myself. I want to manage things alone.

GINA. But why do you want to do that, Hjalmar? You'll only make your life a misery.

HJALMAR. That's my affair. And I think I would like to keep proper accounts, too.

GINA. You?

HJALMAR. Yes, you *do* keep accounts?

HEDVIG. But Mother's so good at it.

HJALMAR. And that's how she gets the money to stretch so far, I imagine. Remarkable that we can live so well on the pittance I've earned this winter.

HEDVIG. Yes, Daddy, but think of all that copying for Graaberg.

HJALMAR. The copying, yes.

GINA. Nonsense, nonsense, that doesn't amount to much. . . .

HEDVIG. Oh, but it does. It's mostly that we live on.

GINA. Oh, how can you say such a thing!

HEDVIG. Why mustn't Daddy know that, Mother?

HJALMAR. So, that's what we live on. Copying for Mr. Werle.

GINA. But you know very well it's Graaberg who pays for it.

HJALMAR. Out of his own pocket?

GINA. Yes, presumably.

HEDVIG. But it's all the same to us, Daddy.

HJALMAR. Of course! It's all the same to us where the money comes from.

GINA. I agree. But since we're on the subject . . .! Hedvig, you haven't done a thing all day today. . . .

HEDVIG. I'd better go in and . . .

GINA. Yes, go on.

[HEDVIG *goes into the living-room.*]

GINA. What happened to you, Hjalmar?

HJALMAR. Do you think Gregers is in his right mind?

GINA. How should I know? I hardly know him.

HJALMAR. If only I knew.

GINA. You heard what Relling said about him.

HJALMAR. Oh Relling, Relling. . . . Let's have the lamp lit.

GINA [*lights it*]. All his life Gregers Werle has been a bit strange.

HJALMAR. Your voice seems to be trembling.

GINA. Is it?

HJALMAR. And your hands are shaking. Aren't they?

GINA. Yes. I don't know why.

HJALMAR. Now you're going to hear what Gregers has said about you.

GINA [*puts her hands over her ears, in horror*]. No, no, I won't listen!

HJALMAR [*pulls her hands away*]. You will hear it.

GINA. You needn't tell me.

HJALMAR. You know what it is.

GINA. I can guess.

HJALMAR. It's true, then. True, true. This is dreadful!

GINA. I realize I ought to have told you long ago.

HJALMAR. You should have told me immediately while there was still time.

GINA. What would you have done?

HJALMAR. Then, of course, I wouldn't have wanted anything to do with you.

GINA. That's what I thought too, at the time. So I said nothing.

HJALMAR. Simple-minded fool that I was, I imagined you were very much in love with me.

GINA. That has come with time, Hjalmar, as sure as I stand here. Oh yes, my dear, I care a great deal for you, more than anyone else does.

HJALMAR. I don't want to hear about it. How do you think I see you now, giving yourself like that to a middle-aged married man?

GINA. Yes. I can't really think now how I could do it.

HJALMAR. Can't you now? Perhaps you've grown respectable with time. But then—how on earth could you get yourself mixed up in a thing like that?

GINA. Oh, believe me, Hjalmar, it isn't so easy for poor girls. These rich men start in a small way with presents and then . . .

HJALMAR. Yes, cash! That's what you think is important.

GINA. It was mostly jewellery and dress material and that sort of thing.

HJALMAR. And you've sent it all back long ago, of course.

GINA. I've worn out the dresses and I sold the gold things bit by bit when we needed money.

HJALMAR. We have lived on that man's money. Everything we have in the house we owe to him!

GINA. I've never had a penny off him from the day we were married and I don't believe I've even clapped eyes on him since.

HJALMAR. But the copying!

GINA. Berta fixed that for me when she started in the house.

HJALMAR. You and Berta, yes, you are both the same.

GINA. Tell me, Hjalmar, haven't I been a good wife to you?

HJALMAR. But what about all the things *you* owe me? Didn't I take you away from that menial job? Haven't I given you a name to bear—yes, a name—for it *shall* be restored to respect and honour again.

GINA. It doesn't make any difference to me.

HJALMAR. Really? Ah yes, I dare say.

GINA. Yes, because I like you just as you are, Hjalmar, even if you never do all the great things you talk about.

HJALMAR. That's your baser nature showing itself. Misunderstood in my own home! You have always misunderstood me.

GINA. But I've been a good wife to you all the same.

[GREGERS WERLE *enters through the hall door.*]

GREGERS [*at the hall door*]. May I come in?

HJALMAR. Yes, come in.

GREGERS. So you haven't done it yet, then?

HJALMAR. I *have* done it.

GREGERS. You *have?*

HJALMAR. I have experienced the bitterest moment in my life.

GREGERS. But also the most sublime, I should think.

HJALMAR. Well, so far we've got it off our chests anyway.

GINA. May God forgive you, Mr. Werle.

GREGERS. But I don't understand.

HJALMAR. What don't you understand?

GREGERS. After laying bare your souls like that . . . so completely . . . this exchange on which you can now build a completely new mode of life . . . a way of living in truth.

HJALMAR. Yes, I know, I know all that.

GREGERS. I was absolutely convinced that when I came in after this, I would find, as it were, a purer light of regeneration over your home, and here I am confronted by this dull, gloomy, miserable . . .

GINA. Very well then. [*She turns up the lamp.*]

GREGERS. Tell me honestly though, Mrs. Ekdal, isn't it a joy for you to be relieved of this burden of deceit?

GINA. I can tell you, Mr. Werle, I haven't had the time to think about the past.

GREGERS. I would have thought it would have been with you every minute of the day.

GINA. I've really had far too much to think of in running the house. And since I've been married, nobody can say but what I haven't been respectable and honest.

GREGERS. Your whole attitude to life baffles me—so different, so fundamentally different, from mine. But *you* now Hjalmar, all this must have brought you some higher resolve.

HJALMAR. Yes, of course it has. That is . . . in a sort of way.

GREGERS. To forgive one who has sinned, to raise up again in love one who has strayed. . . .

HJALMAR. Do you think a man so easily recovers from what I have just been through.

GREGERS. No, not an *ordinary* man, I dare say. But a man like *you* . . . !

HJALMAR. Yes, I know, I know, but it takes time, you know.

GREGERS. You have been too long at the bottom, Hjalmar, bit yourself fast down there. And of course it's always difficult, when you first come up again into the clear light of day.

HJALMAR. You're right there, it is difficult.

GREGERS. Yes, because you do have some of the spirit of the wild duck in you.

[RELLING *comes in from the hall.*]

RELLING. What's this, the wild duck on the carpet again?

GREGERS. Yes, it's the evil spirit of the house. And it's not for nothing that it came from Haakon Werle.

RELLING. Ah, it's Mr. Werle who's under discussion.

HJALMAR. Him . . . and certain others.

RELLING [*turns to* GREGERS]. God damn you!

HJALMAR. You know about it too, then!

RELLING. It doesn't matter what I do or don't know. If it concerns that quarter, you can believe anything.

GREGERS. But am I not supposed to speak . . . I who know all about these things? Could I stand by and see these two dearly beloved people ruined because they were basing their lives on a false foundation?

RELLING. But it has nothing whatsoever to do with you. You can leave my patients alone with your quackery.

HJALMAR. Patients?

RELLING. Oh yes, everybody has need of a doctor sometimes. But you are no judge of that, Mr. Werle.

GREGERS. I know from experience what it is to live with a gnawing conscience, such as has poisoned my life. But here I've found my mission. Now I'm so happy, so happy. Why shouldn't I open the eyes of two people who need so desperately to see?

RELLING. What is it they are going to see?

GREGERS. The truth. The revelation that until today their union has not been a true marriage.

RELLING. Do you think it's going to be any more true hereafter?

GREGERS. I sincerely hope so.

RELLING. Naturally, your sort are always so damned hopeful. Time and again you get led by the nose . . . made fool of. Hasn't that ever happened to you?

GREGERS. To be sure; I've suffered many disappointments.

RELLING. But, nevertheless you go on sincerely hoping.

GREGERS. This is different, quite out of the ordinary. A character like Hjalmar Ekdal.

RELLING. Ekdal . . . !

HJALMAR. That may very well be true, but . . .

RELLING. Oh well, Ekdal, yes. But he already has his mission in life elsewhere, he doesn't need any better marriage than the one he has had up to now.

GINA. Ah, you believe that too, Relling. We used to get on so well. . . .

HJALMAR. You don't understand the claims of the ideal at all.

RELLING. But don't you see, Hjalmar Ekdal can manage things all right, he can't sink right to the bottom. Hasn't he got his great project to grapple with . . . ?

HJALMAR. Yes, the project . . . it's true, I have that.

RELLING. And when it is solved, he will again have brought glory and honour to the name of Ekdal.

HJALMAR. It's to be hoped so anyway.

GREGERS. Yes, this project is all very well, but it is something which is *outside* the individual; a scientific problem pure and simple, a technical thing or whatever you like to call it. And it is inconceivable. that such a project could satisfy an individual like Hjalmar. Or do you think perhaps it *does* satisfy you?

HJALMAR. No, I don't altogether. . . .

GREGERS. Now you see, Doctor Relling. And if it does not fully occupy his personality *now*, when it still hasn't developed to complete freedom . . . Well let me put this question to you. Do you think a great problem can ever be solved by an immature personality?

RELLING. Do you mean that photography cannot be raised to the level of an art as long as the relationship between the photographer and his wife is not a true marriage?

GREGERS. You put it rather crudely. But I have such utter faith in the regenerative powers of a true marriage. . . .

RELLING. Excuse me, Mr. Werle, have you seen many true marriages?

GREGERS. No, I hardly think I've seen a single one.

RELLING. Nor have I.

GREGERS. But I have seen the opposite sort of marriage, and what damage it can do to a person. . . .

RELLING. And it's from these that you draw your conclusions. Well, well, Ekdal, now you know then what it takes to make a great invention.

GINA. But you shouldn't talk so much about this invention, Relling. Because nothing will ever come of it anyway.

HJALMAR. Nothing ever come of it!

RELLING. Now what are you saying!

HJALMAR. You say nothing will come of my project!

GINA. No, I'm pretty sure it won't. You've been waiting all this time to invent something; but you never get any further. . . .

RELLING. These things often happen through a kind of revelation, Mrs. Ekdal.

HJALMAR. She doesn't understand that.

GINA. Yes, revelations are all very well, but surely you need something else too. I think it would be better if you worked with those instruments we have, Hjalmar, and then the others can find the new things.

HJALMAR. Not understood; not understood in one's own home. [*Sees* HEDVIG.] Yes, she understands me. Or don't you believe in me either, Hedvig?

HEDVIG. What am I to believe in, Daddy?

HJALMAR. Naturally you must believe generally in me, believe in my mission in life and believe in my project.

HEDVIG. Yes, I think you'll find it sometime all right.

HJALMAR. Hm. . . .

GINA. Hush, there's a knock.

[*She goes over to the hall door*, MRS. SÖRBY *comes in*.]

GINA. Why Berta, it's you!

MRS. SÖRBY. Yes, it's me.

HJALMAR. If it's something you've got to talk to Gina about, wouldn't you like to . . . [*He points to the living-room*.]

MRS. SÖRBY. Thank you, I'd rather stay here. I've come with a message from Mr. Werle.

HJALMAR. What does he want with us?

GREGERS. Perhaps it's something about me.

MRS. SÖRBY. He wants you to hear it in any case. The first thing is there's going to be a fairly big change in Mr. Werle's domestic and other arrangements.

GREGERS. Aha!

MRS. SÖRBY. Mr. Werle has decided to hand over the business here in town to Graaberg and then he himself is going to move up to the works.

GREGERS. Is he!

HJALMAR. Well, well. So Mr. Werle's going to move up to the works.

RELLING. He won't stand that long, it's so lonely up there.

MRS. SÖRBY. Well, he won't be completely alone, actually.

GREGERS. So he's going through with it after all.

MRS. SÖRBY. Yes.

RELLING. What's he going through with?

HJALMAR. I don't understand a word.

GREGERS. I'll explain. My father is marrying Mrs. Sörby.

HJALMAR. Marrying!

GINA. Well, at last!

RELLING. Surely this is never true.

MRS. SÖRBY. Yes, it is true. He has a special license and is leaving for up there this evening and I mean to go tomorrow. Well, I've told you; now it's over.

RELLING. So this is the end of the affair.

GREGERS. What do you think will come of all this, Mrs. Sörby?

MRS. SÖRBY. Nothing but good, I think. Mr. Werle is by no means as difficult to get on with as some people imagine.

GREGERS. You surely have no grounds for complaint.

MRS. SÖRBY. Oh, no. He can be a bit unreasonable at times, but I have been through worse things than that, Mr. Werle. And it's nice to be provided for.

RELLING. And Mr. Werle is the man to provide for you. He's no beggar.

MRS. SÖRBY. There are plenty who wouldn't need to be beggars if only they'd really put their minds to something.

RELLING. Put their minds ... Tell me, what good do you think that does?

MRS. SÖRBY. Oh yes, a person can be so far gone that he no longer has a mind for anything.

RELLING. Tonight I'm going out with Molvik.

MRS. SÖRBY. You shouldn't, Relling.

RELLING. There's nothing else for it.

[*He goes out through the hall door.*]

MRS. SÖRBY. There's one thing more. There are probably some people who think that Mr. Werle should have done a bit more for an old friend like Lieutenant Ekdal.

HJALMAR. Mr. Werle does a great deal for Father. He pays so generously. . . .

MRS. SÖRBY. Yes, you mean for the copying. But your father's getting old now and soon his eyes won't be able to stand it, so here is a banker's draft as a final settlement. You or Gina can draw 100 crowns every month for your father. . . .

HJALMAR. Gina can?

MRS. SÖRBY. Yes, or you, just as you will. And when your father, well . . . when he doesn't need anything any more, then it passes to Hedvig.

HJALMAR [*recoils as though stabbed*]. To Hedvig!

HEDVIG. Fancy! All that money!

HJALMAR. Hedvig! What do you say to that, Gina?

GINA. Mr. Werle probably thought that . . .

MRS. SÖRBY. He thought this was the nicest way of doing it ... after all Hedvig is still a child, and she can quite well accept it.

HJALMAR. Yes, she has the greatest right to it, if Gina herself won't . . .

MRS. SÖRBY. Gina herself!

HJALMAR. But what about me, me!

HEDVIG. I don't want anything. You can have it all, Daddy.

MRS. SÖRBY. What's happened here?

HJALMAR. Something that should have happened long, long ago.

MRS. SÖRBY. Already.

GREGERS. I quite understand why Father has made this arrangement. He wanted to convince me Hjalmar Ekdal is not the man I imagined.

HJALMAR. Then, he's made a mistake there. Look, Gregers! [*He tears the paper in two.*] There you are, Mrs. Sörby. Will you please give Mr. Werle that back?

MRS. SÖRBY. I won't take it.

HJALMAR [*throws it on the table*]. Then let it be. But tell him anyway that I've torn his deed of gift in little pieces.

GREGERS. And ask your future husband who was wrong—he or I.

MRS. SÖRBY. I shall. Goodbye, Gina, I do hope things turn out all right.

GINA. Same to you, Berta. Goodbye.

[MRS. SÖRBY *goes.*]

HJALMAR [*in a whisper*]. Now you must answer me as if you were on oath: Is Hedvig mine or is she not?

GINA. I don't know.

HJALMAR. You don't know!

GINA. How should *I* know . . . the kind of woman I am?

HJALMAR. And brazen about it, too. Gregers, tomorrow I leave this house.

HEDVIG [*screams*]. No, Daddy, no.

GINA. Surely you'll never do that, Hjalmar!

GREGERS. Must you, Hjalmar?

HJALMAR. I must. I'm going immediately. [*He puts on his top-coat.*] I won't be home tonight. . . .

HEDVIG. Oh, no, no Daddy, you mustn't go.

HJALMAR. Go away. I want nothing to do with you. Ask your mother . . . if you want to. So! [*He takes his hat.*] I'm going now and I'll never set foot here again.

[*He goes out right.*]

HEDVIG [*throws herself on the sofa*]. He's leaving us! Daddy, Daddy's leaving us! Oh Mother, Mother!

GINA. Don't cry, Hedvig. He'll come back.

HEDVIG. No, he'll never come back. He said so.

GINA. Do you think he'll come back, Mr. Werle?

GREGERS. I sincerely believe so. Hjalmar will come back to his home, and you'll see how uplifted he'll be when he returns.

HEDVIG. But what have we done to him? Mother, tell me, what is it? Why doesn't he want anything to do with me? Tell me that. Oh, tell me that!

GINA. Hush, hush, you'll know all about it when you're older.

HEDVIG. Yes, but I won't ever be older if Daddy won't have anything to do with me.

[*She bursts out sobbing.*]

GINA. You mustn't cry, Hedvig. You really mustn't cry. It's bad for you, Dr. Relling says so.

HEDVIG. I can't help it. Oh Mother, Mother get him to come back home again. . . .

GINA. Yes, I'll go after him. Perhaps he's only down below with Relling. [*She throws her shawl round her.*] But you must be quiet, Hedvig, promise me?

HEDVIG. Yes, yes.

GREGERS. Wouldn't it be better to let him fight his bitter fight to the end . . .?

GINA. Oh, he can do that afterwards. The first thing is to get the child quietened down.

[*She goes out through the hall door.*]

GREGERS. Come on now, cheer up, Hedvig. It may be all right yet.

HEDVIG. Why doesn't Daddy want anything to do with me any more, Mr. Werle? You must tell me that.

GREGERS. I can only say the same as your mother. You'll find out one day.

HEDVIG. But I can't go on waiting and being as miserable as I am now.

GREGERS. What right have you or anybody else to be happy? What right, I say?

HEDVIG. Oh, I don't bother myself about that. Because it's so lovely to be happy and gay.

GREGERS. There are higher things than that in life, Hedvig.

HEDVIG. Yes, but that doesn't mean a thing so long as everything comes all right here again at home between Daddy and Mother and me. Do you think everything will be all right again between us?

GREGERS. I hope most sincerely that everything will be all right again in time between your father and mother.

HEDVIG. Yes, but what about me!

GREGERS. You must remember one thing, Hedvig. You are not bound to stay at home for ever.

HEDVIG. Yes, yes I am. I'm always going to stay at home. I'd never dream of leaving Daddy and Mother. Ah, but . . . just think . . . Daddy doesn't want anything to do with me!

GREGERS. You must wait and hope. Your father must first fight out his battle.

HEDVIG. But I can't wait, all miserable like this. Why won't Daddy have anything to do with me any more? Perhaps I'm not Daddy's and Mother's real child? Perhaps they only found me?

GREGERS. Found you? Well, it could be that your father thinks something of the sort.

HEDVIG. Yes, but then Mother could tell him it wasn't true.

GREGERS. But what if he doesn't believe her now?

HEDVIG. But even if it *was* true, couldn't Daddy be just as fond of me for all that? We don't know where the wild duck came from either, and yet we're terribly fond of her.

GREGERS. The wild duck. Yes, you're terribly fond of the wild duck, Hedvig.

HEDVIG. Yes, terribly.

GREGERS. And the wild duck belongs to *you*. Doesn't it?

HEDVIG. Yes, it belongs to *me*. But why . . .?

GREGERS. Have you anything else you're equally fond of?

HEDVIG. Oh no, definitely not! Nothing in the world.

GREGERS. Then you must sacrifice the most precious thing you have. . . .

HEDVIG. The wild duck!

GREGERS. Yes, and get back your father's love instead.

HEDVIG. But how can you know . . .?

GREGERS. He said it himself before he left. Neither you nor the old man would make such a sacrifice for his sake. It is your love for him he doubts, that's why he won't have anything to do with you.

HEDVIG. Oh, if it were no more than that. . . .

GREGERS. Show him that it means more to you than anything else on earth to win him back. Give, give gladly the most precious thing you have in the world.

HEDVIG. Yes, if only that could put everything right again.

GREGERS. You must not doubt the power of self-sacrifice, it is the real ideal in family life, you see. . . .

HEDVIG. Oh, but I can't be bothered about *that*. I don't understand it.

GREGERS. But can't you understand that this would be a deed that would impress itself as something most unusual. And that's just what would make your father see the kinship between you and him.

HEDVIG. Do you think so?

GREGERS. Yes. I certainly think so. And then your father will say: Hedvig is my child in spirit and truth, though she came from the far ends of the earth.

HEDVIG. Or from the briny deep.

GREGERS. Or from the briny deep, if you prefer it.

HEDVIG. And then everything would be all right between Daddy and me again? Oh, that would be so very wonderful.

GREGERS. Everything is so very wonderful when one's life is lifted to a more sublime plane. Well, Hedvig, that which is most precious must be sacrificed. Confide in your grandfather, and get him to do it. Wait until he feels he wants to go hunting, you know. . . .

HEDVIG. Yes, yes, I know all right. . . .

GREGERS. But keep your mother out of it. . . .

HEDVIG. Why Mother?

GREGERS. Well, because she's not likely to understand us.

[GINA *comes in from the hall.*]

HEDVIG. Did you find him, Mother?

GINA. No, I heard he'd called and gone out with Relling.

GREGERS. Are you sure?

GINA. Yes, the woman down in the yard told me. Molvik was with them as well.

GREGERS. At a time like this, when his soul desperately needs to wrestle in solitude. . . .

GINA. Yes, I would have thought so too. God knows where they've gone. Not to Ma Eriksen's anyway.

HEDVIG [*bursts into tears*]. Oh, suppose he never comes home again.

GREGERS. He will come back. And then you'll see just *how* he'll come. Good evening, and sleep peacefully.

[*He goes out through the hall door.*]

HEDVIG [*throws herself on* GINA's *neck, in tears*]. Mother, Mother!

GINA. Ugh! This is what happens when you get mad people in the house.

⟨Act V is dated 9.6.84–13.6.84; the beginning is not greatly dissimilar from the final version, until:⟩

GREGERS. Can you explain to me the mental turmoil going on in Ekdal?

RELLING. I'm damned if I think there's any mental turmoil going on in him.

GREGERS. But do you really think that a personality like his . . .?

RELLING. Oh, personality, personality! I don't know what personality is. Hjalmar Ekdal is a good, kind, decent person whose chief desire is to live as good and comfortable and carefree a life as possible.

GREGERS. Him . . . who has his name and his family honour to reinstate.

RELLING. Oh yes, I know that sort of talk; he gabbled something about it last night. How the devil can he make reparation for what's happened? Tell me that.

GREGERS. Aren't you forgetting the marvellous invention he's working on.

RELLING. Don't say you seriously believe in this invention?

GREGERS. Yes, most certainly I do. Surely you yourself believe in it too.

RELLING. Well, Mr. Werle, you know . . . I may be a bit of a swine, but I'm not a bit of a fool.

GREGERS. But you spoke highly enough yesterday about his efforts.

RELLING. Well, damn it, can't you see why? All this about a remarkable invention, that's the life-lie he lives by.

GREGERS. Life-lie?

RELLING. Yes, of course. Most people go around clinging to an illusion, it helps them to live their lives.

GREGERS. That would be very sad.

RELLING. Who says it ought to be pleasant? That's just the way it is. The remarkable invention is for Ekdal what the demonic is for Molvik.

GREGERS. Isn't it true with him then, either?

RELLING. An idiot like him—demonic? How the devil could you imagine a thing like that? And what's more there isn't even anything like it. But if I hadn't put that idea into his mind, he would have succumbed miserably to self-contempt long ago.

GREGERS. So it's you perhaps who gave him this idea.

RELLING. Yes, I'm his doctor after all; curing him is impossible, but a little lie injected now and again . . . that alleviates things.

GREGERS. That may be. But this is not the case with Hjalmar Ekdal.

RELLING. Isn't it? Take that lie away from Hjalmar Ekdal and straight away you take away his happiness.

GREGERS. Oh, the lie, the lie—possibly. But what about his idealism?

RELLING. Good Lord, man, they are just two different names for the same thing. [*To* HEDVIG *who comes in.*] Well, Hedvig, I'm just going down to see your father.

[*He goes out right.*]

GREGERS. Have you the courage and the strength today?

HEDVIG. Well, I don't know; I don't really think I believe in a thing like that.

GREGERS. Then let it be. Without the proper strength of mind there's nothing to be done.

[*He goes out right.* HEDVIG *goes towards the kitchen; at that moment there is a knock on the door of the loft; she goes over and opens it, and* OLD EKDAL *comes out; she shuts the door after him.*]

EKDAL. There's no fun in being alone in there. What's happened to Hjalmar?

HEDVIG. Wouldn't you like to shoot the wild duck today, Grandfather?

EKDAL. Hush, hush, don't talk like that. It's just that something comes over me. Old sportsman, you know.

HEDVIG. Isn't it in the breast they have to be shot?

EKDAL. Under the wing, if that can be managed. And preferably a little from behind.

HEDVIG. Do you often feel like taking a shot at her?

EKDAL. Needn't be afraid. I can make do with a rabbit.

[*He goes into his room.* GINA *comes from the living-room and begins to tidy up the studio. After a moment the hall door slowly opens;* ⟨'HJALMAR *appears' inserted later*⟩; *he is without hat or top-coat, unwashed and with tousled hair.*]

GINA. Well, so you've come at last!

HJALMAR [*enters*]. I'm going straight off again.

GINA. Yes, yes, I suppose that's all right.

HEDVIG [*from the kitchen.*] Oh, Daddy!

HJALMAR [*turns aside and waves her away*]. Go away, go away!

GINA. Go into the other room, Hedvig.

[HEDVIG *goes.*]

HJALMAR. I must have my books with me. Where are my books?

GINA. What books?

HJALMAR. My scientific books, of course; the technical periodicals I use for my invention.

GINA [*looks in the bookcase*]. Are these them, the ones in paper backs?

HJALMAR. Of course they are.

GINA [*placing them on the table*]. Shouldn't I get Hedvig to cut the pages for you?

HJALMAR. I don't need any cutting done.

GINA. So you haven't changed your mind about moving out and leaving us?

HJALMAR. I should think that was pretty evident.

GINA. What about Grandfather?

HJALMAR. He'll come with me. I shall go to town and make the necessary arrangements. . . . Hm. . . . Has anybody seen my hat on the stairs?

GINA. No, have you lost your hat?

HJALMAR. I had it when I got back, I'm quite certain of that. But I couldn't find it again today.

GINA. As long as you haven't caught cold, Hjalmar.

[*She goes out into the kitchen.* HJALMAR *rakes about in the papers and photographs, finds the torn document of the day before, picks it up and looks at it; he sees* GINA *and puts it down.*]

GINA [*with a breakfast tray, from the kitchen*]. Just a bit of something to warm you up, if you fancy it.

HJALMAR [*glances across*]. Coffee! ... Oh yes, I am in just the right mood for drinking coffee! My manuscripts, my letters and my important papers. [*Opens the living-room door.*] Is she there again? Get out. [HEDVIG *comes.*] Spending these last moments here, I wish to remain undisturbed by people who have no business to be here.

[*He goes into the living-room.*]

GINA. Stay in the kitchen, Hedvig. [GINA *goes into the living-room.*]

[HEDVIG *stands motionless for a moment, biting her lip to stop herself from crying and clenches her hands.*]

HEDVIG [*softly*]. The wild duck!

[*She crosses to the door of the loft, pushes it a little to one side, slips in and shuts the door behind her.*]

HJALMAR [*with some writing-books which he puts on the table*]. Oh, there are thousands of things I've got to hump away with me.

GINA. Yes, it won't be easy for you getting things in order again. But now your coffee's standing there getting cold.

HJALMAR. Hm.

[*He takes a mouthful or two without thinking.*]

GINA. Your worst job now will be finding a room for the rabbits.

HJALMAR. What! Have I to take all the rabbits with me?

GINA. Yes, you know Father couldn't live without his rabbits.

HJALMAR. He'll have to get used to it. The pigeons will have to stay here for the time being, too. I must try and dispense with them. There are many things I'll have to dispense with after this.

[*He takes a piece of bread and butter, eats a little and drinks some coffee.*]

GINA. If only we hadn't let that room, you could have moved in there.

HJALMAR. Me live under the same roof as you and her . . . her . . . that . . .

GINA. Hush, don't talk so loud. Father's in the loft.

HJALMAR. So he's in the loft again?

GINA. But couldn't you move into the living-room for a day or two? You could be all on your own there.

HJALMAR. Never within these walls.

GINA. What about going in with Relling then?

HJALMAR. Don't mention those people to me. It makes me feel sick just to think of them. Ah, no, I must go out into the snow and seek shelter for my father and myself.

⟨Then not greatly dissimilar from the final version, until:⟩

HJALMAR. Of course I shall leave this house as soon as possible. I'm busy packing my things. I cannot live in a broken home.

GINA. Will you give me the key to the chest of drawers, Hjalmar?

HJALMAR. What do you want with it?

GINA. I want to put your shirts in the valise.

HJALMAR. Here! And keep it. I don't need it any more.

[GINA *goes into the living-room.*]

GREGERS. Must you do this?

HJALMAR. Don't you know me well enough to realize that I can't live in a shattered home?

GREGERS. But now is just the time when that home could be built up again on foundations ten times firmer than before—on truth, on forgiveness, on reconciliation.

HJALMAR. Could you really approve of that?

GREGERS. Yes, my dear fellow, isn't that just what I was wanting?

HJALMAR. Yes, but the terrible thing—the absolutely desperate thing about it you see—is that happiness is gone for good! Just think of Hedvig, and how terribly fond of her I was.

GREGERS. And who is so fond of you, too.

HJALMAR. But that's something I just can't believe in after today. Whatever she says, whatever she does, I'll never be able to know whether she isn't behaving like that just because she feels insecure, worrying herself and feeling that she has become a stranger in the house, so to speak.

GREGERS. Hedvig knows nothing of deceit. Supposing she were now to bring you, as a sacrifice, the best thing she possessed—would you still not believe her?

HJALMAR. Oh, what sacrifice could she possibly make which . . . ?

GREGERS. Some small thing perhaps; but for her, the most precious. Let us just suppose that for your sake she gave up the wild duck.

HJALMAR. The wild duck? What would be the point of that?

GREGERS. To give up the most precious thing she knew in the world.

HJALMAR. This is hysterical talk. Even if she gave up the wild duck ten times over, there would still be a sort of hidden gulf between us. Both Hedvig and I would feel it and suffer under it. No, for us, happiness is past. Never again can Hedvig and I be together as father and child.

[*A shot is heard inside the loft.*]

HJALMAR. What! Is he shooting again!

GINA [*comes in*]. I hope he doesn't end up by doing himself an injury.

HJALMAR. I'll look in. . . .

GREGERS. Wait a minute. Do you know what that was?

HJALMAR. What what was?

GREGERS. That was a futile sacrifice which poor Hedvig has made. She got him to shoot the wild duck.

GINA. Are you sure of that?

GREGERS. I know it.

HJALMAR. The wild duck.

GINA. Yes; she's been so wretched and dejected, Hjalmar.

GREGERS. And she couldn't think of anything else but to sacrifice to you the best thing she had.

HJALMAR. And to think that I could have been so hard on her. Where is she, Gina?

GINA [*fighting her tears*]. She's sitting out in the kitchen.

HJALMAR. Things must and shall be put right again. [*He walks over and opens the kitchen door.*] Come here, I want you, Hedvig!—No, she isn't here.

GINA. Isn't she? Then she must have gone out.

HJALMAR. Oh, I do hope she comes back again soon, so that I could tell her properly . . . because really I didn't mean anything by it all.

GREGERS. You didn't mean anything by it all?

GINA. It wasn't like you, either, Hjalmar.

HJALMAR. No, it was mostly on your account, Gregers. Coming here and making these unreasonably large demands upon me. . . .

GREGERS. Do you think that?

HJALMAR. Yes, you don't know me properly, you see; I'm not quite as you imagine me to be—I must have everything nice and easy and comfortable. . . .

GINA. Hjalmar just isn't made to be unhappy. . . .

GREGERS. I'm almost beginning to believe that.

HJALMAR. Yes, and that's why I'm going to stay here, together with Gina and Hedvig, just as things were before. . . .

GINA. That's right.

GREGERS. But my dear fellow, that's exactly what I've been fighting for.

HJALMAR. Yes, but you wanted to make it happen by a lot of hocuspocus, which I didn't understand at all.

GREGERS. Ah, there's no doubt that I'm the one who got things wrong.

HJALMAR. Yes, you see, because we're not like that, neither Gina nor I; but what's become of Hedvig? Oh Lord, I do wish she would come. And then I'll tell her how much I love her. . . .

GINA. Just as much as she loves you, Hjalmar.

HJALMAR. And as much as she loved the wild duck.

GREGERS. The sacrifice has after all not been in vain.

HJALMAR. No. After this, Hedvig shall be the wild duck in our house. . . .

        [OLD EKDAL *appears at the door of his room.*]

HJALMAR. Father!

GINA. Was he shooting in *there*!

EKDAL. What do you mean by going off shooting alone, Hjalmar?

HJALMAR. Wasn't it you who was shooting?

EKDAL. Me shooting?

GREGERS. She's shot it herself, then!

HJALMAR. What is this! [*He runs to the door of the loft, tears it open, looks in and screams.*] Hedvig!

GINA [*going towards the door*]. What is it?

HJALMAR. She's lying on the floor!

        [*He goes into the loft.*]

GREGERS. Hedvig!

GINA. Hedvig! [*From within the loft.*] No, no, no.

EKDAL. What is it? Was it Hedvig . . . ?

HJALMAR [*carries* HEDVIG *into the studio*]. She's shot herself! Call for help!

GINA [*runs out into the hall and is heard shouting*]. Relling! Relling! Dr. Relling!

HJALMAR [*lays* HEDVIG *down on the sofa*]. She's coming round. . . . She'll come round soon. The pistol's gone off. . . .

EKDAL. There were bullets in it. She didn't know that. Didn't know it was loaded.

GINA [*who has come in again*]. Where's she been shot? I can't see anything.

[RELLING *comes in from the hall, closely followed by* MOLVIK, *the latter has neither waistcoat nor collar and his coat is flying open.*]

RELLING. What's going on here?

GINA. Hedvig has shot herself.

HJALMAR. Come here and help!

RELLING. Shot herself!

[*He goes over to the sofa and examines her.*]

HJALMAR. It can't be anything serious; she's hardly bleeding, it can't be. . . .

RELLING. How did this happen?

HJALMAR. Oh, how do I know . . . !

GINA. She wanted to shoot the wild duck.

RELLING. The wild duck?

HJALMAR. The pistol must have gone off.

RELLING. Hm!

EKDAL. Shoot the wild duck. Don't understand a word of it. Don't want to hear any more.

[*He goes into the loft.*]

RELLING. The bullet hit her in the breast. . . .

HJALMAR. Yes, but she's alive!

GINA. Can't you see that Hedvig is dead. . . .

HJALMAR. No, no, she *must* live. Just for a moment. Just long enough for me to tell her. . . .

RELLING. She was hit in the heart. Internal hæmorrhage. She died instantaneously.

HJALMAR. Oh, Gina, Gina. What have I done to you!

GINA. Perhaps I didn't have any right to keep her.

HJALMAR. Did I have any right to take her away from you? From you, after what you have been to us all these years?

GINA. She must be carried in and laid on her own bed. Help me with her, Hjalmar.

[*She and* HJALMAR *take* HEDVIG *between them.*]

HJALMAR [*as they carry her*]. Oh, Gina, can you bear this?

GINA. We must help one another. I brought her into the world, and you took her out of the world—so *now* she's as much yours as mine.

⟨'They carry her into the living-room' crossed out.⟩

MOLVIK [*stretches out his arms and mutters*]. Praised be the Lord! Earth to earth . . . earth to earth. . . .

RELLING [*in an undertone*]. Shut up, Molvik; you're drunk. Go downstairs.

[HJALMAR *and* GINA *carry the body into the living-room*.]

RELLING [*shuts the door after them, crosses to* GREGERS]. That was no accident.

GREGERS. Are you quite certain of that?

RELLING. No doubt about it. After the way the powder burnt her dress. She pressed the pistol right against her dress and fired.

GREGERS. I can almost believe that was the way it happened.

RELLING. And can you claim to be altogether free from blame?

GREGERS. I meant everything for the best.

RELLING. Yes, you wanted to make something you call a true marriage in this house; and then you calculated only for the man and the wife, but the child you forgot ⟨*altered to* 'you cancelled out'⟩.

GREGERS. She couldn't stand the light of truth; it burnt into her eyes.

RELLING. For most people, truth is not always a good thing. Take the lie out of any particular situation, and at once you take away happiness as well.

GREGERS. If that were so, life would not be worth living.

RELLING. Do *you* think it is so important then that life should be lived?

GREGERS. I don't. On the contrary. But my fate isn't to live my life, either. I have another mission.

RELLING. What mission is that?

GREGERS. To be thirteenth at table.

[*He goes.*]

RELLING. The devil it is.

⟨The text of this draft was subsequently heavily revised, both by alterations on the pages of the manuscript itself and by more extensive deletions and additional substitute passages on separate sheets of paper, which then served as the basis for the final text.⟩

Ibsen's Letters[†]

To Georg Brandes

[The Beginning]

Rome, June 12, 1883

*   *   *

My head is full just now with the plot of a new dramatic work in four acts [The Wild Duck]. In the course of time a variety of crazy ideas are apt to collect in one's mind, and one needs an outlet for them. But as the play will deal neither with the Supreme Court nor the right of absolute veto, nor even with the removal of the sign of union from the flag,[1] it can hardly count upon arousing much interest in Norway. I hope, however, that it may win a hearing elsewhere.

*   *   *

To Frederik Hegel

[The Final Draft]

Rome, June 14, 1884

Dear Councilor Hegel, I am pleased to be able to inform you that I finished the draft of my new play [The Wild Duck] yesterday.

It has five acts and, according to my calculations, it will fill some two hundred pages in print, possibly a little more.

I still have to make the fair copy, and I shall begin that tomorrow. However, as customary with me, this will mean not just copying the draft but a thorough revision of the dialogue. And that will take time. Still, providing no unforeseen circumstances prevent

† From *Ibsen: Letters and Speeches,* edited by Evert Sprinchorn. Copyright © 1964 by Evert Sprinchorn. Reprinted by permission of Hill and Wang, Inc., New York, and MacGibbon and Kee, Ltd., London.
1. This disavowal by Ibsen himself did not prevent Dr. Wilhelm Hans from writing: "In old Ekdal Ibsen ridicules his fatherland, which once had had a time of greatness but which now felt happy and content in the idle recollection of this heroic past and wished to hear and know nothing about great future problems. It is old Ekdal's ardent wish to be allowed again to wear his lieutenant's uniform in public, which had been denied him. The restoration of the outward appearance of honor is what is most important to him. With this Ibsen openly plays on the struggle of the homeland patriots for an independent Norwegian flag." (*Ibsens Selbstportrat in seinem Dramen.* München, 1911. p. 146.) See also quotation from Archer, "Ibsen as I Knew Him," p. 209 [Editor].

it, I would say that the complete manuscript should be in your hands by mid-September.

This play does not concern itself with political or social questions or with public matters in general. The action takes place entirely in the area of family life. It will certainly provoke discussion, but it cannot possibly give offense to anyone. . . .

To Sigurd Ibsen

[*Finishing Touches*]

Gossensass, August 27, 1884

. . . Work on my play is rapidly nearing an end. It will be all finished in three or four days. Then I shall read it through carefully and mail it. I am very happy when I work on this play. I keep putting in more and more details all the time; and I hate to part with it—but I'll also be glad. . . .

The German sculptor Professor Kopf from Rome has brought his thirteen-year-old daughter with him. She is as nearly perfect a model for Hedvig in my play that I could hope for. She is pretty, has a serious face and manner, and is a little *gefrässig*.[2] . . .

To Suzannah Ibsen

[*Completion*]

Gossensass, August 30, 1884

Dear Suzannah, Although I do not know when and where my letters will reach you who fly about from one place to another, I must send you the good news that I have just completed my manuscript. The play is of considerable length, longer than any of my later ones. I have been able to put everything I wanted into it and I don't think it could easily be improved. Now it only remains to read it through, which will take two or three days, and then it goes to Hegel. Now I have to send him a preliminary note which must be done before midday, therefore only these lines.

I wrote to Sigurd on the twenty-seventh. The weather here is fine but chilly. Everything goes well. Your letter arrived on the twenty-second. Many greetings to you both from

Your devoted
Henrik Ibsen

2. A bit of a glutton (German) [Editor].

To Frederik Hegel

[*The Characters*]

Gossensass, September 2, 1884

Dear Mr. Hegel, Along with this letter, I am sending you the manuscript of my new play *The Wild Duck*. For the last four months I have worked on it every day, and it is not without a certain feeling of regret that I part with it. Long, daily association with the characters in this play has endeared them to me, in spite of their manifold failings. And I hope that they may find good and kind friends among the great reading public, and more particularly among the actor tribe—for all of them, without exception, are rewarding roles. But the study and representation of these characters will not be an easy task; and therefore the book should be offered to the theaters as early as possible in the season. I shall send the necessary letters, which you will be good enough to dispatch along with the different copies.

In some ways this new play occupies a position by itself among my dramatic works, its plan and method differing in several respects from my former ones. I shall say no more on this subject at present. I hope that my critics will discover the points alluded to. At any rate, they will find several things to squabble about and several things to interpret. I also think that *The Wild Duck* may perhaps entice some of our young dramatists into new paths, which I think is desirable.

* * *

To Hans Schrøder

[*The Casting*] †

Rome, November 14, 1884

Dear Mr. Schrøder, On my return here last night I found your telegram; as a reply to which allow me to note the following.

I myself have no desire to cast my new play, nor could I very readily assume that responsibility, since several members of the company are unknown to me, and, in regard to others, I have no

† *The Wild Duck* was published on November 11 in a first printing of 8,000 copies and proved so popular that a second printing appeared on December 1. The major Scandinavian theaters staged the play during the 1884–85 season, the Bergen theater opening first on January 9, and the Christiania Theater only two days later. The unusual demands that the play made of the actors prompted Schrøder, the head of the Christiania Theater, to write the author for advice.

way of knowing their development except through newspaper reviews, which very often do not give a reliable picture.

However, I have supposed that Hjalmar will be played by Reimers. This part must definitely not be rendered with any touch of parody nor with the faintest suggestion that the actor is aware that there is anything funny about his remarks. He has a warm and sympathetic voice, as Relling says, and that should be maintained above all else. His sentimentality is genuine, his melancholy charming in its way—not a bit of affectation. Confidentially, I would like to call your attention to Kristofer Janson who, frankly, can be charming when he's talking the worse nonsense. This is a hint for the actor in question.

Gina, I think, could be acted well by Mrs. Wolf. But where can we get a Hedvig? I do not know. And Mrs. Sørby? She is supposed to be attractive, witty, and not at all vulgar. Could Miss Reimers solve the problem? Or can Mrs. Gundersen? Gregers is the most difficult character in the play as far as acting is concerned. Sometimes I think Hammer could do it, or perhaps Bjørn B. Old Ekdal can be given either to Brun or to Klausen; Relling perhaps to Selmer. I would prefer to get rid of Isachsen, because he always carries on like a strange actor and not like an ordinary man; but he might perhaps make something out of Molvik's few lines. The two servants must not be neglected. Pettersen could perhaps be given to Bucher, and Jensen to Abelstad, if he is not needed as one of the gentlemen at the dinner party. The guests! Simple supernumeraries cannot be used of course without destroying the whole act. And what about the merchant Werle? There is Gundersen, of course. But I do not know if he is capable of evoking what I want and in the way I want it evoked.

In both the ensemble acting and in the stage setting, this play demands truth to nature and a touch of reality in every respect. The lighting too, has its significance; it differs from act to act and is calculated to correspond to the basic mood that characterizes each of the five acts. . . .

To August Lindberg

[*The Staging*]†

† More than the other Scandinavian directors, Lindberg appreciated the theatrical richness of *The Wild Duck*. After reading it, he said, "I get dizzy thinking about it. Such great opportunities for us actors! Never before have we been faced with such possibilities." To the playwright he wrote, "With Doctor Ibsen's newest play we have entered virgin territory where we have to make our way with pick and shovel. The people in the play are completely new, and where would we get by relying on old theatrical clichés?" Preparing to put the play into rehearsal immediately, he wrote to Ibsen about some details of the staging and got the following reply.

Rome, November 22, 1884

Dear Mr. Lindberg: In reply to your inquiry I hasten to inform you that *The Wild Duck*, just like all my other plays, is arranged from the point of view of the audience and not from that of the actor. I arrange everything as I visualize it while writing it down.

When Hedvig has shot herself, she should be placed on the couch in such a way that her feet are downstage, so that her right hand holding the pistol can hang down. When she is carried out through the kitchen door, I have imagined Hjalmar holding her under her arms and Gina carrying her feet.

I lay much stress in this play on the lighting. I have wanted it to correspond to the basic mood prevailing in each of the five acts.

I am especially delighted to learn that you yourself are likely to take a part in the play. . . .

To August Lindberg

[*The Part of Gina*]†

Rome, February 18, 1885

. . . When I submitted *The Wild Duck* to the management of the Royal Dramatic Theater in Stockholm, I was absolutely certain that the part of Gina would be entrusted to Mrs. Hwasser.

When I learned from the newspapers of the final distribution of parts, I was quite surprised. But it never occurred to me to take exception to the decision of the theater, since I was not familiar with the actress who had been assigned the role of Gina, and naturally I assumed that the management's choice was the best one.

Since then, however, all the reports that have come to me from Stockholm agree that neither Gina nor Mrs. Sørby is being represented in an altogether satisfactory manner.

† Lindberg's production of *The Wild Duck* went into rehearsal at the Royal Dramatic Theater in Stockholm in December and opened on January 30. Recognizing Lindberg's innovations, professional theater people felt that this production was the first in Scandinavia to utilize fully the new "naturalistic" approach to stage direction. The stage was treated as a room with one wall transparent; the actors moved as if they were in a real room; there were real doorcases; the doors had knobs; and there was even a commode with chamber pot and wash basin on stage. Indeed, Lindberg's commode became as famous in Scandinavia as Robertson's doorknobs in England. But the critics were unable to agree on the merits of the production. Their confusion stemmed in part from the fact that Lindberg in trying to avoid "theatrical clichés" in the various roles had slighted some of the leading actors at the theater. They protested to the head of the theater, the charges were echoed in the newspapers, and the reverberations soon reached Ibsen in Rome. Lindberg himself played Hjalmar Ekdal, and though his performance was as much censured as praised by the critics, their accounts suggest that Lindberg's performance was actually a masterpiece of acting and that it was the character as conceived by Ibsen that perplexed the critics.

Whether the Royal Theater has another actress at the moment who would be capable of giving a better interpretation of the latter role I cannot state positively, although I rather suspect it.

But I do feel absolutely convinced that the part of Gina will not be handled properly until it is given to Mrs. Hwasser.

Head of the theater Willman states in the newspapers that such a change in the parts might be possible after the play has been performed a number of times. On the basis of this remark, I hope and trust that *The Wild Duck* will soon be brought before the public in Stockholm in the best production possible.

I beg you not to misunderstand me, my dear Mr. Lindberg. I certainly do not doubt that the present distribution of parts was arranged with the best interests of the play in mind. But it cannot be denied that this was an experiment which did not succeed completely in all respects.

I believe I should make it clear that Mrs. Hwasser is entirely unaware that I am writing this letter to you. I have not heard a single word from her in a long time, either directly or through other persons; nor has she heard from me.

Please accept my warmest thanks for your performance as Hjalmar as well as for all your work in rehearsing and staging the play. From the reports I have heard, all this seems to be exemplary. The triumph of young Miss Seelig [as Hedvig] gladdens me especially. Please convey my regards to her and my best wishes for the future. . . .

To Victor Barrucand

[The Translation]

Munich, March 6, 1891

. . . I also want to say that on principle I am opposed to any translation undertaken by two or more working in collaboration. Moreover *The Wild Duck* presents great difficulties, since one must have an intimate knowledge of the Norwegian language in order to appreciate how thoroughly each person in the play has his own special, individual way of speaking, by means of which his degree of education or learning can be noted. When Gina, for example, is speaking, one can immediately hear that she has never learned any grammar and that she is a product of the lower classes. And similarly in various ways for the other characters. Hence the task of the translator is not an easy one. . . .

Suggested Sources

J. S. WELHAVEN

Søfuglen (1839) †

En Vildand svømmer stille
ved Øens høie Kyst;
de klare Bølger spille
omkring dens rene Bryst.

En Jæger gaar og bøier
sig i den steile Ur,
og skyder saa for Løier
det smukke Kreatur.

Og Fuglen kan ei drage
til Redens lune Skjød,
og Fuglen vil ei klage
Sin Smerte og sin Nød.

Og derfor taus den dukker
dybt i den mørke Fjord,
og Bølgen kold sig lukker,
og sletter ud dens Spor.

I Søens dybe Grunde
gror Tangen bred og frisk;
derunder vil den blunde,—
der bor den stumme Fisk.

The Sea Bird (1839)

A wild duck floats serenely
along the steep isle coast;
the limpid waves are playing
about its pristine breast.

A hunter comes and crouches
against the rocky steep,
and just for sport shoots
the beautiful creature.

And the bird cannot find home
to the comfort of the nest,
and the bird will not bemoan
Its grief and its distress.

And so it plunges silent
deep in the murky fjord,
the cold wave on it closes,
and wipes out all trace thereof.

Deep in the water's bottom
the sea weed flourishes;
there below it will slumber,—
there dwells the silent fish.

Ederfuglen (1851) ‡

Ederfuglen i Norge bor;
der holder han til ved den blygrå fjord.

† From J. S. Welhaven, *Samlede Skrifter* (København: Gyldendalske Boghandel, 1867), Vol. III, p. 55. Translated by Dounia B. Christiani. ‡ From Ibsen, *Samlede Værker* (Kristiania og København: Gyldendalske Boghandel-Nordisk Forlag, 1914), Vol. IV, p. 165. Translated by Fydell Edmund Garrett in *Lyrics and Poems from Ibsen* (London: J. M. Dent & Sons Ltd., 1912; Minneapolis: Augsburg Publishing House, 1912). Reprinted by permission of the publishers.

Han plukker af brystet de bløde dun,
og bygger sig rede både varm og lun.

Men fjordens fisker har stålsat hug;
han plyndrer redet til sidste fnug.

Er fiskeren grum, så er fuglen varm;
han ribber igen sin egen barm.

Og plyndres han atter, så klæder han dog
sit rede påny i en velgemt krog.

Men røves hans tredje, hans sidste skat,—
da spiler han vinger en forårs-nat.

Da kløver han skodden med blodigt bryst;—
mod syd, mod syd til en solskins-kyst!

The Eider-Duck (1851)

The eider's home is in Norroway;
He dwells by the fjord that is leaden-grey.

He plucks the soft, soft down from his breast,
And warm and cosy he builds his nest.

But the cruel fisherman does not spare;
He plunders the nest till all is bare.

The fisher is hard, but the bird holds true;
He strips his own warm bosom anew;

And robbed once more, he will yet make rich
Once more his nest in a secret niche.

But steal this treasure, his third, his last—
One night he spreads his wings to the blast;

With bleeding bosom the sea-fog dun
He cleaves, to the South, to the South and sun!

[The Attic]†

. . . When Ibsen was eight years of age, his father's business was found to be in such disorder that everything had to be sold to meet his creditors. The only piece of property left when this process had been gone through was a little broken-down farmhouse called Venstöb, in the outskirts of Skien. Ibsen afterwards stated that those

† From Edmund Gosse, *Ibsen* (London: Hodder and Stoughton Ltd., 1907; New York: Charles Scribner's Sons, 1907), p. 5. Reprinted by permission of the publishers.

who had taken most advantage of his parents' hospitality in their prosperous days were precisely those who now most markedly turned the cold shoulder on them. It is likely enough that this may have been the case, but one sees how inevitably Ibsen would, in after years, be convinced that it was. He believed himself to have been, personally, much mortified and humiliated in childhood by the change in the family status. Already, by all accounts, he had begun to live a life of moral isolation. His excellent sister long afterwards described him as an unsociable child, never a pleasant companion, and out of sympathy with all the rest of the family.

We recollect, in *The Wild Duck*, the garret which was the domain of Hedvig and of that symbolic bird. At Venstöb, the infant Ibsen possessed a like retreat, a little room near the back entrance, which was sacred to him and into the fastness of which he was accustomed to bolt himself. Here were some dreary old books, among others Harrison's folio *History of the City of London*, as well as a paintbox, an extinct eight-day clock, properties which were faithfully introduced, half a century later, into *The Wild Duck* . . .

[Poverty] †

As long as his father had passed for a rich man, life was full of possibilities; but Henrik Ibsen was a mere eight years old when his childhood world crashed in ruins. He missed the town. He never cared to live in the country later in life either, and at Venstøp the Ibsen family felt themselves sorely oppressed by grief and poverty; oftentimes food was so short that they had to count the potatoes for dinner. The bankrupt's son suffered through feeling himself torn out of his milieu and through having to be ashamed of his father, and neither during school hours nor during recess did Henrik Ibsen achieve any triumphs which could compensate for this sensibility of the family's defeat; only in his ambitious fantasies did he find a sort of redress, and the shows he put on[1] were like an attempt to realize the daydream that one day he would win power over people and make himself a praiseworthy name.

At Venstøp there had lived before Knud Ibsen's [Henrik's father] time a widefaring naval officer, about whom there were thrilling legends and who had left curious old books up in the attic. There Henrik Ibsen found engraved pictures from far-off lands, and these excited his imagination and increased his desire to draw and paint. . . .

† From Francis Bull, *Norsk Litteraturhistorie* (Oslo: H. Aschehoug & Co., 1937), Vol. IV, p. 270. Reprinted by permission of the publishers. Translated by Dounia B. Christiani.

1. Magic shows which the boy Ibsen put on from time to time with his younger brothers, according to his sister Hedvig, despite his usual unsociability and stage fright [Editor].

[Hedvig] †

Many personal recollections of the playwright found a place in this drama. Poor old Ekdal, who had formerly been wealthy and honored, was modeled on Ibsen's father. It is told of Magdalene Thoresen, the vivacious pastor's wife of Bergen, that she used to say jokingly to her black-bearded, silent son-in-law: "Come here, Ibsen, let me kiss you! You are so dæmonic!"—one personal reminiscence employed in the character of the drunken theologian Molvik; perhaps there were others too. Gregers' principle of doing things for himself, brought into play when he pours water into his smoking stove, draws comments from Gina such as Mrs. Ibsen may have employed when her husband insisted on polishing his own shoes or sewing buttons on for himself.[1] But for Ibsen the rarest memory was that of Hedvig in the attic poring over heirlooms left there by ancestral sea captains. In this play he erected for his sister, for whom Hedvig was named, a beautiful monument that makes the charming, devoted little girl of Skien immortal.

[Boccaccio's Falcon] ‡

Staring too fixedly . . . at the Wild Duck has its dangers, and in

---

† A. E. Zucker, *Ibsen the Master Builder*, New York: Holt, Rinehart and Winston, Inc. Copyright 1929, © 1957.

1. John Paulsen, who tells about Ibsen's self-help in *Samliv med Ibsen* (1906), emphasizes that the playwright's wife fixed up his sewing on the sly. Mrs. Ibsen, by all accounts a rather depressed woman totally unlike her vivacious stepmother, could hardly have contributed anything to Gina's characterization. One suspects that the long-suffering Aline Solness, if anyone, is modeled on her.

Could there be in Gina, "a few years" older than Hjalmar, traces of the servant girl, ten years his senior, who bore young Ibsen an illegitimate son? There is a haunting if tenuous suggestion in Ibsen's killing off Hedvig on her fourteenth birthday. By some accounts he had to support the boy till his fourteenth year, by others, through his fourteenth year; only rarely is the term given as fifteen (see Chronology, p. 219), although this was specified in a Norwegian law of 1821. (Compare Ibsen's note, "14 Hedvig, their eldest daughter, 14–15 years," McFarlane, p. 433). Ibsen was deeply ashamed of this indiscretion and tried to keep it a dark secret. There is no record that he ever saw this son, and the only trace of him in his writings is Peer Gynt's bastard troll.

The Three Ibsens, by Bergliot Ibsen, the daughter of Bjørnstjerne Bjørnson and wife of Ibsen's legitimate son, Sigurd, contains some further biographical data relevant to *The Wild Duck*. Ibsen and his father did not write to each other for twenty-five years (p. 12). On his father's death in 1877, Ibsen wrote to his uncle that he had not kept in touch with his parents because "I could do nothing for them, till recently" (p. 59). Ibsen did not attend the wedding of his only recognized child because he was ill and could not make the trip to Norway, it is given out; only Mrs. Ibsen and her brother accompanied the bridegroom (p. 101). A propos the menu Hjalmar brings home: When Sigurd Ibsen, at twenty-two and a half, got his Ph.D. and was finally allowed to make a trip alone, Ibsen enjoyed hearing what he could afford to eat; in a letter home, Sigurd gave the complete menu, with prices, of both the lunch and dinner at the Paris restaurant he frequented (pp. 70, 73).

Finally, there is a distinct resemblance between Ibsen's failure to pass the matriculation examinations (see Chronology, p. 219) and Hjalmar's getting into the university, as Relling says, "after a fashion" [Editor].

‡ James Walter McFarlane, "Revaluations of Ibsen," in *Ibsen and the Temper of Norwegian Literature*, ed. McFarlane (London: Oxford University Press, 1960). Reprinted by permission of the publisher.

straining the vision the analogy itself becomes strained. Looking around for a moment instead at the company it keeps, one becomes aware of another bird which has been strangely disregarded, one which along with Chekhov's Seagull seems to be—no matter what ornithology might say—a bird of a feather: Boccaccio's Falcon, that which appears in the ninth story of the fifth day of the *Decameron*. There is even some suggestion that the resemblance is not altogether accidental, the link between the two being Paul Heyse, German critic and author, whom Ibsen met in 1875 while living in Munich. Ibsen frequently attended the weekly meetings of the Crocodile Society, of which Heyse was a prominent member, and they saw much of each other without ever becoming close friends. A few years earlier, in 1871, Heyse had sketched his theory of the *Novelle*, his so-called *Falkentheorie*, derived from a study of Boccaccio's story; and it would be surprising if this did not on some occasion provide the society with something to discuss. . . .

BOCCACCIO: The Decameron

[Fifth Day, Novella IX] †

Federigo degli Alberighi being in love, without meeting with any return, spends all his substance in seeking to gratify his lady, till he has nothing left but one poor hawk, which he gives to her for dinner when she comes to his house; she, learning this, changes her resolution, and marries him, by which means he becomes wealthy.

The queen, now observing that only herself and Dioneo were left to speak, spoke pleasantly to this effect:—

As it has come to my turn, I shall give you a novel something like the preceding one, that you may not only know what influence the power of your charms has over a generous heart, but that you may learn likewise to bestow your favours of your own accord, and where you think most proper, without suffering Fortune to be your directress, who disposes blindly and without the least judgment whatsoever.

You must understand, then, that Coppo di Borghese Domenichi (who was, and perhaps still is, a person of great respect and author-ity in our city, whose amiable qualities, rather than his noble birth, had rendered him worthy of immortal fame) in the decline of life used to divert himself among his neighbours and acquaintances by relating things which had happened in his days, which he knew how to do with more exactness and elegance of expression than any

† From Giovanni Boccaccio, *The Decameron* (London: Gibbings and Co., Ltd., 1911), Vol. III, pp. 98–108.

other person;—he, I say, amongst other pleasant stories, used to tell us that at Florence dwelt a young gentleman named Federigo, son of Filippo Alberighi, who, in feats of arms and gentility, surpassed all the youth in Tuscany. This gentleman, as usually happens, fell in love with a lady called Madam Giovanna, one of the most agreeable women in Florence, and, to gain her affection, used to be continually making tilts, balls, and such diversions; lavishing away his money in rich presents, and everything that was extravagant. But she, as careful of her honour as she was fair, made no account either of what he did for her sake or of himself. Living in this manner, his wealth soon began to waste, till at last he had nothing left but a very small farm, the income of which was a most slender maintenance, and a single hawk, one of the best in the world. Yet loving his mistress still more than ever, and finding he could subsist no longer in the city in the manner he would choose to live, he retired to his farm, where he went out a-fowling, as often as the weather would permit, and bore his distress patiently, and without ever making his necessity known to anybody.

Now, one day it happened that, as he was reduced to the last extremity, this lady's husband, who was very rich, chanced to fall sick, and, feeling the approach of death, made his will, leaving all his substance to an only son, who was almost grown up; and, if he should die without issue, he then ordered that it should revert to his lady, whom he was extremely fond of; and when he had disposed thus of his fortune he died. She now, being left a widow, retired, as our ladies usually do during the summer season, to a house of hers in the country, near to that of Federigo, whence it happened that her son soon became acquainted with him, and they used to divert themselves together with dogs and hawks, when he, having often seen Federigo's hawk fly, and being strangely taken with it, was desirous of having it, though the other valued it to that degree that he knew not how to ask for it. This being so, the lad soon fell sick, which gave his mother great concern, as he was her only child: and she ceased not to attend on and comfort him, often requesting him, if there were any particular thing which he fancied, to let her know it, and promising to procure it for him if it were possible. The young gentleman, after many offers of this kind, at last said, "Madam, if you could contrive for me to have Federigo's hawk, I believe that I should soon be well." She was in some suspense at this, and began to consider how best to act. She knew that Federigo had long entertained a liking for her, without the least encouragement on her part; therefore she said to herself, "How can I send or go to ask for this hawk, which I hear is the very best of the kind, and what alone maintains him in the world? Or how can I offer to take away from a gentleman all the pleasure that he has in life?" Being in this perplexity, though she was very sure of having it for the asking, she stood without making any reply; till at last the love of her son so far prevailed that she resolved at all events to make him easy, and not send, but go herself, to bring it. She then replied, "Son, set your heart at rest, and think only of your recovery; for I promise you that the first thing I do to-morrow morning will be to ask for it, and bring it to you." This afforded him such joy that he immediately showed signs of amendment.

The next morning she went, by way of a walk, with another lady in company, to Federigo's little cottage to inquire for him. At that time, as it was too early to go out upon his diversion, he was at work in his garden. Hearing therefore that his mistress inquired for him at the door, he ran thither, surprised and full of joy; whilst she, with a great deal of complaisance, went to meet him; and, after the usual compliments, she said, "Good morning, Federigo; I come to give you some recompense for the trouble you have formerly taken on my account, when your love carried you beyond reasonable bounds: it is in this wise,—I mean to dine with you in a homely way, with this lady, my friend." He replied, with a great deal of humility, "Madam, I do not remember ever to have received any hurt or loss by your means, but rather so much good that if I were worth anything at any time it was due to your singular merit and the love I had for you; and most assuredly this courteous visit is more welcome to me than if I had all that I have wasted returned to me to spend over again; but you are come to a very poor host." With these words he showed her into his house, seeming much out of countenance, and from thence they went into the garden, when, having no company for her, he said, "Madam, as I have nobody else, please to admit this honest woman, a labourer's wife, to be with you, whilst I set forth the table."

He, although his poverty was extreme, was never so sensible of his having been extravagant as now; but finding nothing to entertain the lady with, for whose sake he had treated thousands, he was in the utmost perplexity, cursing his evil fortune and running up and down like one out of his wits. At length, having neither money nor anything he could pawn, and being willing to treat her as honourably as he could, at the same time that he would not make his case known, even so much as to his own labourer, he espied his hawk upon the perch, which he seized, and finding it very fat, judged it might make a dish not unworthy of such a lady. Without further thought, then, he twisted its neck, and gave it to a girl to truss and roast carefully, whilst he laid the cloth and the napkins, having a small quantity of linen yet left; and then he returned, with a smile on his countenance, into the garden, telling her that what little dinner he was able to provide was now ready. She and her friend, therefore, entered and sat down with him, he serving them all the time with great respect, when they ate the hawk. After dinner was over, and they had sat chattering a little together, she thought it a fit time to tell her errand, and she spoke to him courteously in this manner:—

"Sir, if you call to mind your past life, and my resolution, which perhaps you may call cruelty, I doubt not but you will wonder at my presumption, when you know what I am come for: if you had children of your own, whereby you might understand how strong our natural affection is towards them, I am very sure you would excuse me. But, though you have none, I who have am bound by the natural laws of maternity, the force of which is greater than my own will, and indeed my duty: I am therefore constrained to request a thing of you which I know you value extremely, as you have no other comfort or diversion left in the extremity of your fortunes; I mean your hawk, which my son has taken such a fancy to that unless I bring him back with me I very much fear that he will die of his disorder. Therefore I entreat you, not for any regard you have for me (for in that respect you are no way obliged to me), but for that generosity with which you have always distinguished yourself, that you would please to let me have him, by which means you will save my child's life, and lay him under perpetual obligations."

Federigo, hearing the lady's request, and knowing it was out of his power to serve her, began to weep before he was able to make a word of reply. This she first thought was his great concern to part with his favourite bird, and she was about to say that she would not accept it; but she restrained herself, and awaited his reply when he should become more composed. At last he said, "Madam, ever since I have fixed my affections upon you, Fortune has still been contrary to me in many things, and I have often complained of her treatment; but her former harshness has been light and easy compared with what I now endure, which banishes all my peace of mind. You are here to visit me in this my poor mansion, whither in my prosperity you would never deign to come; you also entreat a small present from me, which it is no way in my power to give, as I am going briefly to tell you. As soon as I was acquainted with the great favour you designed me, I thought it proper, considering your superior merit and excellency, to treat you, according to my ability, with something more choice and valuable than is usually given to other persons, when, calling to mind my hawk, which you now request, and his goodness, I judged him a fit repast for you, and you have had him served roasted on your dish. Nor could I have thought him better bestowed, had you not now desired him in a different manner, which is such a grief to me that I shall never be at peace as long as I live;" and upon saying this he produced his feathers, feet, and beak. She began now to blame him for killing such a bird to entertain any woman with, inwardly praising the greatness of his soul, which poverty had no power to abase. Thus, having no farther hopes of obtaining the hawk, she thanked him for the respect and good-will he had showed towards her, and returned full of concern to her son, who, either out of grief for the disappointment or through the violence of his disorder, died within a few days.

She continued sorrowful for some time; but, being left rich and young, her brothers were very pressing with her to marry again; and, though this were against her inclinations, yet, finding them still importunate, and remembering Federigo's great worth and the late instance of his generosity in killing such a bird for her entertainment, she said, "I should rather choose to continue as I am; but, since it is your desire that I take a husband, I will have none save Federigo degli Alberighi." They smiled contemptuously at this, and said, "You simple woman! what are you talking of? He is not worth one farthing in the world." She replied, "I believe it, brothers, to be as you say; but know that I would sooner have a man that stands in need of riches than riches without a man." They, hearing her resolution, and well knowing his generous temper, gave her to him with all her wealth; and he, seeing himself possessed of a lady whom he had so dearly loved, and such a large fortune, lived in all true happiness with her, and was a better manager of his affairs for the time to come.

Criticism

Essays in Criticism

E. M. FORSTER

Ibsen the Romantic†

"My book is poetry, and if it is not poetry, then it will be."—Ibsen to Björnson.

Ibsen was a poet during the earlier part of his life. He began as a lyricist, and his first plays are either in verse or are inspired by an imaginative contemplation of the past. When he was about forty, a change occurred, the importance of which has been differently estimated. Certain critics, both friendly and hostile, regard it as a fundamental change. They argue that with *The League of Youth* the real or realistic Ibsen begins to emerge, the singer dies, the social castigator is born, the scene clarifies and darkens, and ideas come to the front which do not necessarily contradict previous ideas, but which are given a prominence that entirely alters the dramatic emphasis. We pass from the epic to the domestic. Peer Gynt becomes Hjalmar Ekdal, and Brand as Gregers Werle tears the spectacles of illusion from his eyes, and they work out their tragedy, not among forests and fjords, but in a photographic studio opening into a sort of aviary. The aviary contains a few dead Christmas trees, also a water trough, some rabbits but no bears, one wild duck and that a damaged one. We could not be further from romance, the critics say, and turn, if they are friendly, to the character drawing, the technique, and the moral and social issues; if they are hostile, to the squalor. "Somewhere in the course of the battle of his life Ibsen had a lyric Pegasus killed under him," writes Brandes. "Novel and perilous nonsense," wrote the *Daily Telegraph*. The critics agree in thinking that the poetry, if ever there was any, has gone.

Has it gone? Can the habits of forty years be set aside? Of twenty years—yes; most people are romantic at twenty, owing to lack of experience. As they grow older life offers various alternatives, such as worldliness or philosophy or the sense of humor, and they usually accept one of these. If, in spite of more solid tempta-

† From E. M. Forster, *Abinger Harvest*, copyright 1936, 1964 by E. M. Forster (New York: Harcourt, Brace & World, Inc.; London: Edward Arnold Ltd.) Reprinted by permission of the publishers.

tions, they still cling to poetry, it is because a deep preference has to be satisfied. Ibsen was a poet at forty because he had that preference. He was a poet at sixty also. His continued interest in avalanches, water, trees, fire, mines, high places, traveling, was not accidental. Not only was he born a poet—he died one, and as soon as we try to understand him instead of asking him to teach us, the point becomes clearer.

He is, of course, not easy to understand. Two obstacles may be noted. In the first place although he is not a teacher he has the air of being one, there is something in his method that implies a message, though the message really rested on passing irritabilities, and not on any permanent view of conduct or the universe. In the second place, he further throws us off the scent by taking a harsh or a depressing view of human relationships. As a rule, if a writer has a romantic temperament, he will find human relationships beautiful. His characters may hate one another or be unhappy together, but they will generate nobility or charm, they will never be squalid, whatever their other defects. And the crux in Ibsen is that, though he had the romantic temperament, he found personal intercourse sordid. Sooner or later his characters draw their little knives, they rip up the present and the past, and the closer their intimacy the better their opportunities for exchanging pain. Oswald Alving knows how to hurt his mother, Rosmer his mistress, and married couples are even more favorably placed. The Helmers, the Tesmans, the Wangels, Solnesses, Allmers, Borkmans, Rubeks—what a procession, equally incapable of comradeship and ecstasy! If they were heroic or happy once, it was before the curtain rose, and only survives as decay. And if they attain reconciliation, like the Rentheim sisters, the curtain has to fall. Their intercourse is worse than unfriendly, it is petty; moral ugliness trespasses into the aesthetic. And when a play is full of such characters and evolves round their fortunes, how can it possibly be a romantic play? Poetry might perhaps be achieved if Ibsen's indignation was of the straight-hitting sort, like Dante's. But for all its sincerity there is something automatic about it, he reminds us too often of father at the breakfast table after a bad night, sensitive to the defects of society as revealed by a chance glance at the newspaper, and apt to blame all parties for them indiscriminately. Now it is the position of women that upsets father, now the lies people tell, now their inability to lie, now the drains, now the newspaper itself, which he crumples up, but his helpers and servers have to retrieve it, for bad as are all political parties he must really see who got in at Rosmersholm. Seldom can a great genius have had so large a dose of domestic irritability. He was cross with his enemies and friends, with theater-managers, professors, and students, and so cross with his countrymen for not volunteering to help the Danes in 1864 that he had to go to Italy to say so. He might have volunteered in person—he was in the prime of life at the time—but this did not occur to him; he preferred instead to write a scathing little satire about a Norwegian mother whose son was safe at the front. And it is (if one may adopt the phrase) precisely the volunteer spirit that is absent from his conception of human relationships. He put everything into them except the strength of his arm.

"Not a great writer . . . almost great, but marred by this lack of generosity." How readily the phrases rise to the lips! How false they are! For this nagging quality, this habitual bitterness—they are essential in his greatness, because they beckon to the poetry in him, and carry it with them under the ground. Underground. Into the depths of the sea, the depths of the sea. Had he been of heroic build and turned to the light and the sun, his gifts would have evaporated. But he was—thank heaven—subterranean, he loved narrow passages and darkness, and his later plays have a romantic intensity which not only rivals the romantic expansion of their predecessors, but is absolutely unique in literature. The trees in old Ekdal's aviary are as numerous as a forest because they are countless, the water in the chickens' trough includes all the waves on which the Vikings could sail. To his impassioned vision dead and damaged things, however contemptible socially, dwell for ever in the land of romance, and this is the secret of his so-called symbolism: a connection is found between objects that lead different types of existence; they reinforce one another and each lives more intensely than before. Consequently his stage throbs with a mysteriousness for which no obvious preparation has been made, with beckonings, tremblings, sudden compressions of the air, and his characters as they wrangle among the oval tables and stoves are watched by an unseen power which slips between their words.

A weaker dramatist who had this peculiar gift would try to get his effect by patches of fine writing, but with Ibsen as with Beethoven the beauty comes not from the tunes, but from the way they are used and are worked into the joints of the action. *The Master Builder* contains superb examples of this. The plot unfolds logically, the diction is flat and austere, the scene is a villa close to which another villa is being erected, the chief characters are an elderly couple and a young woman who is determined to get a thrill out of her visit, even if it entails breaking her host's neck. Hilda is a minx, and though her restlessness is not so vulgar as Hedda Gabler's it is quite as pernicious and lacks the saving gesture of suicide. That is one side of Hilda. But on the other side she touches Gerd and the Rat-Wife and the Button-molder,[1] she is a lure and

1. Gerd is in *Brand*, the Rat-Wife is   is in *Peer Gynt* [Editor].
in *Little Eyolf*, and the Button-molder

an assessor, she comes from the non-human and asks for her king-
dom and for castles in the air that shall rest on solid masonry, and
from the moment she knocks at the door poetry filters into the
play. Solness, when he listened to her, was neither a dead man nor
an old fool. No prose memorial can be raised to him, and consequently Ibsen himself can say nothing when he falls from the
scaffolding, and Bernard Shaw does not know that there is anything
to say. But Hilda hears harps and voices in the air, and though her
own voice may be that of a sadistic schoolgirl the sound has nevertheless gone out into the dramatist's universe, the avalanches in
Brand and *When We Dead Awaken* echo it, so does the metal in
John Gabriel Borkman's mine. And it has all been done so compe-
tently. The symbolism never holds up the action, because it is part
of the action, and because Ibsen was a poet, to whom creation and
craftsmanship were one. It is the same with the white horses in
Rosmersholm, the fire of life in *Ghosts*, the gnawing pains in *Little
Eyolf*, the sea in *The Lady from the Sea*, where Hilda's own stepmother voices more openly than usual the malaise that connects
the forces of nature and the fortunes of men. Everything rings true
and echoes far because it is in the exact place which its surroundings require.

The source of Ibsen's poetry is indefinable; presumably it comes
from the same place as his view of human nature, otherwise they
would not harmonize as they do in his art. The vehicle in which
poetry reached him—that can easily be defined; it was, of course,
the scenery of western and south-western Norway. At some date
previous to his Italian journey he must have had experiences of passionate intensity among the mountains, comparable to the early
experiences of Wordsworth in the English lakes. All his life they
kept returning to him, clothed in streams, trees, precipices, and hal-
lowing his characters while they recriminated. In *Brand* and *Peer
Gynt* they filled the stage; subsequently they shrank and concentrated; in the two last plays they again fill the stage and hasten the
catastrophes by a shroud of snow. To compare Ibsen with Wordsworth is to scandalize the faithful in either camp, yet they had one
important point in common: they were both of them haunted until
the end of their lives by the romantic possibilities of scenery.
Wordsworth fell into the residential fallacy; he continued to look
at his gods direct, and to pin with decreasing success his precepts to
the flanks of Helvellyn. Ibsen, wiser and greater, sank and smashed
the Dovrëfjeld in the depths of the sea, the depths of the sea. He
knew that he should find it again. Neither his satire nor his character drawing dwelt as deep; neither the problems he found in human
conduct nor the tentative solutions he propounded lay at the roots
of his extraordinary heart. There, in that strange gnarled region, a

primeval romanticism lurked, frozen or twisted or exuding slime, there was the nest of the Great Boyg. The Great Boyg did not strive, did not die, lay beneath good and evil, did not say one thing more than another:

> Forward or back, and it's just as far;
> Out or in, and it's just as strait.

What do the words mean, and, apart from their meaning, are they meant to be right? And if right, are the prayers of Solveig, which silence them for a moment, wrong? It is proper that we should ask such questions as these when focusing on the moral and social aspect of his work, and they have been brilliantly asked and answered by Bernard Shaw. But as soon as we shift the focus the questions go dim, the reformer becomes a dramatist, we shift again and the dramatist becomes a lyric poet, listening from first to last for the movements of the trolls. Ibsen is at bottom Peer Gynt. Side whiskers and all, he is a boy bewitched:

> The boy has been sitting on his mother's lap.
> They two have been playing all the life-day long.

And though the brow that bends over him can scarcely be described as maternal, it will assuredly preserve him from the melting ladle as long as books are read or plays seen.

BRIAN W. DOWNS

The Wild Duck†

I

The two plays by Ibsen which lie between A *Doll's House* (1879) and *The Wild Duck* (1884) are *Ghosts* (*Gengangere*, 1881) and *An Enemy of the People* (*En Folkefiende*, 1882). About *Ghosts* and the manner with which it links up to, and supplements, A *Doll's House*, everything needful for present purposes has already been touched upon, except the great scandal which it provoked. Ibsen's staunch defender, Jonas Lie, said that *Ghosts* was 'a major operation with the knife plunged straight into the unmentionable'—rotten marriages, sexual misconduct, venereal disease, elimination of the unfit, etc. Small wonder that the public exposure of such things, particularly in a form commonly associated with social entertainment, was fiercely and widely resented. Ibsen

† From Brian W. Downs, *A Study of Six Plays by Ibsen* (Cambridge: Cambridge University Press, 1950), pp. 147–77. Copyright © 1950 by Cambridge University Press. Reprinted by permission of the publishers.

had invited the public to a party for which they had had to pay, and then thrown a stink-bomb into their midst.

The reception of *Ghosts* gave its author the theme of his next play without any of the outward and inward searching and sifting he found necessary at other times. If he was to be accused of malodorous practices he would examine more fully than his critics the justification for indulging in them. So he invented Dr. Thomas Stockmann, the large-hearted medical officer to a Spa Committee, who publicly discloses the grave scandal that the Spa's water supply is tainted, and is ignominiously deprived of his livelihood as an Enemy of the People: at the same time, Ibsen made it clear that, to all but those who are 'to Themselves—Enough' and in fact in the eyes of everybody outside the Spa, Thomas Stockmann was doing his duty and that in principles and personality, he was, for all his precipitancy and tactlessness, much to be preferred to those who hounded him out of office.

No play by Ibsen has greater concreteness than *An Enemy of the People* with its small seaside town struggling to raise itself in the world as a health resort, its Rate-Payers' Association and mean local newspaper, its municipal panjandrum and the effluvium from the wealthy citizen's tannery which causes all the mischief. The scale of things may be petty—and Ibsen was not above rubbing in his disdain of Scandinavian conditions by deliberately making it so—but the implication is not utterly provincial: Bath[1] or Aix-les-Bains might find itself in a similar quandary. The story, lacking all 'prehistory', suggestions of abstruse symbolism or unnecessary question marks, is straightforward; yet at the same time it constitutes an answer to the critics of *Ghosts*, and, to that extent at least, is a parable. Never were Ibsen's theme and methods to be so simple again; and one way and another, the parabolic gained ground.

Never again, it may be added, did Ibsen attack specific abuses as he had done in the four plays published between 1877 and 1882; a partial explanation for this may be found in the termination of the great struggle between prerogative and the will of the Norwegian people (which, however, still fills the background of *Rosmersholm*, 1886) and the inauguration of a new political era by the rise to power of Sverdrup and the 'Left' in 1884.

II

The title for *The Wild Duck* was certainly suggested to Ibsen by one of the finest poems of his compatriot Welhaven, '*Søfuglen*' (The Sea-bird). Welhaven's Sea-bird is not only a wild duck, but the fate also that overtakes it is clearly reproduced in the play.

---

1. The novelist-physician Smollett did in fact try to play the part of a Stock- mann in the Bath of the eighteenth century.

Injured by a sportsman, prevented from reaching its nest and unwilling to make moan, it dives into the deeps to where the weed grows broad and fresh and the mute fish dwells. It is just possible that from the mouth of his friend Jens Peter Jacobsen, the Danish translator of Darwin, or otherwise, Ibsen learnt of Darwin's observation: 'We have seen how soon the wild duck, when domesticated, loses its true character, from the effects of abundant or changed feeding, or from taking little exercise.'[2] For the wild duck of the play is certainly becoming acclimatised in its unfamiliar surroundings; and in so far as this acclimatisation represents a kind of degeneration and Ibsen was intent in his play to show the effects of degeneration through a parable—two debatable propositions—he may have chosen precisely this exemplification, to which Darwin introduced him, with the poetic associations which Welhaven had imparted to it.

The original conception must have differed considerably from the play which ultimately became *The Wild Duck*. The earliest notes on it we have make, for instance, no mention at all either of the duck herself or of the menagerie in which she queens it. We find there, however, the idea of the family that has come down in the world, even if it comprises a somewhat larger number of persons, one of whom, the son, is a photographer;[3] the family probably played fatuously with the idea of their eventual rehabilitation. They were in contact, too, with another family, that of a merchant. Here again there is a notable difference. For the son of this last-named family, for Halfdan Walle, Ibsen apparently took for his model the author Alexander Kielland.[4] Kielland, after Ibsen himself, Bjørnson and Jonas Lie the greatest Norwegian writer of the time, was a scion of a famous patrician mercantile family of Stavanger: his grandfather had been reputed the richest man in Norway. In a very short space of time Kielland had made a considerable name for himself both with short stories (e.g. *Novelletter* of 1878 and 1880) and with novels which not only described faithfully and warmly his own social environment, but very plainly revealed also an unmistakable radical outlook. Like others, Ibsen was fascinated by the contrast between the man who had all the appearance and manner of a great merchant prince and the understanding, if unsentimental, sympathy which he bestowed on the humble of spirit and estate. He was inclined to think of him as a 'sybarite'—this is the word he used—the complete Kierkegaardian aesthete, who derived an additional pleasure in his luxurious life by

2. Darwin, C., *Variation of Animals and Plants under Domestication, II* (1868), p. 278. It would indeed be possible to argue that this sentence re-echoes also in *The Lady from the Sea*.

3. Rather perplexingly called Gregers at this stage, his *vis-à-vis* having the name Halfdan.

4. Referred to as 'A.K.' or 'A.K-d' in the notes.

the contemplation of others' misery. One of Ibsen's notes sketches him lying cosily tucked up in bed after a good supper, revelling in the thought of tired, cold wayfarers plunging through the splashing rain outside. We may conjecture—but it is no more than a conjecture—that in the original conception of *The Wild Duck* this sybarite was to amuse himself by contemplating the misfortunes of his former school friend, the photographer, and probably playing Providence to him and his squalid family (somewhat after the manner in which old Werle does so in the finished play), and that the disaster was caused by this purely aesthetical, quite unidealistic activity. That scheme, however, would not work and had to be abandoned; but the names Walle or Werle, Ekdahl or Ekdal, Gina, Hedvig, Graaberg and Pettersen were perpetuated; the two groups of personages, the contrast between the opulent group and the down-at-heel persisted and oddly enough, the elder Walle or Werle probably took over many of his son's characteristics just as the latter took over the photographer's Christian name; and the matter-of-fact physician was presumably developed out of the schoolmaster Nanne, who may originally have combined the functions of Relling and Molvik.

The changes in conception just indicated took place mostly between the early days of 1883 and April 1884, when, at Rome and on the 20th of that month, Ibsen began the first complete draft (subsequently much altered) of Act I. The drafts of all five acts were completed by 13 June: Ibsen then took up his quarters at Gossensass in the Austrian Alps, where *An Enemy of the People* had been finished off, and in July and August made the fair copy, which was sent off to Messrs. Gyldendal of Copenhagen on 2 September. Publication in a slightly smaller edition (8000 copies instead of 10,000) than the first edition of *Ghosts* and *An Enemy of the People* took place on 11 November; a second edition was called for three weeks later, but remained on the publisher's hands for thirty years.[5]

Competition for the *première* was very keen. In the event the prize fell to the Christiania Theatre, which presented it on 9 January 1885, with Ibsen's old friends Gundersen, Brun and Fru Wolf as Old Werle, Old Ekdal and Gina respectively, Hammer as Gregers, Reimers as Hjalmar, Isachsen as Relling, Frøken Krohn as Hedvig.[6] The earliest performances in Finland, Denmark (at Aalborg) and Sweden were given the following January 16, 25 and 30 respectively. The theater's 'censor', Erik Bøgh, though as a rule well disposed towards Ibsen, had reported adversely on *The Wild*

5. In the interval, however, there were some collected editions of the works, the first in 1898.

6. Johanne Dybwad (then still Frøken Juell) did not take up the part of Hedvig till 1889.

Duck,[7] yet on 22 February 1885 the Royal Theatre at Copenhagen gave it most successfully with great realism of staging and a magnificent cast: the brothers Emil and Olaf Paulsen played Hjalmar and his father respectively, Betty Hennings was the Hedvig,[8] and young Karl Mantzius Dr. Relling. Emil Paulsen, it may be observed, was a fine comedian, and so much prominence was given to the ludicrous elements in *The Wild Duck* that, for all the brilliance of the presentation, Ibsen felt constrained to protest mildly that he had written a 'tragi-comedy' in which word the 'tragi' was as important as the 'comedy'—otherwise Hedvig's death, as he said, would become 'incomprehensible'.[9] Olaf Paulsen excelled in parts like Falstaff, and this should be borne in mind by those theatrical producers who take the opposite view to that reprobated by the author and who seek to sink the play in gloom.[1] At its first presentation, *The Wild Duck* produced in the more discerning little more than puzzlement. Its superficial formlessness and the mixture of the tragic and farcical had, in the long run, a pervasive effect on dramatic technique, to which, in their different ways, Hauptmann's *Ratten*, Shaw's *The Doctor's Dilemma*, Chekhov's dramas and many plays of the Dublin Abbey Theatre[2] bear witness. It has never been *widely* popular, but general consensus of the best opinion to-day would probably consider it 'the Master's masterpiece'—at any rate if the dramatic poems were set aside.

III

In a letter sent to his publisher, Frederik Hegel of Gyldendal's, at the same time as the manuscript of *The Wild Duck*, Ibsen had written: 'In some ways this new piece occupies a place apart in my dramatic production; the method of procedure differs in certain respects from the previous.' The novel method of procedure reveals itself at once when the attempt is made to summarise the extremely elaborate antecedent data which, though they are fraught with the weightiest consequences, exhibit little of the precision of Nora Helmer's forged bill or Consul Bernick's successful use of Johan Tønnesen as his scapegoat.[3] The facts in themselves are nowhere really established; they sink into virtual irrelevance; what matters is the construction which the personages of the play with or without warranty put upon them. For convenience they may be

7. In particular he insisted that the drunken parson, Molvik, must be omitted; that was not done. Wherever (as in Denmark) he was in a position legally to enforce his wishes, Ibsen refused all tampering with his texts.

8. Ibsen said of this production 'Fru Hennings *is* Hedvig but the others fall short'.

9. *Cit.* Centenary Edition, x, 38.

1. *The Wild Duck* was first acted in Germany in 1887, in France in 1891 and in Britain in 1894.

2. It is amusing to find that a blowzy old woman in Walter Macken's *Galway Handicap* (1947) is called 'Winnie the Wild-Duck'.

3. In *Ghosts*, it may be noted, the true nature and origin of Oswald's illness are left somewhat uncertain.

arranged in three groups which, however, are closely related: (i) Old Ekdal's disgrace, (ii) the home life of Haaken Werle during his wife's lifetime, and (iii) Hjalmar Ekdal's marriage to Gina Hansen. A fourth group of data concerned with the earlier relations of Gregers Werle, Dr. Relling and Berta Sørby has only subsidiary importance.

(i) Twenty years or so before the action of *The Wild Duck* begins, Lieutenant Ekdal and Haaken Werle, then comparatively young men, were in partnership together in Højdal, a remote part of Northern Norway where the latter still owns certain 'works'. Ekdal was convicted and condemned to imprisonment and loss of military rank for having unlawfully felled (and presumably appropriated) timber on Crown property, availing himself of an unreliable map which he himself had drawn. His partner was involved in the prosecution but acquitted. So much seems certain. But about Werle's complicity there is a difference of opinion. His servant Pettersen, who seems to be no respecter of persons, harbours no suspicions of it nor seems to have heard of discreditable rumours: 'They say that he [Ekdal] once played Mr. Werle a very nasty trick.' But Werle's son, Gregers, who, it may be borne in mind, has spent sixteen or seventeen years in the district where the criminal transactions took place, is persuaded that his father was an accomplice and construes his later acts of charity to the Ekdal family as the expiations of a bad conscience. Hjalmar Ekdal looks upon his father as a martyr, but at first bears Haaken Werle no grudge; Relling, who apparently knows something about this old story, remarks that Lieutenant Ekdal was always 'an ass'.

(ii) Haaken Werle's marriage, of which Gregers was the fruit, was an unhappy one. The spouses were at odds, and Gregers always took his mother's side. She had weaknesses and according to the testimony of a former maid (on whom she laid violent hands) occasionally had 'crazy fits'; if she was an alcoholic addict, that would fit the descriptions. Her husband, on the other hand, exposed to unending domestic scenes, ran after the said maid with dishonourable intentions, but whether he was actually unfaithful to his wife is not made explicit.

(iii) When Fru Werle died, the widower continued his pursuit of Gina Hansen—through the comparatively decent intermediacy, it may be noted, of her mother—and 'had his will of her'. Soon after this she married Hjalmar Ekdal, who also had enjoyed extra-marital relations with her and who, his university career broken off by his father's disgrace, had recently been trained as a photographer and installed in his own studio at Haaken Werle's expense. That the latter furthered the marriage of Hjalmar and Gina in any other way is not stated. Gina's child, Hedvig, born in wedlock, had been conceived before, but the paternity is left uncertain; Gregers unquestionably assumes that she is his half-sister, and the assumption is supported by the fact that both she and Haaken Werle suffer from a serious affliction of the eyes.[4]

This then is the complex relationship to one another of most of the principals at the beginning of Act I, when old Werle, a highly prosperous merchant, is giving a sumptuous dinner in honour of his son Gregers and his return home after a long absence. Gregers has insisted on the inclusion of Hjalmar Ekdal among the guests (though this brings the number at dinner up to thirteen); they had been friends in the old days of their fathers' partnership, but had maintained no correspondence: so Gregers is quite unfamiliar with the Ekdal's circumstances and even with the identity of Hjalmar's wife. He learns something about all this during an after-dinner talk interrupted by a painful episode when the shabby, shambling figure of Old Ekdal has to make its way through the reception rooms from Werle's office where he has been fetching the copying work— grossly overpaid—on which he subsists. Gregers is indignant at what he considers Hjalmar's tame, not to say cowardly, acceptance of the situation and further outraged at the offer of a partnership in the firm which his father then makes to him. Gregers looks upon the offer and the festive celebration of his return as a mere *façade* which he is to embellish and by which his father wishes to cover up any suspicion of family disunion, as well as the marriage on which he now proposes to enter with the present housekeeper, Berta Sørby.

Not all the reasons transpire on account of which, at the outset of *The Wild Duck*, Gregers has travelled up from the Højdal works to the capital.[5] His father's invitation does not by itself exhaust them; for the offer of a partnership comes, apparently, as a surprise to him, while, at the same time, he has made no plans to return. His talks with Hjalmar Ekdal and his father in the first act, however, furnish him with a definite purpose: to open Hjalmar's eyes to his true position and thus induce him radically and immediately to change it: for, having as high an opinion of his friend's character as of his abilities, he cannot but believe that only sheer ignorance can account for his continuing to put up with something that he, Gregers, looks on as dishonourable.

The second, third, fourth and fifth acts are laid in an environ-

4. On the other hand, Lou Andréas-Salomé argued with some ingenuity that, if Hedvig's artistic leanings which make her wish to be an engraver are inherited, they are more likely to have come from Hjalmar Ekdal than from Haaken Werle (Andréas-Salomé, L., *Henrik Ibsen's Frauengestalten*, 1892, p. 88).

5. The general stage-direction of the finished play says no more than that 'The first act passes in Werle's house, the remaining acts at Hjalmar Ekdal's'; but the original draft declared that the action took place in Christiania, and I think that this should be assumed.

154 · *Brian W. Downs*

ment strikingly different from the opulent—not to say the ostenta-
tious—luxury of Haaken Werle's study; they play in Hjalmar
Ekdal's third-rate photographic *atelier*, which commonly serves also
as his family's living-room. Some necessary professional apparatus
and litter apart, it is snug, if cheap and shabby, and not greatly in
demand for its ostensible purpose. A remarkable feature is the
extension of this room—which is at the top of the building and has
a convenient sky-light—into a large, derelict attic, harbouring not
only more usual lumber, but in addition, a small forest of decaying
Christmas-trees and a quantity of livestock.

Owing to his neglect of it, Hjalmar Ekdal's business scarcely
thrives, and an additional source of income accrues from the sub-
letting of rooms in his house. One of these Gregers Werle, calling
shortly after Hjalmar has returned from the dinner-party, proposes
to take, and Hjalmar's wife, Gina, who knows Gregers of old,[6]
reluctantly consents to the arrangement. The following act, the
third, takes place next morning and is largely taken up with the
lunch-party which Hjalmar gives for Gregers and to which he
invites also his other lodgers, the doctor Relling and the parson
Molvik. His indignation exacerbated both by fuller appreciation of
Hjalmar's environment—not least, by the make-believe wild life in
the attic—and by a last friendly overture which his father calls to
make, Gregers invites his old friend for a long walk and, in the
course of it, reveals to him Gina's intrigue with Werle senior and
the dubious nature of the latter's benefits to the Ekdal family. Gregers purposed thereby, no doubt, to perform 'the miracle of mira-
cles', whereby a true marriage should come about between Hjalmar
and his lowly, but loyal wife; the effect of his interference, however,
is only to rouse in Hjalmar a sullen resentment at the disturbance
in his mental habits—a resentment which is heated to a warmer
glow by the receipt, in Act IV, of a deed of gift from Old Werle
for the benefit of Ekdal senior and, after his death, for that of
Hedvig. Firmly convinced now that the little girl is not his, but
Haaken Werle's child, Hjalmar repulses her and joins Relling and
Molvik on a drunken tour through the town. In the course of the
following morning (Act V) he returns home to arrange for the final
removal of himself and his old father. But the project is shattered
by the death of Hedvig, who, urged by Gregers to sacrifice to her
father's love what she holds dearest in the world, has gone into the
attic to shoot the wild duck and has turned the pistol against her
own breast.

6. Gina was Haaken Werle's housekeeper and mistress after Gregers had
left home, it seems; but she was a servant girl in the house before. From the
first, her aversion to Gregers is very
marked and significant, though different interpretations may be put upon
it. Perhaps, like Relling, she knew
him as an inveterate mischief-maker.

As four of *The Wild Duck's* five acts play amid a physical confusion and squalor for which the author's earlier plays scarcely show a parallel,[7] so the level of the characters shows in almost every respect a marked degradation. Thomas Stockmann was an uncommon doctor to find in a small provincial town, and much of the point of *Pillars of Society* would be missed if Consul Bernick were not conceived as an *entrepreneur* of great energy and initiative; Fru Alving was a remarkable woman, and it may not be irrelevant to remember that, in some ways, Nora Helmer was something of a study of her in her youth. No one quite of their calibre—unless a partial exception be made in favour of Dr. Relling—takes a chair round the lunchtable in Hjalmar Ekdal's studio, nor is there even an indication that Haaken Werle, for all his wealth, is a commercial *matador* like Carsten Bernick.

The diminished scale of the figures becomes even more obvious when we compare the two most fully portrayed characters, Hjalmar Ekdal and Gregers Werle, with their forerunners Peer Gynt and Brand. Hjalmar is the complete egocentric who cloaks his lack of principle and purpose, not (as Peer Gynt did) with scraps of proverbial wisdom, but with the kind of sentimental rhetoric he had learned in post-prandial orations, and who always finds himself in positions into which more purposeful individualities and the drift of circumstances have pushed him. He could never have seized the opportunities that would make him master of an ocean-going steam-yacht; his utterly fatuous working at a great invention (which from first to last has been a suggestion foisted upon him from outside) lacks the grandeur both of Peer Gynt's dizzy ride on the reindeer and of his project of a super-Faustian 'Gyntiana'; his affection for his father and for Hedvig is mainly self-dramatising patronage of the grey- (or white-) haired veteran maimed in the battle of life and of the trustful child on whom eternal darkness is about to descend: he lets the former fuddle himself whenever others furnish the necessary liquor, and has no scruples in allowing the latter to strain her eyesight when it suits his convenience. The genuineness of Peer's devotion to Solveig becomes plain when it is contrasted with Hjalmar's using of Gina as a mere drudge not even worthy of sentimental allocutions. It is, alas, only too likely that even Hedvig's death will, as Relling prophesies, mean nothing more to him than a new repertoire of fine phrases.

Gregers Werle, like Parson Brand, is a man with a mission. But he is the idealist even more fatally run to seed than Brand's distorted image, the 'regenerated' Einar. The 'mission' which he con-

---

7. In some ways *An Enemy of the People*, culminating in the disorderly public meeting, anticipates this: but the squalor of Aslaksen's printing office is largely professional untidiness.

ceives to have been laid upon him is almost as nebulous as Hjalmar's great invention, though it may possess[8] the merit—for what that is worth—of being self-imposed. He is the 'superior' person who, whenever he sees his fellow-men going the common rounds of their daily lives, immediately thinks that they ought to be doing something different and, of course, 'better'.[9] He does not stop at thinking, but proceeds to exhortations, which, as far as one can judge, are of a negative or very nebulous character: his victims are to rouse themselves, give up their old habits and assumptions, search their hearts, take moral soundings, judge themselves and their neighbours, all in the name of an 'ideal' which is not further defined. In the end, as Gregers himself comes to admit, his mission amounts to no more than being the self-invited thirteenth round the dinner-table, a cause of discomfort at the time and of calamity thereafter.

With both Gregers and Hjalmar Ibsen insists on the formative influences undergone in youth as he did with Brand and Peer Gynt. Gregers was the child of unhappily married parents, brought up in a divided home, where his mother filled him up with her wrongs, set him in incurable antagonism against his father,[1] made him abhor moral uncleanness as strongly as he everywhere suspected its existence and inspired him with the ambition to eradicate it. Hjalmar owed his education mainly to two foolish maiden aunts who, on the one hand, by their adulation destroyed any personality he may have been born with—this, at any rate, is Relling's view—and on the other hand gave him a great conceit of his abilities, which the admiration of co-evals like Gregers and of others, won by his gift of the gab and his pleasing address, confirmed.[2]

Gregers's antipode is Relling, a medical man who, for all his practical psychology, has come down in the world, perhaps through dissipation. Where Gregers generalises, he considers every case on its merits; where Gregers dimly envisages a general good, his aim is the happiness of the individual; Gregers spreads *malaise* and disaster, he on the other hand brings ease and healing—at any rate to

8. I say 'may possess' because, as we shall see, Gregers's fantasies over the wild duck are quite unoriginal and, for anything we know to the contrary, his grand mission may well have been imposed upon him by his dead mother.

9. There is an obvious anticipation of this in Fru Linde of *A Doll's House,* whose activities, however, seem to meet with the author's approval.

1. Gregers's relations to his father are fully expounded in Freudian terms by Nissen, I., *Sjelelige Kriser* (1931), p. 98. Fru Werle's grievances may have been imaginary, at least in part.

2. The most recent editor of Ibsen (Koht, H., Introduction to *The Wild Duck* in Centenary Edition, x, 10) be-

lieves that traits for Hjalmar Ekdal's character were contributed by an unsuccessful artist, Magnus Bagge, who once gave him drawing-lessons, Kristoffer Janson who was parodied as Huhu of *Peer Gynt,* and Edward Larssen, who took the earliest known photograph of Ibsen. The last identification is very likely in view of the fact that the figure who ultimately became Hjalmar is indicated in the early notes as 'E. L.'. Koht further draws attention (*ibid.* p. 23) to Mr. Micawber, who seems to me much more plausible as a likely model for Hjalmar than his suggestion Alceste (of Molière's *Misanthrope*) for Gregers Werle.

others: with himself, as his barely indicated love-affair with Berta
Sørby suggests, he would appear to have been less successful. The
guiding principle on which he acts will come up for consideration
later. Though his readiness to talk about that principle and the
pregnancy of his observations approximate him in some degree to
the stage-*raisonneur* (such as Fjeldbo of *The League of Youth*,
another doctor), Relling, positive and very clear-sighted, is rather a
unique type in Ibsen's gallery of portraits: the schoolmaster Arn-
holm in *The Lady from the Sea* and the engineer Borghejm of
Little Eyolf have none of his force and individuality. He was
almost certainly suggested by the figure of Dr. Borg, who in Strindberg's novel, *The Red Room*,[3] exhibits many of the same characteristics and fulfils a similar function.

Another sensible and balanced mind is that of Gregers's father.
In view of two major points for which Ibsen admits only a purely
subjective interpretation—the timber-fraud and Hedvig's paternity
—a verdict of his character is difficult to reach (and is in fact
unnecessary to pronounce). In general, he has received short shrift
from the commentators, particularly the seniors among them, as an
adulterer, domestic tyrant and swindler, whose main strength lies in
his banking-account; but it is permissible to judge him much more
favourably, as a man more sinned against (both by Old Ekdal and
by his wife) than sinning, who certainly is not exempt from sins,
but who voluntarily pays for them and uses tact and imagination—not to mention generosity—in the mode of payment. His
contemplated marriage with Fru Sørby may strike a severe moralist
as 'repulsive';[4] on the other hand, it is repugnant neither to natural
nor to human law, it is entered upon under certain quite good
moral guarantees, it injures none and it will undoubtedly subserve
the lasting happiness and solid usefulness of the contracting parties.
It is difficult to think—provided always that the general depressed
level of the play is kept in mind—that Ibsen disapproved of this
union, though something of the same sort for a Rebecca West or
Arnold Rubek might have seemed definitely less desirable.

A propos of the Copenhagen production, a warning was given
not to repeat Hjalmar's mistake and take too sentimental a view of
his father. He has certainly suffered shipwreck, either through the
wickedness of others or through his own incompetence rather than
through sheer criminality, but with his ungrateful cadging, his fur-
tive drunkenness and his antics amid the Christmas trees in the
attic, he is as despicable and ludicrous as he is pitiable. I cannot
help thinking that Ibsen made a trifling mistake by putting in his

---

3. *Röda Rummet*, 1879; it rightly
caused a considerable literary sensation
in Scandinavia. Ibsen knew it (Paulsen, J., *Samliv med Ibsen, II*, 1913, p.
224).

4. 'Abstossend' is the epithet of Har-
nack, O., *Essais und Studien* (1899), p.
351.

mouth (twice) the phrase: 'The forests avenge themselves.' It does not seem to me an expression at all consonant with his usual speech and is either farcically inappropriate or else cloudily portentous.

The remaining characters may be passed in review more summarily. The drunken reprobate Molvik, the servants and the bookkeeper speak for themselves. Gina's vulgarity—perhaps a trifle overdone in Archer's translation?—is vulgarity of speech only: she is competent, loyal, considerate and affectionate without in any way advertising these qualities and, though with all the burdens of a household and a business on her she is overworked, she should not, I think, give the impression of a downtrodden slattern: otherwise Relling would have done something for her and even Gregers might have perceived that Hjalmar was not the only victim of the situation. Her friend Berta Sørby, the veterinary surgeon's widow, stands on a higher level of intelligence and culture, perfectly capable as she seems to be holding her own in the best mercantile society of Norway.

For Hedvig Ibsen seems to have drawn on his recollection of his sister with the same name, the only member of his family with whom he maintained some sort of friendly relations and who followed his own career with sympathy. She is no childish heroine. There is nothing very unusual about her individuality or ways, except that she is, perhaps, a little young for her years in her continual absorption in make-believe and completely uncritical acceptance of her environment.[5] No more, I think, should be made of Relling's allusions to her puberty than an occasional proneness to a certain excited violence, which goes some little way to accounting for her suicide.[6]

IV

The pathos of Hedvig's fate has led those for whom it is the most moving and the most arresting thing in *The Wild Duck* to look upon her as the heroine of the play and, as a not unnatural corollary, to identify her in some measure with the wild duck itself: for, after all, it is a not unusual practice to name a drama after its foremost character. Hedvig may be the most admirable personage presented in the play, but that in itself does not guarantee the validity of the theory; the virtuous Kent is not the hero of *King Lear*, nor the blameless Cassandra of *Agamemnon*; neither can it rightly be maintained that the play fundamentally is 'about'

5. Bjørnson thought that she would have seen through Hjalmar before this and therefore refrained from her self-sacrifice. It will be remembered that she has not gone to school nor mixed with others of her age.

6. Relling's very positive pronouncement is intended to put the purposive nature of her act beyond doubt.

Hedvig, that her fate is the constant preoccupation either of the other personages or of the spectators: she is a victim like Ophelia in *Hamlet*, and almost an accidental victim.

The same, to be sure, can be said of the wild duck, but is there really any other close parallel between them? Does the wild duck's fate mirror that of her owner and, in doing so, give it a wider significance? They who incline to such a view remark that both of them live in a world of pretences for which they are not responsible and that they are the noblest, the least corrupted denizens of that world. Both perish. But further the parallel cannot be extended, and the dissimilarities are greater than the resemblances. Nothing goes to show that Hedvig has been wounded or maimed or even that the environment of pretence in which she has been brought up is marring desirable potentialities in her. We do not exclaim: 'What a nice, what a happy, what a noble little girl this would be *if she had not got* such a horrible home.' Nothing indicates a distortion in her nature except her reported playing with fire, which Relling expressly puts down not to anything in her environment, but to the stage which she has reached in her natural physical development. And where are we to find the application of the wild duck's plunge to the bottom of the sea and her recovery by Haaken Werle's incredibly clever dog?

Why does Hedvig shoot herself? Accident, as has been noted, should be ruled out. Hers is an intentional act, induced by the notion of sacrifice which Gregers has put into her head: to regain her father's love she is to offer up what she holds dearest in the world. She does not hesitate in designating as the sacrificial victim her pet, the maimed wild duck: she will get her grandfather, Old Ekdal, to shoot it dead. The construction that, on further reflection, as a conscious perseverance in Gregers's idea, Hedvig considered her own life to be even more precious than the wild duck must, I think, be rejected, even if unconsciously her act may conform to it. The act is a violent, perhaps hysterical one of self-destruction, the cause of it despair at Hjalmar's rejection of her as an interloper[7] and the manner suggested by the mocking rhetorical question she overhears: 'Hedvig, are you willing to renounce that life for me? [*Laughs scornfully.*] No thank you! You would soon hear what answer I should get.'

Hedvig loves the wild duck partly because it has been wounded and is thriving again under her care, partly because it is the rarest, most aristocratic denizen of the attic and her very own property, partly because there are about it the romantic, fairy-tale associations of having lived its wild life a long way away and, at the time it was

7. The terrible Racinian *réplique;* 'Er det mig?' 'Does that mean me?'

wounded, having 'been down in the depths of the sea.' Even if Hedvig were capable of conceiving a 'symbol'—which, of course, she is not—there is nothing to suggest that the wild duck is a symbol to her in any deeper sense any more than that a boy's passion for his rocking-horse is a symbol to him of his pride of possession or love of mastery.

The other characters' attitude towards the bird is not quite so straightforward. For old Ekdal she is part, the most authentic part, of the surrogate wild life in which he can still see himself leading the primitive sportsman's existence where he had been happiest; for Hjalmar, similarly, one of the distractions enabling him to escape from a reality that otherwise would depress him by its squalor and his own conviction of failure. But it is Gregers, with his proneness to read sermons in stones, who weaves speculative phantasies about the wild duck, not merely as one (if the most outstanding) of the elements in the make-believe wild life of the attic—which he dislikes as a sham and an obfuscation of reality—but in herself. It is not an exuberant imagination that makes him do this; significantly, the ideas are put into his head by others, first by his father, when, before the wild duck has ever been mentioned, he says *à propos* of Old Ekdal 'there are people in the world who dive to the bottom the moment they get a couple of slugs in their body, and never come to the surface again', and then by Old Ekdal himself, who, after repeating the hunters' lore that, when a wild duck is shot, it plunges to the bottom and bites itself fast to the weed and rubbish there, recalls that this particular wild duck, having done this, was retrieved by an 'amazingly clever dog' belonging to Haaken Werle, who then made a present of the bird to the Ekdal family. Gregers immediately fastens on the parallel between this story and the carefree, naïve life of Old Ekdal, which was shattered by the action of his old partner, but continued in a kind of twilight, amid filth and rubbish, barely conscious, half dead. He sees himself as the incredibly clever dog who dives down and restores submerged creatures to light and renewed utility above. He does more than perceive analogies of this order, he voices them:

GREGERS. My dear Hjalmar, I almost think you have something of the wild duck in you.

HJALMAR. Something of the wild duck? How do you mean?

GREGERS. You have dived down and bitten yourself fast in the undergrowth.

HJALMAR. Are you alluding to the well-nigh fatal shot that has broken my father's wing—and mine too?

GREGERS. Not exactly to *that*. I don't say that your wing has been broken; but you have strayed into a poisonous marsh, Hjalmar; an insidious disease has taken hold of you, and you have sunk down to die in the dark.

HJALMAR. I? To die in the dark? Look here, Gregers, you must really leave off talking such nonsense.

GREGERS. Don't be afraid: I shall find a way to help you up again.[8]

It is clear that, to Gregers, Hedvig's wild duck is a symbol, which can possess, as the most thoroughgoing symbolists seem always to hold, an active property of its own in relation to what it is held to symbolise. For, in inducing Hedvig to kill her pet, he intends to destroy the bogus, 'lying' make-believe which poisons the atmosphere of her family.

We must, however, beware of identifying the calamity-fraught notions of Gregers Werle with Ibsen's own. Like many another author, especially when a comparatively concentrated literary form, like the dramatic, enjoins economy, Ibsen could give prominence to a single phrase or object or concept (where in real life a number of rather similar phrases or objects or concepts would more usually occur), without necessarily attaching any unique and thus mysterious significance to the one chosen as representative; and an occasional, not over-recondite, coincidence or parallel[9] can have its uses for giving unobtrusive emphasis. Because only the orphanage is mentioned during the eighteen hours or so in which *Ghosts* plays, we are not to suppose that Fru Alving had kept her late husband's memory alive in no other ways. Aslaksen (of *The League of Youth*) no doubt had many other stock-phrases besides 'the local situation', and Ballested (in *The Lady from the Sea*) was capable of painting other subjects than expiring mermaids. Nor would Ibsen disdain a small telling phrase or *motif* which in its context suggests something bigger, more comprehensive and of wider applicability than itself, which 'strikes overtones' as some phrase it, such as Falk's killing of the song-bird in *Love's Comedy* and Nora's remark on coming out of her room to engage her husband in her great debate: 'Yes, I have changed my frock now.' Many others have done the same: one thinks of the purple carpet in Aeschylus's *Agamemnon*, which stands for the equality with the gods arrogated unto himself by the victorious leader of the Greeks.

Undeniably, however, Ibsen exhibits a liking for such overtones which does not characterise all tragedians, not even all poetic tragedians. However far we may go with Mr. Wilson Knight in conceiving each of Shakespeare's plays as one 'extended metaphor', their allusiveness must be reckoned to a different order—unless we interpret Fortinbras and his share in *Hamlet* as representing all

8. IV, 57; Archer, VIII, 300. There is a further allusion to this conversation, IV, 73; Archer, VIII, 333.

9. Perhaps one can range under this head the mess which Gregers, with his doctrinaire determination to do everything for himself, makes of his room in trying to cope with an unfamiliar stove; this may imply some self-criticism of Ibsen, who, we know, insisted on sewing on his own buttons, but did it ineffectively.

that part in the hero's nature which he aspires to perfect, but is temperamentally debarred from, or look upon Desdemona's handkerchief as a symbol of domestic disarray. At the beginning of the present chapter it was noted how the fortunes of Dr. Thomas Stockmann constitute a parable of the unpopular reformer; and, of course, the two great 'dramatic poems'—to which different criteria apply than to a comedy like *An Enemy of the People*—are, by their nature, such elaborate parables of two different types of humanity that they are not infrequently referred to as 'allegories'. In *The Pretenders*, similarly, the contrast between three historical figures, King Haakon Haakonsson, Earl Skule and Bishop Nicholas, is carried so far and so deep as to embrace a universally valid commentary on leadership.

It is important to observe, nevertheless, that an ear insensitive to overtones can still derive the impression of a symphonic whole from the works just mentioned, perhaps even make out the essential themes. The fate of Haakon Haakonsson and his competitors, of Peer Gynt, of Brand and of Dr. Stockmann can give us all the emotions we expect in great drama, even if we take no interest in leadership or Kierkegaardian ethics or municipal corruption. If we choose to regard the plays in question as being in their essence 'symbolic', as contributions to the elucidation of such general questions, we do so to some extent at our peril; as the author has furnished us in each instance with a complete and satisfying work of art we must not hold him responsible for the constructions it may please us to put upon it. The symbolism is, so to speak, detachable.

But the pervasiveness of the wild duck, the repeated references to it and the way in which so many of the human beings round about are preoccupied with it raise a presumption that this single small object, which is not even seen, possesses an importance of a novel order. After all, the play is called *The Wild Duck*. The wild duck and its associations can scarcely be dismissed *prima facie* as 'detachable' in the sense just argued. Should not a significance be attached to it greater than the aggregate of things which it means to the various personages who mention it, something overriding all the small 'lessons' and 'morals' which those who will can derive from almost any work of art, a significance for which the author himself can be made responsible? The same question presents itself more or less insistently with *Rosmersholm* and the 'White Horses' after which that play was originally named, with Ellida's love of bathing in *The Lady from the Sea*, with the vine-leaves in Løvborg's hair of which even so prosaic a person as Hedda Gabler makes mention, with the tower on Master Builder Solness's new house, with the great statuary group on which Rubek of *When We Dead Awaken* had founded his fame. Is any paramount importance to be attached to the fact that little Eyolf's crutch is seen floating

after he is drowned or that the night on which John Gabriel Borkman dies should be a specially cold one? Has at the end of Ibsen's
career the symbolism, in Mr. Tennant's phrase,[1] become
'organic'—something, so to speak, without which the plays would
fall to pieces as artistic and intellectual constructions, be nothing
but trivial and rather painful anecdotes? Mr. Tennant declares:

> Ibsen gave the play the name *Vildanden* and I maintain that it
> was not a title chosen because of the association such a name
> would arouse but because the wild duck is the chief protagonist
> of the play. . . . The play is not called *Vildanden* because Hedvig's
> fate was like that of a wild duck, nor because the wild duck, under
> the censorship of morals, conventions or religion, is the distorted
> expression of elementary urges. It is because the wild duck by
> its mere presence so affects the conditions of Gregers, Hjalmar and
> Hedvig by the various associations it suggests that it bears the
> sole responsibility for the final catastrophe.[2]

We may say at once that, if Mr. Tennant is right, *The Wild
Duck* is all but unique among Ibsen's plays. Almost too obviously
the lofty tower which Solness has constructed bears the 'responsibility for the final catastrophe'; but Løvborg's vine-leaves, Little
Eyolf's crutch and Rubek's statue certainly do not, and the White
Horses of Rosmersholm are only a minor item in Rosmer's and
Rebecca's preoccupations. But, even for *The Wild Duck*, Mr. Tennant, I think, overstates his case. The catastrophe, Hedvig's death,
is brought about by Hjalmar's unkindness to her, which Gregers's
doctrinaire interference unnaturally stimulates, and a play ending
similarly could have been constructed by omitting the wild duck
altogether (as indeed Ibsen seems at first to have conceived it) or
by, so to speak, putting its various functions in commission instead
of concentrating them in a single focus. Very likely, such a play
would have been less effective than *The Wild Duck* we have. But
the fact that Ibsen seems to have contemplated it at first goes some
considerable way to proving that the symbolism again is 'detachable'.

In general, Ibsen was disdainful of symbolic explanations.
Among all the contemporary critics of his play he seems to have
preferred Edvard Brandes (Georg Brandes's journalistic brother)
who consistently denied that symbolism; and he declared scornfully:[3] 'Yes, to be sure, the explainers. They don't always do their
job well. They like symbolising,[4] because they have no respect for
reality.' He added, to be sure: 'But if you really put a symbol into

1. Tennant, P. F. D., 'Critical Study
of the Composition of Ibsen's *Vildanden*', in *Edda*, xxxiv (1934), p. 327.
2. *Loc. cit.* p. 325; I have corrected
some misprints.
3. *Auct.* Lothar, R., *Henrik Ibsen*
(2nd ed. 1902), p. 126.

4. Sometimes the 'symbolising' is no
more than bad style, as when I. Nissen
says that 'Dr. Relling *symbolises* the
recognition that once damage and lies
have supervened it is often necessary to
acquiesce' (*Sjelelige Kriser*, 1931, p.
78).

their heads, they turn it into something trivial and use bad language.' One will probably not be far out in concluding that for the plays as a whole—with the possible exceptions of the two great 'dramatic poems',—the interpretation on the plane of actuality is primary and sufficient, and that such 'symbols' as occur in them, like the sea in *The Lady from the Sea* or the wild duck in the play now under review, are added graces which conveniently (and perhaps poetically) resume in themselves from time to time a series of associations. But these associations are always, to begin with, in the minds of the actors in the plays, and, if the spectator adopts them too, he does so at his own pleasure and risk, with no guarantee that the author himself accepts responsibility for their authenticity.

v

If in one way (to put it at its lowest) the wild duck serves to hold together the play called after her, in another way Relling does so too. Whatever it is, his is a somewhat more limited function. For he has next to nothing to do with the sphere of which Haaken Werle forms the centre: his activities are confined to the Ekdal household. Not unlike Gregers Werle, he is a man with a mission, though he would probably have repudiated any such ascription to him other than the good physician's principle to do his best for his patients, for each according to his diathesis and complaint. In the play, he is called in to examine Hedvig after her suicide; but otherwise, his ministrations belong entirely to the psychological and moral realm; and, though he proceeds with professional empiricism, he acknowledges a therapeutic principle. It is formulated as keeping the 'life-lie[5] alive' in his 'patients', to maintain them, in other words, in the atmosphere of illusion where they thrive.

GREGERS. Oh, indeed! Hjalmar Ekdal is sick too, is he!

RELLING. Most people are, worst luck.

GREGERS. And what remedy are you applying in Hjalmar's case?

RELLING. My usual one. I am cultivating the life-illusion in him.

GREGERS. Life-illusion? I didn't catch what you said.

RELLING. Yes, I said illusion. For illusion, you know, is the stimulating principle.[6]

He has contrived to keep some glimmer of self-respect alive in his companion, the debauched theologian Molvik, by persuading him that his alcoholic outbreaks are the manifestation of the

---

5. The Dano-Norwegian *løgn* has a somewhat wider connotation, it seems, than the English *lie*. In one of Amalie Skram's novels a girl mutely hands over to her mother less than she has received, whereupon the latter exclaims: 'That is a lie.'

6. V, 91; Archer, VIII, 369.

'dæmonic nature' in him craving for satisfaction from time to time. He has not invented the notion of the 'hunting-ground' in the attic for Lieutenant Ekdal's benefit—the old man hit on it himself—but he encourages and approves of it. It is he, however, who has put into Hjalmar's head the belief that he has it in him to make a great discovery in the science of photography and thereby to redeem the decayed family honour. Relling's only concern is the happiness of his patient—though it may be noted that that happiness nowhere involves the unhappiness of others: but concepts like the good of society or the moral efficacy of the individual are not only excluded but repudiated.

Relling accordingly stands as the poles apart to the man of principle, Gregers Werle, who is in every way antipathetic to him. He rejects ideals in themselves;

> RELLING. While I think of it, Mr. Werle, junior—don't use that foreign word: ideals. We have the excellent native word: lies.
> GREGERS. Do you think the two things are related?
> RELLING. Yes, just about as closely as typhus and putrid fever;[7]

and particularly because the impossible demands which they make are the direct cause of individual dissatisfaction and unhappiness. 'Life would be quite tolerable', he exclaims at the very end of the play: 'Life would be quite tolerable, after all, if only we could be rid of the confounded duns that keep on pestering us, in our poverty, with the claim of the ideal.'[8] Pragmatically he is justified: as long as it was he who was in control of the situation in Hjalmar's house, all went well; but, from the moment he is ousted by the idealist, *malaise*, unhappiness and disaster ensue.

Relling being thus justified according to the most reliable test available, how far may we identify Ibsen's own attitude with his? 'Ideals' are seen as the hostile agent, standing in the way of human happiness. Has Ibsen finally come round to this view? If we make the identification of Relling and Ibsen, is there not a grave inconsistency between the position which the latter takes up in *The Wild Duck* and that to be inferred from the earlier plays, where truth, honesty, candour, straight-dealing, the resolute facing of facts, everything indeed repugnant to the 'life-lie', seem to be exalted? Undoubtedly there is a great difference. But we have noted before, in connection with *Brand* and *Peer Gynt* particularly, how Ibsen could make his work embody two opposing points of view, could impartially scrutinise them and show them as issuing in similar results; he realised more and more clearly that everything, even

---

7. V, 92; Archer, VIII, 371.   8. V, 106; Archer, VIII, 400.

truth,[9] was relative, that it was impossible to make universally valid demands,[1] and he was insistent that every factor must be weighed, all circumstances of an individual case taken into account. This is in a way a consequence of self-criticism. If Ibsen felt that he had been too hard on Brand, he redressed the balance by subjecting to similar castigation one who had none of the qualities of Brand, seeing himself or part of himself in both. Similarly he could see himself, the author of *Pillars of Society*, *A Doll's House* and *An Enemy of the People*, going about the world with the demands of the ideal in his pocket just like Gregers Werle among the cottagers at Højdal. Could he be sure that he had produced nothing but good? Were there not, to put it at its lowest, circumstances in which a Relling would be absolutely right in rounding upon him? The Lie, against which Falk[2] so exuberantly declared war, may sometimes have its justification.

In the circumstances that must be taken into account in any verdict upon *The Wild Duck*, there is one of particular importance which has already been glanced at. The personages in the play are by comparison with their predecessors of a diminished stature, they are much more ordinary people. Is it fair, the inference seems to be, is it proper in the last analysis, is it profitable to ask such ordinary people to raise themselves to the moral level of a Thomas Stockmann or Helene Alving, not to mention a Brand and an Agnes? In other words, may not 'ideals' be a luxury and as such inaccessible to the great mass of humanity? The pragmatical test represented by *The Wild Duck* seems to return the answer Yes.

They who scan a work of art for ideals are themselves idealists in the popular accepted meaning of the term: they attribute the best motives and await the highest in mankind. A conclusion like that to which Relling attains, in much of which Ibsen himself seems also to concur, is profoundly repugnant to them or if not repugnant, at least grieving. It is on that account, no doubt, that *The Wild Duck* has been called the most pessimistic of Ibsen's plays[3] and that the pessimism vulgarly attributed to all tragedies is confirmed in his case.

Before proceeding to a discussion of *The Wild Duck* as a tragedy and to a fuller consideration of Ibsen's pessimism, we might for a moment pause to ask whether the thesis that ideals are not for the common man is taken up again. Relling, it has been said, is a unique figure in Ibsen's gallery of portraits. In his next work he characteristically put this variant of the *raisonneur* in quite a differ-

---

9. Note in this connection Dr. Stockmann's exaggerated claim that very few truths have a life of more than twenty years (IV, 338; Archer, VIII, 135).
1. Letter to C. Caspari of 27 June 1884 (*Breve*, II, 136).

2. In *Love's Comedy* [Editor].
3. E.g. by Georg Brandes (in 1898), *Henrik Ibsen*, p. 145, English translation (1899), p. 99.

ent light with Ulrik Brendel, the peripatetic philosopher full of ideals and talk who does as little good to others as he does to himself. But Brendel is dwarfed by Rosmer and Rebecca, in whom there are potentialities of true greatness, and the scale of the figures is nowhere again quite so much reduced as in *The Wild Duck*. The protagonists of *Rosmersholm* and *When We Dead Awaken* certainly, of *Little Eyolf*, *The Master Builder* and *John Gabriel Borkman* almost certainly, are personalities of uncommon endowments, whose frustration stirs emotions again akin to that of Brand, Earl Skule and Bernick and of Mrs. Alving and Hjørdis.

The mention of Hjørdis, however, gives one pause in calling to mind Hedda Gabler, who in a very similar fashion, when her own life has lost its meaning, plays with the lives of men; a diminution of stature in *her* case is undeniable; mere *ennui* has in her taken the place of Hjørdis's tragic despair. *Hedda Gabler* and *The Lady from the Sea* stand nearest to *The Wild Duck* from the present point of view. But *The Lady from the Sea* is a comedy to which another scale must be applied than those of tragedy and tragicomedy, and in *Hedda Gabler* we may give Eilert Løvborg the benefit of taking him for a genius, even if we cannot, with some admirers, go so far as to look upon Hedda Gabler herself as a grand creature gone wrong.

If these arguments are accepted, *The Wild Duck* will be seen to stand isolated at any rate among those plays to which we can attribute a tragic ending. This may be the 'novelty' to which Ibsen drew his publisher's attention, although by the 'method of procedure' he mentioned at the same time he much more probably meant that grouping of the personages and incidents round the doubly mysterious Wild Duck herself.[4]

VI

If Hjalmar be regarded as a diminished, even less heroic, Peer Gynt and Gregers Werle as a smaller Brand who has fostered his idealism in similarly remote and barren tracts, the tragedy of *The Wild Duck* proceeds from an impact of these two characters, and the smash-up of Hjalmar's domestic felicity, with the death of Hedvig, has a two-fold cause. The catastrophe is most obviously induced by Gregers, who, presenting the demands of the ideal, first undermines the mutual confidence on which the Ekdal household is reared, replaces its security by disquieting doubts about its past and its future, turns a collectively and individually happy family into an unhappy one, and also puts the idea of a blood sacrifice into Hedvig's head. In the second place and more particularly, however, as we have seen, Hedvig's substitution of herself for the Wild

---

4. The grouping of *Ghosts* round the Orphanage is not unlike this, however.

Duck as the sacrificial victim is due to Hjalmar's thoughtless cruelty towards her. Such cruelty does not seem an obvious attribute of an easy-going, comfort-loving nature like his; but in the circumstances it proceeds naturally from his complete egoism, his inability to realise the bearings of the situation in which he finds himself and from the angry *malaise* engendered by his uncertainty.

Hjalmar has been very suddenly thrust into this situation through the interference of Gregers, and the situation from which the tragedy ensues is therefore fortuitous. It is not every Peer Gynt who runs up against a Brand, and most of the Peer Gynts of this world proceed happily to their obscure graves. If the second phase of Gregers's interference—his action upon Hedvig—had not supervened upon the first, all might still have been well, especially if the practised healer Relling had remained at hand to soothe and guide. In fact we see the reintegration of Hjalmar's shattered family life taking place before our eyes at the beginning of the fifth act when he consents to sit down to lunch and to postpone his removal from the house to a more convenient season. And Relling's bitter prophecy: 'Before a year is over little Hedvig will be nothing to him but a pretty theme for declamation', from which it is impossible to dissent, indicates that in so far as he is concerned that process of reintegration will continue, though of course to a lesser completeness.

Besides the grotesque, the comic elements associated with the attic menagerie and inherent in the character of Hjalmar and his father, Ibsen thus had a double justification for describing his play as a tragi-comedy and withholding the full designation of tragedy: the fortuitous juxtaposition of Hjalmar and Gregers and the evanescent effect on the former of the catastrophe that overtakes him.

There is, however, another—at least one other—aspect from which the 'tragedy' of *The Wild Duck* may be explored. The catastrophe is undeniably the catastrophe of Gregers. He has had a great chance of the sort for which he has been waiting, the chance to have justice done to his old friend's family, which, rightly or wrongly, he believes to have been outrageously treated, and to raise at any rate some of his fellow men to that high moral level on which he thinks that all should have their being; and nothing but evil has ensued upon these selfless efforts. Cannot, therefore, *The Wild Duck* be construed as the idealist's tragedy? Undoubtedly it can (subject to the overriding consideration that it should be the idealist's, the active moralist's, constant preoccupation to take the circumstances of every case into account and that he must take full responsibility if he fails to do so). But it seems as if Ibsen wished to minimise this aspect of *The Wild Duck*—and by so doing to refrain from casting a justifying glow around those activities of his own which resemble Gregers Werle's. For one thing, he withheld from Gregers not only the greatness and nobility with which he endowed Brand, but all amiability as well: Gregers is animated by no real love for mankind in general or of Tom, Dick and Harry in particular, and no one cares for him. In the second place, important as he is in the scheme of *The Wild Duck*, he never holds the centre of the stage: he is an ominous rather than a sinister figure, standing at the side, fatally involving others in the darkness of his personality. Moreover, his final exit deprives him of the last opportunity of assuming heroic stature: he expresses no regret—beyond the apology that he always acted with the best intentions—no contrition or repentance like that of Brand or Peer Gynt. He betrays no resolve, like Nora, to think things out in the light of fresh knowledge and, in a new life, make good the ill he has committed, turn himself into a real benefactor of his kind. If he really intends to commit suicide, he slinks off as one who just sees that he has no luck on his side. Neither in Gregers nor in Hjalmar does calamity induce a purgation—yet another card in the hand of those who contend for Ibsen's pessimism.

* * *

Up to a point every tragedy must be pessimistic, and dramatists whose preferences lie with tragedy are pessimists, since they exhibit 'heroes', men and women of superior abilities, coming to grief by a process which is made to appear inevitable. Ibsen accordingly must, like his brethren, suffer the presumption of being a pessimist. Paradoxically enough, however, a common ground for the imputation in his case is one that should lessen it on considerations proper to tragedy in general. It is contended that he takes a 'low view' of humanity and that the men and women whose sad fate is unfolded in his plays precisely lack all superior abilities, that, in brief, they are not true heroes, that he is incapable of creating true heroes. Certainly, if the ascription 'heroic' be confined solely to those who, like Don Rodrigue the Cid, perform almost superhuman feats or, like Orestes, feel themselves called upon to cope with intractable situations or, like Lear, run through a whole gamut of torments, very few indeed of Ibsen's personages would qualify for it: none, indeed, after Haakon Haakonsson and Brand. His Hedda Gablers fail to do their duty, his Bernicks and Borkmans are swindlers, his Rosmers and Allmerses[5] weaklings. But an argument so based is surely two-edged. If the personages whom Ibsen presents are no prehistoric champions strayed into the modern world, all the more credit is due to them for exhibiting will-power, endurance and resignation, and, on occasion, for repenting their trespasses. That his

5. Respectively in *Hedda Gabler*, *Pillars of Society*, *John Gabriel Bork-* *man*, *Rosmersholm*, *Little Eyolf* [Editor].

characters are 'low' does not make Ibsen a pessimist. Is Arnold Bennett a pessimist—and Dickens with his unrivalled gallery of 'low' portraits?

Where, however, 'lowness' connotes not merely lowly birth, defective breeding and small knowledge of the world, but an ignoble outlook which by its prevalence puts on an appearance of universality, there is rather better reason in identifying its presentation with pessimism. But, as has been pointed out, The Wild Duck stands unique among Ibsen's plays in the unrelieved earth-of-the-earthiness of the characters amid the illiberal life which they lead and in the apparent approbation with which the frustration of ideals is treated. Dr. Relling is par excellence, however, the advocate of moral relativity; he is the last man to hold that what he prescribed for the Ekdal household or the cottagers of Højdal is a universal panacea.

All the same, Ibsen viewed humanity through no rose-tinted spectacles. Even if The Wild Duck be left out of consideration, a high proportion of the men and even of the women he presents are individually poor stuff and the society into which they coalesce seems to be fatally unable to rise above their highest common factor. Think of the hypocrite and knave Engstrand in Ghosts with his precious daughter, the hypocrite and fool Manders, and Oswald, who may be a good-for-nothing through no fault of his own, but none the less remains a good-for-nothing; think of the mixture of intrigue and bullying which characterises Peter Stockmann in An Enemy of the People, the malicious old rascal Morten Kiil, the sweepings of the educated class who people the newspaper office, the poltroons who vote solid at the public meeting—and so the list might be extended. There is scarcely a single play with a range of decent, kindly and intelligent folk.

Not that the majority of Ibsen's characters are in any notable degree villains, criminals or even considerable sinners; they are just stuff for the Button-Moulder's ladle. With Kierkegaard, Ibsen said: 'I do not complain that mankind is wicked, I complain that it is abject', and no doubt, as Sophocles felt that 'not to have been born is best', so he thought that the extinction of the human race could be no great calamity. In the notorious poem 'Til min Ven Revolutionstaleren'[6] he declared that, if he could, he would have torpedoed the Ark. Ibsen's tragedy is manifestly tinged with a deeper pessimism than that, shall we say, of Schiller or Voltaire or perhaps even Sophocles.

It is true, too, that for all the background of fjord, sea, waste upland, rain, snow and radiant glacier which Ibsen takes every

6. Samlede Værker, Kristiania og København 1914. Vol. IV, p. 260 [Editor].

befitting opportunity to suggest,[7] there is little to be seen in his work of serene or starry vault of heaven. None of his personages is sustained by any religious faith and in their misery they do not, as Chekhov's so often do, look forward in a selfless rapture to some happy future for mankind or even to a half-mythical Moscow. But neither does his work leave an impression, as does that of Hardy, of a vast constrictive universe which, by its very power and its indifference to what human creatures do or plan, puts on an appearance of hostility. His Boyg is a much more narrowly localised monster, whom one can evade if one cannot overcome. Ibsen may be an unmetaphysical genius, as indeed most great dramatists seem to be; the fact acquits him of the charge of postulating a universe whose creatures are doomed to ineluctable misery. He may have known of Schopenhauer and Hartmann, but he did not subscribe to their constructions.[8]

Existence, as Ibsen exhibits it, is a strenuous and hazardous business, to live and be happy involves perpetual exposure to evil chance and constant struggle either with rivals (as in *The Pretenders*) or with character (as in *Peer Gynt* and *Brand*) or with the conventional restrictions of present-day society (as in *A Doll's House*) or with a crushing misfortune (as in *Little Eyolf*) or with the 'trolls within' (as in *The Master Builder*, indeed in all the last plays from *Rosmersholm* onwards); but the strenuousness of the strife, before which only two of Ibsen's figures lay down their arms, not only breeds in a Nora or a Brand or a Rebecca West strength, even nobility of character, but betrays also a conviction that the prize is attainable. Except Hedda Gabler and Rosmer all believe that it may be possible for them to survive and be happy, and their fate may weaken that conviction in others, but does not destroy it. 'Life would be tolerable,' says Relling, 'if. . . .'

ALAN REYNOLDS THOMPSON

Ibsen As Psychoanatomist†

Because of the limited time at my disposal I must pass by a group of Ibsen scholars—what the newspapers might call a hot-bed of them—who have been recently fruiting in Cambridge

---

7. He often produced a comparable effect by the lighting which he prescribed. Writing to Lindberg about *The Wild Duck* he observed: 'I lay great weight on the lighting in this piece. I have wished it to correspond to the fundamental mood which prevails in each of the five acts' (*cit.* Centenary Edition, X. 36).

8. He asked himself the question, nevertheless, whether human evolution might not have taken the wrong path (*Efterladte Skrifter*, III, 1909, p. 142).

† From *Educational Theater Journal*, Vol. III, No. 1 (March 1951), pp. 34–39. Reprinted by permission.

University.[1] Regretfully I must also omit discussing the recently published memoirs of Ibsen's daughter-in-law,[2] which throw a new and warmer light on the dramatist and his home life during his later years.[3]

What has most interested me in the recent literature is the work of two Norwegian critics who have approached the great dramatist and his characters psychologically. In so doing they are following Ibsen's own practice, which he described in his familiar quatrain:

What is life? a fighting
    In heart and in brain with Trolls.
Poetry? that means writing
    Doomsday-accounts of our souls.

His works were, as he said, self-anatomies. He anatomized his own soul, and he built his characters on dynamic motivation so full and searching that modern students, aided by our systematic psychologies, can only deal with them as though they were real people with real complexities—and complexes. I might therefore call Ibsen a psychoanalyst, using the word in its literal sense of soul-searcher, except that Freud and his school have put a virtual copyright on that word. Incidentally, it is rather surprising that the Freudians have not done more with Ibsen, and that what they have done is generally disappointing, at least to a student of drama.[4] The books I wish to discuss follow Adler rather than Freud, and their emphasis is on the inferiority complex and its compensatory drive for power rather than on the so-called libido. I hasten to say that I do not propose to take sides in the now ancient quarrel between the Founding Fathers of analytical psychology; I can only report that the two Adlerites have done a much better job on Ibsen than any Freudians I have found.

The two take as their central view that Ibsen was a divided soul

1. Brian W. Downs, *Ibsen, the Intellectual Background* (Cambridge, 1946);———*A Study of Six Plays by Ibsen* (Cambridge, 1950); Miss M. C. Bradbrook, *Ibsen the Norwegian* (London, 1948); P. F. D. Tennant, *Ibsen's Dramatic Technique* (Cambridge, 1948)

2. Bergliot Ibsen, *De Tre* [*Those Three,*—referring to Ibsen, his wife, and his son Sigurd] (Oslo, 1948).

3. A recent example of Teutonic philosophizing, mostly about *The Master Builder*, is Ludwig Binswanger, *Henrik Ibsen und das Problem der Selbstrealisation in der Kunst* (Heidelberg, 1949).

4. A partial list of papers by psychoanalysts dealing wholly or in part with Ibsen follows. (I am indebted for aid here to Mr. W. David Sievers.)

Freud, Sigmund. "Some Character-Types met with in Psycho-analytic Work." [Rebecca West] *Collected Papers,* IV (London, 1925).

Goitein, W. Lionel. " 'The Lady from the Sea.' A Fresh Approach to an Analysis of Ibsen's Drama." *Psycho-Analytical Review,* XIV, 1927, pp. 375–419.

Jeffreys, Harold. "Ibsen's 'Peer Gynt': a Psychoanalytical Study." *ibid.,* XI, 1924, pp. 361–402.

Jelliffe, Smith Ely, and Louise Brink. "The Wild Duck." *ibid.,* VI, 1919, pp. 357–378. [The present editor found these pages to deal with *The Lady from the Sea,* not *The Wild Duck.*]

Schatia, Viva. "Henrik Ibsen's Doll's House." *ibid.,* XXVI, 1939, pp. 33–38. "Peer Gynt—a study of Insecurity." *ibid.,* XXV, 1938, pp. 49–52.

Wisdom, J. O. "The Lust for Power in Hedda Gabler." *ibid.,* XXXI, 1944, pp. 419–437.

who suffered throughout his life from inner conflicts, and who ana-
lyzed himself and utilized his understanding of his own conflicts
when developing the dramatic conflicts in his plays.

* * *

The two books which principally concern us were published in
Oslo in 1931 and 1945. I shall take up the later one first. Its title
may be translated as *Symbolism in Henrik Ibsen's Plays.*[5] The
author's name is Arne Duve.

This study follows Adler's view that each individual constructs
an imagined goal to strive for, and that this "line" or "style of
life," when understood, explains the ways and directions of his
strivings. Ibsen's "style of life," writes Mr. Duve, "was a search for
compensation and self-assertion . . . The kernel of all his drama is
the desire to free himself from all the bonds that hemmed him in
from his earliest childhood. His dramas are unconscious demands
to be quit of all the sense of guilt and anxiety that shut him out
from spiritual freedom and earthly happiness. He is in a greater
degree than any other the poet of the sense of guilt. This binds his
life and poetry together in a clarifying unity."[6]

Mr. Duve makes much of a very early memory which Ibsen
recorded in the few pages of reminiscences he wrote for an early
biographer.[7] Henrik must have been about three years old when
the nursemaid took him up into the church steeple and held him
out of an opening there, so that he looked far down into the street.
From the window of the Ibsens' house across the street Henrik's
mother saw her child there and fainted with terror.

According to Adler we remember early events which suit our
life-goal. Mr. Duve considers this memory very significant. Ibsen
does not say whether he was terrified while being held out up there.
Probably he was. Certainly he always was subject to vertigo like his
hero Solness. At the same time, for him as for Solness, looking out
from a high place meant the glory of superior vision. This the adult
Ibsen sought for and symbolized over and over again. Mr. Duve
may be more fanciful when he suggests also that seeing his mother
below meant to the child that he could reach her love and comfort
only by falling, which meant death. It is true, however, that again
and again the patterns of his dramatic actions follow this symbolism:—the Ibsen hero makes an egotistical "climb" toward a fictitious life-goal or—as the 19th century expressed it—Ideal. But this
climb separates him from love and human happiness. At the pinna-
cle of the climb the hero falls, freezes, or is overwhelmed. Reconciliation of the claim of the Ideal and the claim of love could only be

5. Arne Duve, *Symbolikken i Henrik
Ibsens Skuespill.* (Oslo, 1945).
6. Op. cit., p. 7; my translation.

7. In Henrik Jaeger, *Henrik Ibsen.
A Critical Biography.* (English translation: Chicago, 1901).

made by death, for Ibsen never found it possible to reconcile them in himself. His sympathies were torn both ways; hence his ambiguity and his irony.

Mr. Duve explains how Ibsen must have become thus self-divided. The education of his time set up an ideal of "purity," enforced by rewards and punishments, which often burdened children by a conscience that destroyed joy, made sexuality seem evil, and led to hatefulness, guiltiness, frustrations, and neuroses. Mr. Duve writes:

> Ibsen's inner split made him regard life and poetry as in absolute opposition. His deep tragedy is that he could never win through to the synthesis life *and* poetry, for that would have meant redemption and happiness for him. As his fate as artist is based upon an inner conflict, it is mirrored throughout his writing. He *could* not seize life with full hands, and the opposition to a healthy and full unfolding of life finds expression in an anxiety about sex that runs like a red thread through all his work. Instead he had to seek compensation and outlet for his activity and powers of love in artistic efforts.

This analysis seems to me well-founded. Ibsen found partial release by projecting his conflicts dramatically in protagonists who choose art and deny life. More or less symbolically veiled, they are projected in all his plays. Mr. Duve's main concern is to unveil the symbols psychoanalytically. Some of his interpretations strike me as far-fetched, and in any case they are rather remote from the concerns of the stage artist. The main line of interpretation, however, is illuminating.

In his earlier works Ibsen idealized his climbers. One of them, in a poem written in 1859, sings:

> Up here on the fells must be freedom and God,
> Men do but grope, in the valley.[8]

But already the poet has doubts. This singer also observes that his heart is turning to stone. Ibsen said that his hero Brand was himself in his best moments; yet that stern preacher ends his life beneath an avalanche while a Voice from heaven proclaims that God is *deus caritatis*. Julian the Apostate dies with the historic words that the Galilean has conquered. Nevertheless, in his earlier works Ibsen felt that the quest, at least, was noble. He held to the sentiments, we might say, of Longfellow's *Excelsior*.

With *The Wild Duck*, however, the doubts dominate. Here the Claimer of the Ideal is not merely destestable but ridiculous, and life-lies are declared to be the only salvation for ordinary mortals.

8. "Pa Vidderne," translated as "On the Fells" by Fydell Edmund Garrett in *Lyrics and Poems from Ibsen* (London and New York, 1912).

Thenceforward Ibsen might regret the hopelessness of climbing, but he never again romanticized it. In my opinion those who think that he admired his later idealists are mistaken. Rosmer, Solness, Allmers, and Rubek, as well as John Gabriel, are all self-deluded egoists who have committed "the unpardonable sin" of killing the love-life in a human soul. Conventional stage interpretations, if I am right, entirely miss the point of these plays.[9]

Only one Ibsen play has a psychologically happy resolution—*The Lady from the Sea.* Here for once the protagonist by giving up her fictitious dream can turn to love and spiritual harmony. And here for once is a man capable of offering real love. "Dr. Wangel's love," writes Mr. Duve, "frees her own powers of love." Other critics who emphasize the talk about free will and responsibility I think are concerned with a side issue.

The earlier of our two Norwegian studies seems to me the more valuable for the stage interpreter; hence I put it last. It is by Ingjald Nissen; its title may be translated as *Spiritual Crises in People's Lives,* and it has a clarifying subtitle: *Henrik Ibsen and Modern Psychology.*[1]

Following Adler, Mr. Nissen observes that all men strive for security, and that children, being feeble, are prone to anxiety because of their inferiority. This feeling leads them to defense mechanisms and overcompensations. If the feeling is strong, it may become an "inferiority complex." The neurotic who suffers from this complex follows a negative system of defenses, a fictitious goal of life. The healthy person finds a positive course of action in the real world.

Like many other artists, Ibsen suffered from a deep sense of inferiority, if not a complex, and he made his life's work as compensation. At first he was a sole child, the one object of his parents' regard; then the birth of the first of four younger children dethroned him. His early memories were of a big house where his father played jovial host and important man. Then the father went bankrupt and the family was disgraced. (Henrik was eight years old then.) Added to this calamity were what seem to have been the clashing personalities of the parents. Knut Ibsen had a satirical temper and a caustic tongue, which Henrik in turn cultivated later. The mother enwrapped the boy in piety, from which he struggled, but only at the cost of an enduring sense of guilt.

As a child he was lonely and unpopular, and turned inward to solitary games. He wanted to be a magician, the man who mystifies; a doctor, the man who knows the secrets of life; a painter, the man

9. See Weigand, *op. cit.,* and chapters on Ibsen in my books, *The Anatomy of Drama* and *The Dry Mock* (Berkeley and Los Angeles, 1942 and 1946; 1948).

1. Ingjald Nissen, *Sjelelige Kriser i Mennesekets Liv. Henrik Ibsen og den Modern Psykologi.* (Oslo, 1931).

who sees. (Later, in his plays, he combined the capacities of all three.) Poverty made immediate pursuit of any such ambition impossible, and at sixteen he found himself a druggist's apprentice in a distant village, too poor to buy an overcoat, and miserably lonely. Two years later the servant girl at the druggist's—a girl ten years his elder—bore him an illegitimate son. For the next fourteen years, during the time of his greatest financial stress, he had to pay for this child's upbringing.

Ibsen buried this episode in silence. That he was profoundly ashamed of it is suggested by Peer Gynt's disgust at himself when the Green-Clad One claims him from Solveig. Ibsen had been reared on Puritan sentiments of purity and romantic idealizations of women, as his early verses show. His introduction to sexual love was being seduced by a housemaid and made the father of a bastard. The effect of this experience must have been profound, but it has never been adequately assessed.

The pattern of Ibsen's life was thus set. I cannot follow with Mr. Nissen the way in which it shaped his later career or trace the motivation of many of his characters with reference to it. I have time for only one or two examples.

The Wild Duck, as we have noted, contrasts the neurotic's world of defense mechanisms and the real world. Of this great drama of "life-lies" the critic writes: "Ibsen works here with nearly all the points of view to which individual psychology has later given scientific form, and one may marvel at the clarity and understanding with which Hjalmar Ekdal's strivings for power and compensation are worked out."[2] It is a pity that we cannot follow the critic's detailed analysis, for the fair-haired photographer is one of the most amusing and fascinating characters in all drama.

Psychoanalytically observed, a number of the later characters show features unobserved by earlier critics, but convincing, once they are noted. Thus both Hjalmar and Gregers show signs of homosexuality, and Hjalmar is clearly impotent—married fifteen years, and Hedvig not his daughter. Indeed, if such immature sexual adjustments as homosexuality and neurotic impotence are understood to be the results of unconscious evasion of adult responsibility, similar features are clear in the character of Rosmer, the pious seeker after a world of what he calls "happy noblemen." Thus viewed he appears as a weakling who like Gregers seeks to compensate for his feeling of inferiority to a dominating and virile father by excessive idealism.

* * *

It has become clear that we can no more fully understand Ibsen's plays without understanding Ibsen than we can understand

2. Op. cit., p. 78.

Strindberg's without understanding Strindberg. And this psychological approach has the merit that it makes all of Ibsen's work coherent. The plays make sense as they have not done previously. And they manifest a startling vitality for our time.

Ibsen himself insisted that he was a poet of human souls—souls faced with "the contradiction between ability and desire, between will and possibility."[3] It follows that his plays should be interpreted to emphasize the conflicts of the divided souls he portrays. Moreover, Ibsen never resolved his own conflicts, and his plays characteristically end in discord. The discords he sounded are our own; our ears are burdened by them; they have not lost their significance.

There is a special value for theatre people in realizing the extraordinary depth and subtlety of Ibsen's psychological understanding. Despite the fascination for the psychiatric shared by so many modern writers and audiences, and despite the advantages in understanding that post-Freudian literature has supplied, I know of no recent play that even approaches Ibsen's later works in power and depth. He is not out of date in this; we have simply not caught up with him.

Finally, notwithstanding his unresolved discords, Ibsen was never an utter pessimist or a nihilist, like too many moderns. The positive message of all his works from the first to the last is that no individual can have a whole soul alone; that a whole and healthy soul grows only by love—the shared love of man and woman.

No doubt you recall Dr. Stockman's curtain line, that "the strongest man in the world is he who stands most alone." Most of the critics who quote that line have failed to notice the tableau that Ibsen arranged for the audience to see as the curtain falls on *An Enemy of the People*. There is the good doctor in the middle, with his wife on one side of him and his daughter on the other. That tableau is Ibsen's quiet joke at the expense of his hero. That tableau symbolizes Ibsen's positive meaning for us.

OTTO REINERT

Sight Imagery in *The Wild Duck*†

It may be a little early to speak of an Ibsen renaissance, but hardly to risk the guess that one is in the making. In England, Brian Downs, P. F. D. Tennant, and Muriel Bradbrook have chal-

3. Preface to the Second Edition of *Catiline*.
† From *Journal of English and Germanic Philology*, Vol. LV, No. 3 (July, 1956), pp. 457–62. Reprinted by permission of the publisher.

lenged the critical stereotype of a dated shocker who with fatal skill froze the form of subsequent drama in a rigid mold of naturalism. Here in America Eric Bentley has judiciously reassessed his accomplishments for modern times. In his native Norway attention is turning away from biography and bibliography, and a long conspiracy of uncritical veneration broken. There is growing recognition that his importance is not just historical, that his dramas have endured remarkably well in spite of a host of less talented imitators, that there are poetic qualities even in his most realistic plays. What has become antiquated is, not the plays themselves, but Shaw's and Archer's kind of distorting championship of them in *The Quintessence of Ibsenism* and *The Old Drama and the New*. Ibsen the artist is at last about to assume his rightful place before Ibsen the social reformer and Ibsen "the father of modern drama."

This is as it should be. But what perhaps should be said today is that his literary achievement is not accounted for when reference has been made to the retrospective technique and exposition by innuendo, to rotten ships, burning orphanages, poisoned bath waters, and white horses. Impressive as his command of dramatic structure and symbol was, he was in addition a genuine poet. My purpose here is to call attention to a pattern of imagery in *The Wild Duck* that serves the same integrating and value-defining functions as similar patterns in Shakespeare's mature plays and in much metaphysical and modern poetry. Ostensibly representational and simply communicative, the language of the dialogue operates on an imagistic level as well, reinforcing and clarifying the meaning of the action, embodying the dramatic metaphor.

Blindness, it will be recalled, is an important plot element in *The Wild Duck*. It is when he learns about Old Werle's approaching blindness that Hjalmar Ekdal concludes that little Hedvig is not his own but Werle's child, since she too is losing her sight. And his repulsion of Hedvig precipitates the catastrophe, the girl's pathetic suicide. To readers of Ibsen there is nothing unusual in this. Once again we find him using a fact of biological heredity both as plot device and as symbol of the visitation of the past upon the present.

What has not been clearly recognized is that images of sight and blindness occur throughout the play, constituting a substratum of ironical values beneath the naturalistic surface. The images help to define the play's action: the struggle between Gregers Werle and Dr. Relling for control over Hjalmar Ekdal's destiny becomes a conflict between two views—one "idealistic," dim, and distorted; one "realistic," clear, and accurate—of modern Everyman's diminished nature. In the strict economy of Ibsen's art the validity of Relling's realistic view is stated only by negative implication. It is vindicated by the setting of Gregers' idealistic view of Hjalmar and

Hjalmar's view of himself (the two are almost identical, since Hjalmar takes the cue for his concept of himself from Gregers) in a context of imagistic irony.

It is a commonplace in Ibsen criticism to regard the theme of *The Wild Duck* as a corrective to the themes of Ibsen's earlier social problem plays. Whereas *Pillars of Society, A Doll's House, Ghosts,* and *An Enemy of the People* grant, if not happiness, then at least moral insight and salvation to individuals who have the courage of their convictions, *The Wild Duck* presents the sorry results of a psychopath's idealistic dedication to a self-assumed mission of truth. The play is neither a tragedy nor a farce but a little bit of both, and as a result its tone is both unique and puzzling. One can understand why even admirers of Ibsen found it vaguely irritating on its first appearance. It is the least "edifying" play Ibsen ever wrote, and certainly the least sublime. That it is also, quite possibly, his best play is something to think about for people who try to reduce Ibsen to a radical crusader whom time and events have turned respectable and a little dull. It is the sodden cynic Dr. Relling who speaks the theme of the play: "Take the life illusion away from the average man, and you take his happiness too." Because Gregers Werle meddles with Hjalmar Ekdal's life illusion, i.e., his concept of himself, Hedvig sacrifices herself for the sake of her worthless father. Hjalmar's selfish, phrase-mongering existence would have been pleasant enough and would have given his wife and daughter happiness enough—if only Gregers had not insisted that the Ekdal marriage needed to be re-established on a foundation of truth. As usual, Ibsen propounds no general dogma here. He is not denying the value of truth. He is questioning the absolute value of a painful truth.

What is one man's truth is another man's poison. It is this skeptical, relativistic theme that Ibsen allows ironical play in the images of sight and blindness. Hjalmar Ekdal is not the kind of man who can live comfortably with an unpleasant truth, and the ruin of the Ekdal happiness is the result of Gregers Werle's mistaken view of Hjalmar's character.

But Gregers goes through the whole play thinking of himself as a man who, if he does nothing else, at least *sees.* His self-hatred, conditioned by a neurotic mother and a miserable adolescence, is modified on this one point only: he prides himself on his ability to see the truth and on his courage to bring it out into the open. In Act I he turns down his father's offer of reconciliation with the words, "I have seen too much of you" (literally: "I have seen you from too close up"). Gregers' choice of phrase is ironic, since there *is* something myopic about his view of his father, and Werle's answer suggests, at an early point in the pay, the dubious validity of his son's vision: "You have seen me with your mother's eyes ... But you should remember that those eyes were—clouded at times." In a play premised on heredity it is not overly ingenious to take this to mean that Gregers' sight is affected, figuratively speaking, by inheritance from both his father and his mother. To his father's offer Gregers opposes his confidence in his clearsightedness: "Now at last I see a mission to live for." The mission, we soon learn, is "to open Hjalmar Ekdal's eyes. He shall see his situation as it is; ..." Ibsen's curtain speeches frequently carry a load of ulterior meaning, and it is Gregers who delivers the curtain speech in Act I: "Look, father; the chamberlains are playing blindman's buff with Mrs. Sørby." The speech is a cruel taunt to a man who is about to go blind, a veiled insult to his father's wife-to-be, a declaration on Gregers' part that blindman's buff is not a game *he* chooses to play—and an anticipation of the kind of game he is, in fact, about to involve the Ekdals in. On the first morning of his residence with the Ekdals he tries to light the stove in his room but succeeds only in filling the room with smoke. Before the play is over he has reduced the Ekdal home to a similar dark and messy state. But to him it is Hjalmar, not himself, who is living in darkness, like a wild duck that has dived down from the light of the sky. " ... you are being corrupted by an insidious disease," he tells Hjalmar, "and you have plunged to the bottom to die in the dark." But he does not apply to Hjalmar the advice he gives concerning the real wild duck: "Be sure it never sees the sea and sky." Rather, when he has revealed the truth about Gina's past to Hjalmar and expects to see "a splendor of revelation" surrounding husband and wife, he is both baffled and anguished when they don't proceed to put the shattered pieces of their lives together. The obtuse idealist is unaware of the portentous implications of the symbol he employs to enforce his own vision of Hjalmar's moral plight. When he at last succeeds in having Hedvig "open [her] eyes to what gives life its worth," the result is her pointless suicide. Coming from the lips of the blind bungler Gregers proves himself to be, his rejection of Relling's realistic estimate of Hjalmar's character marks a climax of irony: "After all, I don't consider myself completely blind."

Hjalmar, too, thinks he sees, and his occupation would seem to support his claim. It is the business of a photographer to see straight and to record his vision objectively. But, significantly, he has not himself chosen his occupation, and it is Gina who actually carries on the daily business. Every afternoon he spends hours on the sofa with his eyes shut—i.e., fast asleep—while his family believes, and he believes himself, that he is visualizing a great photographic invention. His "badness of vision" is, like Gregers', established in the first act, when his father passes through Werle's study where his dinner guests are assembled. Ill at ease among his social superiors Hjalmar refuses to acknowledge his shabby and doddering old father, and is consequently forced—there is a kind of poetic justice in the incident, though Hjalmar is, of course, unaware of it—to pretend to less powers of observation than even "the near-sighted gentleman" who asks him if he knows Old Ekdal. In his misery Hjalmar mutters that he "didn't notice. . . ." But spiritual blindness does not prevent Hjalmar, any more than Gregers, from referring to himself as a person of superior insight, a lover of light. When Gina, fearful of what Gregers may tell her husband about her past, tries to stop Hjalmar from going out with Gregers, Hjalmar complacently assumes that it is his friend and not himself who is in trouble and answers that Gregers needs "a friend's wakeful eyes." Just prior to the climactic scene with his wife, in which he forces her to confess to the old affair with Werle, he asks in a characteristically pregnant speech: "Let me have the lamp lit!" He reproaches Gina that she never "casts a probing glance" at her past, and he silences Relling's warning that the old stories are better left buried with, "You've never had an eye for the claims of the ideal, Relling." Once Gregers has "opened his eyes" he looks back upon the years he has lived in illusion as one long blindness. Werle becomes a man who "has once blinded a trusting fellow being," but he finds comfort in the justice of Werle's own approaching blindness, and concludes sententiously: "It is useful, at times, to plunge oneself into the night side of existence." When he learns about Werle's gift letter to his father and Hedvig, he exclaims: "Oh, what vistas, what perspectives open up before me!" He thinks he has had "his eyes opened" to Hedvig's disloyalty to him. "It is Hedvig who stands in the way," he tells Gregers. "She it is who is shutting out the sun from my whole life." Blind as he is to Hedvig's love for him, he is forced to close his eyes to the ugly facts of the surface truth he *does* see. He sends her away with a "I can't stand to look at you," and is deaf to Gina's plea for the heartbroken girl: "Look at the child, Ekdal! Look at the child!" He doesn't, and the shot in the attic follows.

Gregers' use of sight imagery thus points up his blindness to Hjalmar's true character and to the true nature of the Ekdal family's modicum of happiness. Hjalmar's use of such imagery emphasizes his blindness to Gina's and Hedvig's loyal devotion. The more they think they see the more lost they are in darkness. Hjalmar's stupid cruelty to Hedvig leads to her death, and Gregers' faith in the greatness of Hjalmar's soul remains unshaken even after the catastrophe. Both are incapable of seeing beneath the surface of facts; both are blind to their own reality.

It might be tempting, once the function of this sight imagery is recognized, to extend the pattern and find it analogous to the sight-blindness ironies of *Oedipus Rex* and *King Lear*. But such analogy would not be valid. The painful discovery of truth does not, in *The Wild Duck*, coincide with any loss of physical sight; neither Hjalmar nor Gregers corresponds to an Oedipus or a Gloucester. It might even be argued that neither of them ever attains any real insight. Relling's prophecy of what the dead Hedvig will mean to Hjalmar a year hence is undoubtedly correct, and Gregers leaves the play with no more than a sense of bringing people bad luck. And there is nothing wrong with the eyesight of Dr. Relling, the most perceptive character in the play: he is not a Tiresias. Nor do the two characters who *do* go blind, Old Werle and Hedvig, discover any new truth in the course of the play. For all the reasonableness of his adjustment to life it is difficult to consider Werle a representative of spiritual enlightenment, and his relatively minor part in the play disqualifies him in any case for the part of foil to his son and Hjalmar. With her sensitivity and imagination and capacity for love Hedvig is, in a sense, a source of light, but she is, after all, a child, only dimly comprehending the strange adult doings around her. And her unwavering devotion to Hjalmar and worship of him, beautiful though her sentiments are, are hardly the attitudes of a clearsighted girl. If anything, her physical blindness is simply a symbol of her blindness to her father's obvious moral shortcomings.

But if *The Wild Duck* is not tragedy in the great tradition transposed to a modern middle class setting, it does, like the older plays, make use of responsible images. It is a poetic achievement. It succeeds in expressing its sardonic and tender wisdom about the little souls of men in a form that combines the rich suggestiveness of metaphorical language with the insistent and solid actuality of naturalism. The sight imagery never becomes intrusive; the ironies do not call attention to themselves by breaking through the surface of commonplace idiom. But they are there, and their presence makes for moral spaciousness. Their suggestion of values more true than mere facts, truer than the idealist's misty generalities, proves that the poet in Ibsen was active even in his most sordid play.

MARY McCARTHY

The Will and Testament of Ibsen†

GINA. Wasn't that a queer thing to say—that he'd like to be a dog?

HEDWIG. I tell you what, Mother. I think he meant something else by that.

GINA. What else could he mean?

HEDWIG. Well, I don't know; but it was as though he meant something else all the time—and not what he said.

This short catechism—from the second act of *The Wild Duck*—is at first sight only a sort of road sign to the audience to look out for curves ahead. Hjalmar Ekdal's wife and daughter are discussing his friend, Gregers, the meddling fanatic who has inserted himself into the family speaking a dark language and pressing what he calls the claim of the ideal. In the scene just before he has expressed the wish to be a dog—an "extraordinarily clever dog. The kind that goes to the bottom after wild duck when they dive down and bite fast hold of the weeds and the tangle down in the mud." Translated out of this idiom into plain speech, this means that Gregers sees himself as the rescuer of the household which his father (the hunter) has wounded and sent down into the depths. These depths, ironically, are located in an attic, where Hjalmar, who plays the flute and has a windy, "artistic" personality, also plays at being a professional photographer and inventor while his wife does the hard work. In the neighboring garret room, behind a curtain, Hjalmar's disgraced, drunken old father, wearing a brown wig and his lieutenant's uniform, plays at being a hunter with an old double-barreled pistol, some barnyard fowls, pigeons, rabbits, and a real wild duck. Father and son "go hunting" in this make-believe forest, which is rather like photographers' scenery. Hedwig, the percipient little girl, who is not Hjalmar's real daughter but the illegitimate child of Gregers' father, is going blind. This blindness is a metaphor for the state of darkened self-deception in which the little family lives. Gregers believes that he has the duty to *open Hjalmar's eyes* to the true facts of his marriage. At the house of Gregers' father, who is also losing his sight, they are drinking Tokay wine and playing Blind Man's Buff.

In short, as Hedwig indicates to her uninstructed mother, the dramatist means something else all the time and not what he says. Everything, Hedwig precociously understands, is symbolic. The real wild duck is the child, Hedwig, who picks up Gregers' "loaded" suggestion and shoots herself. The tragic climax of *The Wild Duck* is brought about, thus, by an act of over-interpretation. Gregers, for once, was speaking literally when he said to the little girl: "But suppose, now, that you of your own free will, sacrificed the wild duck for *his* sake?" But Hedwig, confused and terrified the next morning by her supposed father's harshness (for Hjalmar's eyes have at last been opened), thinks that she has finally grasped Gregers' under-meaning and, presuming that she is the "sacrifice" alluded to, goes into the garret room and puts the pistol to her breast.

This ending, like so many of Ibsen's dramatic finales ("The mill race! The mill race!"), seems a little heavy and strained, like the last crashing chords of movie music. Yet it is utterly just. The child's suggestibility has a semantic grounding. She has been led by the Higher Critics around her to look for the real reality under the surface of language—that is, to schematize her life as she lives it. Gregers, with his "claim of the ideal," Hjalmar, with his talk of "a task in life," are both inveterate schematizers, one a truth-speaker, the other an aesthetician. As his wife says of Hjalmar, "Surely you realize, Mr. Werle, that my husband isn't one of those ordinary photographers." Everything has conspired to make Hedwig distrust the *ordinary* way of looking at things. In a peculiarly sinister scene in the third act, Gregers has been talking to Hedwig about the garret room where the wild duck lives. She tells him that sometimes the whole room and all the things in it seem to her like "the ocean's depths," and then she adds: "But that's so silly."

GREGERS. No, you mustn't say that.
HEDWIG. It is; because it's only an attic.
GREGERS. (*looking hard at her*). Are you so sure of that?
HEDWIG. (*astonished*). That it's an attic?
GREGERS. Yes. Do you know that for certain?
(*Hedwig is silent, looking at him with an open mouth.*)

Gregers preaches mysteries. Hjalmar's daily conversation is a flow of oratory. He always speaks of his brown-wigged bald father as "the white-haired old man." And his pretended "purpose in life" is a sort of parody of Gregers' "purpose to live for." Hjalmar too conceives of himself as a savior, the rescuer of his father. "Yes, I will rescue that ship-wrecked man. For he was ship-wrecked when the storm broke loose on him. . . . That pistol there, my friend—the one we use to shoot rabbits with—it has played its part in the tragedy of the House of Ekdal." Again, a flight of metaphors, more disjointed and *ad libitum* in Hjalmar's case, a fact which points to the difference between the two rhetoricians. Hjalmar improvises idly on the instrument of language, but Gregers is in earnest, with his single unifying metaphor of the duck and the bird dog and the hunter, which he pursues to the fearful end.

The men are poet-idealists; Hedwig is a budding poetess. Gina, the uneducated wife, belongs to the prosy multitude that was patronized earlier in the century by Wordsworth: "A primrose by the river's brim, A yellow primrose was to him. And it was nothing more." "That there blessed wild duck," she exclaims. "The fuss there is over it!" When Gregers, true to his metaphor, speaks of the "swamp vapor" that is morally poisoning the Ekdal household, Gina retorts: "Lord knows there's no smell of swamps here, Mr. Werle; I air the place out every blessed day."

The Wild Duck was written in the middle of Ibsen's career, after *Pillars of Society, A Doll's House, Ghosts, An Enemy of the People* and before the sequence of plays beginning with *Rosmersholm*. Ibsen regarded it as a departure from his earlier work, and it is often taken to be a satiric repudiation of "the Ibsenites" or even of Ibsen himself as a crusading social dramatist. In the figure of Gregers Werle, an ugly man in a countrified gray suit who appears on his mission of truth to rip the veil of illusion from a satisfied household, it is certainly possible to see a cruel self-portrait of the dramatic author who sought to "let in the air" on the stuffy Norwegian community, to expose its hypocrisy and commercial chicanery, its enslavement to a notion of duty and to a sentimentalized picture of family life. Gregers Werle's harping on the concept of "a true marriage," which shall not be based on lies and concealment, is certainly a mocking echo of the doctrines of *Ghosts* and *A Doll's House*. Moreover, Gregers Werle has been a radical before the opening of the play, and Ibsen, though he was a stock figure of respectability in private life, looked upon himself as a radical, even an anarchist, and throughout his plays, up to the very end, there is a doctrinal insistence on freedom and the necessity of self-realization that today has a somewhat period and moralistic flavor, as though the notion of duty, reappearing in the guise of Duty to Oneself, had become, if anything, more puritan, more rigid, more sternly forbidding, than the notion of duty to God or family or bourgeois custom. If Gregers Werle is Ibsen in his tendentious and polemical aspect, then indeed he is a demon that Ibsen is trying to cast out through the exorcism of this play—a grotesque and half-pathetic demon, in that he will never understand anything concrete, a demon, in fact, of abstraction who bursts into the play with his ugly face and ugly name like some parochial incorruptible Robespierre whose activities are circumscribed by a sad fate to the reform of a single bohemian family. But if Gregers Werle represents the demand for truth in its ultimate, implacable form, then the message of the play is, as some critics have said, cynical and nihilistic, since the converse of Gregers is a Dr. Relling, a lodger downstairs who believes that lies and illusions are necessary to human survival.

A softer reading of Ibsen's intention suggests that Gregers represents only the eternal interfering busybody, but this reduces the play to a platitude—an object-lesson in what happens when an outsider tries to tell married people how to run their lives. Shaw's opinion was that Gregers is simply a particularly dangerous case of idealism and duty on the rampage, and according to Shaw's thesis Ibsen spent his life doing doughty battle against the joint forces of duty and idealism—the vested interests of the day. But Ibsen was a more divided nature than Shaw allowed for, and the battle was within.

Ibsen is not an attractive personality, and his work has, intermittently, a curious confessional closet-smell, as though he were using his play-writing as a form of psychotherapy. This is especially noticeable in *The Master Builder*, where the hero is Ibsen in a symbolic disguise. The master builder (read sound dramatic craftsman) has first built churches (the early poetic plays), then houses for people to live in (the social dramas), and is finally erecting houses with steeples (the late, symbolic plays). This hero, Master Solness, is very darkly motivated; there has been a fire, years ago, through which, indirectly, he and his wife lost their children, but which, at the same time, permitted him to start on his successful career as a builder and real-estate developer. Now he is obsessed with jealousy of younger men in his profession, and he is suffering from a failure of nerve, which is connected with the fire, perhaps, or with his wife's compulsive sense of duty and her invalidism or with his abandonment of church architecture. The play is strangely thin, more like a scenario with several writers contributing suggestions in a story conference than like a finished play, and throughout its jerky development, there is a sense of something elusive, as though Ibsen, again, like Gregers Werle, meant something else all the time and not what he said. There is the same odd feeling in *Rosmersholm*, which is full of disjointed references, like the talk of an insane person—what are those white horses, really, and what is the mill race, and what is that quest for total innocence, on which the play seems to turn and yet not to turn?

The idea of guilt for some sin of the past, a sin, even, of the fathers, plays a great part in Ibsen. Like many of his characters, he has a secret in his early life—a poor girl whom he got in trouble and left to fend for herself. Hereditary disease, illegitimacy, the death of children haunt the Ibsen world; they are all in *The Wild Duck*. In the early plays, the guilt or the sin is localized; we know what the protagonist has done, in the past, which will spring the trap on him. But in the later plays, starting with *Rosmersholm*, the guilt has become diffuse, and it is no longer clear what is the matter. A kind of corny symbolism replaces the specific fact in the mechanism of the plot—white horses, steeples, trolls, a sailor, a mermaid, and the sea and a ring. And these symbols, which are only vague portents, correspond to a vague ache or yearning in the breasts of the principal characters, who talk about themselves distractedly, as though they were relating their symptoms in a session of group analysis. *Hedda Gabler* is an exception; next to *The Wild Duck*, it is Ibsen's most successful play. Hedda does not discuss herself; the General's daughter is too haughty for that. Instead, she behaves, and the subject of the play is visibly present, as it was in *The Doll's House*, as it still is in *The Wild Duck*. Her suicide at the end is less convincing than her burning of the manuscript, and her burning of the manuscript is less convincing than the transfixing moment in the first act when she pretends to think that the aunt's new hat, lying on the sofa, is the servant's old bonnet. But Ibsen is not very good at making big events happen; he is better at the small shocking event, the psychopathology of everyday life. Hedda and her husband's aunt's hat, Nora, when she nonchalantly pushes off the sewing on her poor widowed friend, Christine, Hjalmar, when he talks himself into letting Hedwig with her half-blind eyes do his retouching for him so that he can go off and play hunter with his father in the attic, Hjalmar cutting his father at the Werle soirée, Hjalmar eating butter obliviously while his hungry daughter watches him. These are the things one knows oneself to be capable of. If the larger gestures are less credible in Ibsen, this is possibly because of his very success in the realistic convention, which implies a norm of behavior on the part of its guilty citizens within their box-like living rooms. The realistic convention requires credibility, that is, a statistical norm; the audience must believe that the people on the stage are more or less like themselves, no worse and no better, in short, they are ordinary, restrained by cowardice or public opinion from stooping too low or rising too high. The faculty for determining likelihood or credibility becomes more and more highly developed—a sensitized measuring instrument—as a society becomes more homogeneous and parochial and less stratified in terms of class.

But this very ordinariness, this exaction of truth to life, is a limitation on an artist, especially on one with "titanic" ambitions, like Ibsen. And this is where symbolism enters, as a device to deepen or heighten the realistic drama while keeping it within the frame of the three-wall stage. Symbolic thinking was already natural to him, as *Peer Gynt* and *Brand* indicate. Here, however, it was used in the old-fashioned way, to sustain a philosophical argument, that is, to make abstractions concrete and visible, with the text of the play serving as a kind of libretto to the music of the thought behind it. But starting with *Pillars of Society*, Ibsen began to reverse the process—to make the concrete abstract, in the "coffin-ships," whose rotting hulls are supposed to symbolize the whole of Norwegian society. But the temptation of this new, allusive method (the method described by Hedwig in the passage quoted) was that it led to grandiosity and cunning or more precisely, to the kind of schematic thinking exemplified by Gregers Werle; this schematic thinking being really a form of God-identification, in which the symbolist imposes on the concrete, created world his own private design and lays open to question the most primary facts of existence, i.e., whether an attic is "really" an attic or is not in fact a swamp or something else. The allusive, hinting language employed by Gregers is the language of all messianic individuals and interfering, paranoid prophets. And like Hjalmar's sentimental flow of metaphor, it is the language of bad art, art that is really religion or edification. This type of symbolism is often found in sermons and in addresses by college presidents, who liken the institution to a ship, themselves to the pilot at the helm, etc.

Ibsen sees all this in Gregers, and he sees, furthermore, that Gregers is incurable. In his last speech of the play, Gregers has merely shifted metaphors: "GREGERS (*looking in front of him*). In that case, I am glad my destiny is what it is. RELLING. May I ask—what *is* your destiny? GREGERS (*on the point of going*). To be thirteenth at table." This cryptic and portentous remark means something more than it says, evidently—either that the speaker is going to commit suicide or that he sees himself from henceforth as the odd, unassimilable man, the bird of ill omen, and that he finds a mysterious satisfaction in the picture.

Odious, baneful creature. And yet one cannot throw off the feeling that Gregers is something more than a repudiation of an earlier stage in the author's development. As in *The Master Builder*, where Solness is fond of likening himself fatly to a troll, there is a sense of confession here which lingers in that last remark and far from rounding off the play leaves it hanging, like an unanswered doubt. The fact is, in any case, that Ibsen, if he did unburden himself of a certain amount of self-dislike through the medium of Gregers, did not follow this up with any reforms. Quite the contrary. In the light of the later plays, this confession appears as a sort of indulgence bought for all future sins. The wild duck in the attic is revived as the carp in the pond of *The Lady from the Sea*, and here it is the sympathetic characters who hint that the carp is "really" a symbol of themselves in their brackish village. The pietistic talk of a "task" or a "purpose in life," which has already been heard in A *Doll's House*, is not silenced by the pistol shot in *The Wild Duck*; it breaks out again, irrepressibly, in *Rosmersholm*, in *The Lady from the Sea*, and even in *Hedda Gabler*; once more it is the sympathetic characters who voice the notions of Gregers and Hjalmar and who allegorize themselves as instruments of a hidden Will. The plays grow more grandiose as the symbolic content inflates them, and the scenery changes to cliffs and mountain tops that evoke the painted canvas settings of Hjalmar's photographic studio.

No doubt there is a good deal of bathetic "studio" art in all the great late nineteenth-century writers, with the exception of Tolstoy. It is in Dickens and George Eliot and Dostoevsky, certainly; they paid for being titans and for the power to move a mass audience by a kind of auto-intoxication or self-hypnosis that allowed them to manipulate their emotion like a stage hand cranking out a snowstorm from a machine containing bits of paper. This effect of false snow falling on a dramatic scene is more noticeable in Ibsen than in any of his great coevals, and he left it as his legacy to the American school of playwrights, to O'Neill and now Tennessee Williams, Arthur Miller, and William Inge. (Shaw, who considered himself indebted to Ibsen, never learned anything from him, for he did not work in the realistic convention, though he may not always have been aware of the fact.) If Ibsen's followers are not better than they are, this may be partly because the master, compared to the great architect-novelists of his period, was only a master builder. The "Freudian" character of his symbols has often been remarked upon, and perhaps his most important contribution was clinical: he was the first to put a neurotic woman—Hedda, Ellida Wangel, Mrs. Solness, Nora—on the stage.

But his work, viewed as a whole, seems at once repetitive and inchoate. Twice, in *Hedda Gabler* and *The Wild Duck*, he created a near-masterpiece. The rest of his career appears as a series of false starts and reverses in an interior conversation that keeps lapsing into reverie. The goal of all Ibsen's heroes and heroines— self-realization—looms throughout his plays like one of his symbolic mountain peaks, which the toiling author himself could never reach.

ROBERT M. ADAMS

Ibsen on the Contrary†

A museum-culture, such as we live in, is forever digging up forgotten or semi-forgotten artifacts, dusting them off vigorously, giving them a new coat of varnish, oohing and aahing over them briefly, and then setting them on the top shelf of Case 17 in Room K to gather dust for another generation or two. That is where Ibsen is to be looked for these days—on a respectable eminence in a glassed case under half a century's dust. He was once a thunderstorm in the theater, and outside as well. A compatriot gently suggested during a friendly discussion that his work, though obviously great and certain to last a very long time, might not endure absolutely forever; Ibsen leaped from his chair in cold fury and flung it after the man's

† From *A Norton Critical Edition of Modern Drama*, edited by Anthony Caputi (New York: W. W. Norton & Co., Inc., 1966), pp. 344–53. An earlier version was published in *The Hudson Review*, Volume X, No. 3, Autumn 1957, under the title "Henrik Ibsen: The Fifty-first Anniversary."

retreating head: "Rob me of eternity, and you rob me of every-thing!" Well, so far he has his eternity; but at the price of persisting, rather like a mummied head in an anthropological museum—shrunken, dried, *miniaturized*.

In fact, the flood of explanatory writing which, in the last decade of the nineteenth century and the first decade of the twentieth, set out to moderate Ibsen's strangeness and domesti-cate his art under the rubric of honest naturalism has done its work all too fully. The modern reader knows Ibsen, or thinks he knows him, too well by half. He is established in the public mind as an author of middle-class tragedies, a man who tried to transplant the art of Sophocles into the social milieu of Wil-liam Dean Howells. It is hard to see why a first-class dramatic artist should want to undertake any such enterprise; therefore, Ibsen was not a first-class dramatic artist. The only flaw in this argument is its major premise. Ibsen in the great plays was not a simple bourgeois realist; the effect at which he was aiming was not Sophoclean, or in fact tragic, except in the most atten-uated sense, a sense in which it hardly differs at all from the word "gloomy.' Judged in its own terms, the effect at which he did aim is concentrated, rigorously economical, dramatically shattering. Above all, it is nothing so formal as trying to do in one social milieu what had already been done perfectly well in another.

If this argument is to be made within the scope of an article, we must not waste more than a paragraph on such fiddle-faddle as the notion that *Ghosts* is a play about venereal disease or that *A Doll's House* is a play about women's rights. On these terms, *King Lear* is a play about housing for the elderly and *Hamlet* a stage-debate over the reality of spooks. Venereal dis-ease and its consequences are represented onstage in *Ghosts*; so, to all intents and purposes, is incest; but the theme of the play is inherited guilt, and the sexual pathology of the Alving family is an engine in the hands of that theme. *A Doll's House* repre-sents a woman imbued with the idea of becoming a person, but it proposes nothing categorical about women becoming people; in fact, its real theme has nothing to do with the sexes. It is the irrepressible conflict of two different personalities which have founded themselves on two radically different estimates of real-ity. *Rosmersholm* describes the same conflict but assigns oppo-site roles to the sexes.

What, then, is the purpose of that bourgeois décor, lovingly detailed and meticulously accurate, which marks the plays of Ibsen's middle period? Miss Mary McCarthy (in *Partisan Review*, Winter, 1956) touches on one aspect when she says, approximately, that Ibsen's characters do little revealing things well and big dramatic ones badly. Precisely so. The bourgeois décor is a device of focus; by looking through it as well as at it, one sees, as through bifocal lenses, the immense moral differences that divide saint and satyr. In our nineteenth-century world they occur as the bank clerk's wife and the bank clerk; or perhaps as the country doctor and the small-town official. They are not, or do not at first seem, very far apart—husband and wife, brother and brother. Their gestures are not grandiose, they are limited, with the awkward charm of people who do not quite know who they are. But the audience can know exactly who they are. If you look at them under the ultra-violet light of Ibsen's satiric glance, their true characters will appear, like ancient writing on a palimpsest: Apollo under the frock coat; Hecate in a bustle; dog, swine, bull, crow, and boar behind the respectable features. Steady and impervious as they seem in their own eyes, the characters of Ibsen are in the eyes of the playwright and his chosen audience deliriously transparent; and the high comedy which attaches to Torvald Helmer or Hialmar Ekdal stems precisely from this combination (to which the inspiredly stupid seem most adaptable)—perfect bland solidity in themselves and absolute transparency in the eyes of others. Miss McCarthy talks of a shocking moment when Hialmar eats bread and butter in front of his hungry daughter; but that, though it might be someone else's shock, is not Ibsen's. Hedvig is not hungry; if she wanted to eat, there is not only bread and butter but herring salad for her. Actually she is not even present at the famous breakfast. But the point is elsewhere. Hialmar has a mighty mission to perform, and is on his way to perform it when he encounters that fatal bread and butter; and the joke is the person he reveals himself to be, even as he tries to talk himself into another identity. He is one of Nature's *noshers*[1].... The telling little gesture reveals how unsuited he is to make a big one.

Like some other great writers who come to mind, Ibsen was not a man of many ideas or for that matter of wide technical virtuosity. Skeletally viewed, the plays from *Catiline* to *When We Dead Awaken* (and that covers half a century) all have a single underlying tension, are all efforts to work out the terms of a single dichotomy. Ibsen was trying all his life to find a stage-language for the sort of moral insights which appear at their clearest in the capering tetrameters and fantastic episodes of *Brand* and *Peer Gynt*. The saint and the satyr are clear to see in this diptych; and it is a commonplace that Ibsen

---

1. A Yiddish term for one who likes to snack.

repeated the characterizations many times. With varying accents and under different circumstances, Parson Manders, Peter Stockmann, Hialmar Ekdal, Torvald Helmer, Parson Strawman, Stensgård, and Rebecca West represent the spirit of Peer Gynt; with the same qualifications, Mrs. Alving, Thomas Stockmann, Gregers Werle, Nora Helmer, Falk, Rosmer, and Lona Hessel[2] represent the spirit of Brand. Bourgeois realism is simply one, perhaps the most successful, of half a dozen different vehicles through which Ibsen tried to adjust his moral insights to the requirements of dramatic presentation. The so-called "middle-class dramas" all reverberate to the urgent note of a single conflict. The tension which explodes in the last act of A *Doll's House* is heard as a high, thin scream of agony throughout *Ghosts*. Shouted boisterously from the housetops in *An Enemy of the People*, it is magnificently inverted and buried in *The Wild Duck*, and raised to the cold, silver-gray tonality of tragic resignation and acceptance in *Rosmersholm*. In a familiar but handy jargon, it is the conflict between the ethical and the acquisitive personalities.

Ibsen's attitude toward this glacial schism in human nature, for which he found a terminology in Kierkegaard and an evidence in the slightest acts of everyday life, was ambiguous enough to satisfy the most passionate present-day pursuer of literary ambiguities. *Brand* is clearly a celebration of the heroic ethical personality as contrasted with the meeching conformity of the acquisitive, self-centered easy-goers who find it comfortable to adjust all mottoes to the middle of the road. The respectable official and the bohemian artist are at one in repudiating the claim of the moral absolute; from this perspective one can glance forward to observe the artistic element which lies latent even in a clod like Torvald Helmer, a retoucher of life *par excellence*, a notary built precisely out of the debris of a poet. Against all this formless mish-mosh of the esthetic and acquisitive, these meager patchwork compromisers, Brand sets himself heart and soul. He will not have a God of Love, a muzzy-minded old forgiver of sins. But in the crashing chord of the last macaronic verse,

Han er *Deus Caritatis!* (He is the God of Love!)

God himself speaks to repudiate Brand. It is an ambiguous repudiation, to be sure; for in the very act of affirming His char-

<hr>

2. Parson Manders and Mrs. Alving are in *Ghosts*, Peter and Thomas Stockmann in *An Enemy of the People*, Torvald and Nora Helmer in A *Doll's House*, Parson Strawman and Falk in *Love's Comedy*, Rebecca West and Rosmer in *Rosmersholm*, Stensgård is in *The League of Youth*, Lona Hessel in *Pillars of Society* [Editor].

ity, the Lord wipes out the man who had questioned it; yet, though Brand is demolished, it cannot be said that any of the compromises against which he has struggled are reconstituted. Unresolved contradiction speaks here as clearly as in *Peer Gynt*, the hero of which is repeatedly exposed as an unscrupulous, acquisitive, esthetic rascal who in the pursuit of lies and acquisitions loses himself. Unpeeled, like an onion, he turns out to consist of wrappings without a center. Yet at the last moment, when he is completely lost, he is found, in the love of Solveig. Once again, it is an ambiguous reversal; the Button-Moulder is put off for a moment only by a symbol too glimmering and insubstantial to have much positive meaning. Both plays end in a tightly knotted sequence of reversals which defy logical restatement.

For the matter of that, the entire career proceeds on the basis of logical antitheses (the very last words of Ibsen's life were "On the contrary"). *The Wild Duck* caricatures the peddler of ethical truth whom *An Enemy of the People* glorifies; the crooked argument between Mrs. Sörby and Old Werle turns out to be the nearest thing to a true marriage anyone in *The Wild Duck* can achieve; Parson Manders of *Ghosts* is a flatulent old fool, but he contains, even if he does not know, an ultimate truth about the fitness of the Alving household for freedom and happiness. The ethical way can and does destroy the esthetic; and vice-versa, too. Only a few rare and strongly assured souls can hope to survive the general disaster. A child could choose with more precision and decision than Ibsen ever displayed between the alternatives which he proposed to himself. A shopgirl could find more attractive alternatives to choose between. Any mealy-mouthed purveyor of platitudes could combine Ibsen's attitudes by watering them down to bring him safely within the confines of the great commonplace—"Truth without love is vain," or some such shuffling together of high-sounding incompatibles. But the man himself defies these comfortable formulations; he was one of the great disquieters, and if he could not bring himself to a smug reconciliation of "love" and "truth," for example, it was because he knew better than the smug what these commitments imply. It was the sense that Ibsen was somehow in touch with moral categories larger and deeper than those commonly available to men that made him an international culture-hero to the late nineteenth century. He provided no answers, though his tone was always dogmatic; he asked, instead, terrible searching questions, at the top of his voice, with perfect scorn for anyone who did not know the answers, and only a little hesitation at his own ability to find them. As with Goethe, whom he resembles in so many ways, there is always an uneasy possibility that the inclusive-inconclusive Ibsen is a vast, vague Germanic fraud. The possibility cannot be talked out of existence, or exorcised with big names; yet if Ibsen was a mere windy trickster, it is odd that contemporaries as acute and diverse as James, Joyce, and Shaw should have been taken in by him.

But the inconclusive quality of Ibsen's philosophy, which is not in itself particularly novel or individual, has a special effect on the patterning of his dramas. At least until we come to those of the last period, starting with *Rosmersholm*, they are not arranged to provide an acting-out of guilt, a release, a lustration; they end with an assumption of new guilt, a full appreciation of one's total responsibility—and sometimes with a sharp repudiation of the audience itself for having been an audience assisting at an esthetic performance when it should have been acting and judging in an ethical one. After twenty years of struggle and failure, Ibsen's first international success was *Brand*; but he spoke of the play with disgust and disappointment (which it is hard not to think somewhat unreasonable), saying that he had written merely a play when he wanted to produce an action, a moral deed (Koht, *Life of Ibsen*, II, 27). The stage is not, perhaps, an inevitable place to express distaste for pretending—or is it? Where and how else could a determined disquieter produce more disquiet?

The sardonic view which Ibsen takes of all his characters—of Nora as well as Torvald Helmer, of Oswald as well as Helen Alving, of Thomas as well as Peter Stockmann, of Dr. Relling and little Hedvig Ekdal as well as of Gregers Werle and Hialmar—is one major reason why the effect of his plays is not pronouncedly tragic. Mockery alienates; and none of Ibsen's characters is quite exempt from the corrosive effect of his mockery. There is, then, relatively little identification; the audience does not transfer its feelings into the protagonist; and hence, when the protagonist "falls," there is almost no tragic release in the patterning of the plays. A *Doll's House* ends by deliberately outraging the audience's dumb, hopeful, and generous character; the slamming of that door is as deliberate as the last, sneering chorus of *The Threepenny Opera*. *The Wild Duck* ends, in total impasse, on an unresolved and ironic discord. Even *Ghosts* (which provides a less obvious example) does not leave the viewer "with calm of mind, all passion spent"; quite the contrary. It winds him up to a pitch, and leaves him there. The audience has not seen the humbling of a pride which it shares with the protagonist; it has not even seen the unintended consequences of a wrong decision brought instructively home to the person who made it. Both these actions are well within the range of emotional patterning which we usually call "tragic." But the fate of Mrs. Alving, while it has certain didactic overtones connected with failure to make up one's mind, does not really purify the emotions or exemplify a general rule at all. After showing us clearly that to live in a slavish and dishonest manner is contemptible, it shows with equal clarity that to live freely and honestly is ruinous. Act II burns up the orphanage, Act III burns up Oswald. It is a fate imagined by a man who hated humanity for adopting shoddy consolations in place of the truth that kills, a man whose fundamental idea was to "torpedo the Ark." Ibsen's play strikes us with much the same sickening impact as the blow which stuns a bullock in an abattoir. Humanistically speaking, the ending of *Ghosts* is altogether unhealthy; but then its aim is not to render an image of man, no, nor of woman either, as wise, healthy, and virtuous. It aims to nose out a corpse in the cargo, it seeks to demonstrate to the entire human condition a sickness unto death and beyond it.

The personal element so deeply buried in Ibsen's plays has sometimes come in for objections, both moral and artistic; but how they can be made to bear against Ibsen without hoisting Dostoevsky and Dante and Dickens as well is not clear. Conceivably there are potent objections to be raised against the bitterly destructive uses to which Ibsen turned his moral categories; but they are practical, not esthetic, objections. Like many late-nineteenth-century prophets, Ibsen thought the masks of moral idealism infinitely corrupting for the people who wore them; but he saw also that the mask-remover, the unmasker of masks, wears his own and specially deceptive disguise. The demand for truth as he presented it is infinite; it corrodes all false-faces and social forms. Now and then he saw that in particular circumstances his special appetite for guilt might be too much for pathetic humanity to bear; but as a rule this did not bother him much. It might even corrode out the inner life of his stage-characters, reducing Hedda Gabler, for instance, to a destructive monster, and Ulric Brendel to the mere animation of an open emptiness. Still, the ultimate demand and the helpless parody of a response were elements in the human condition as he saw it. A melancholy paradox, that Ibsen had no one to communicate this vision to except the shambling human race itself, and no way of communicating it except the ancient game of "Let's dress up and pretend."

There is of course something vulnerable about any man who preaches suicide but does not commit it, who professes his scorn for his art but continues to produce it. On this score, the allegory of *The Wild Duck* is quite as unsparing as Ibsen's worst enemies. But the paradox is larger than Ibsen's individual character. By refusing to turn back before the hard or even the impossible questions, he enlarged our definition of what a stage can be and perhaps even our sense of what a man can ask himself to become.

From the technical point of view, there is doubtless much more to be said against Ibsen's lurking presence in the dramas. Especially in the later series, something stiff and stolid tends to emerge from Ibsen's allegory. Independently of staging, without regard for pronouncedly "symbolic" interpretations, the thought sometimes gets too turgid for the action. *The Master Builder* is an example of this allegory which lays its dead hand over the drama's framework, and makes us feel constrained in the presence of something pompous. Hilda Wangel and her dream-kingdom of Appelsinia: it is all very mock-mystifying, and the more one knows about little Fraülein Bardach from Vienna and her frigid Berchtesgaden flirtation with Herr Doktor Ibsen, the more the whole play seems like a piece of put-together pseudo-profundity. Aside from this stiff, self-conscious quality, too, confessional allegory imposes major limitations on possible stage-effects; instead of a transparency and a solidity we get two side-by-side solidities. Still, it is impossible to write off the last dramas at a stroke. *Little Eyolf* may not, perhaps, be a stage action at all, but its low, devout melancholy, its endless twistings, turnings, and variations on the themes of human weakness and human guilt can be deeply moving.

Yet, to return to the main plays and the confessional, "symbolic" element as it undeniably occurs in these stage actions; at its best it provides a kind of indirect and satiric light which fills the simplest objects and most natural actions with luminous and perfect meaning. The Christmas tree and the letter stuck in a mailbox in *A Doll's House*; or the range and shading of sentiment about photography in *The Wild Duck*; or Engstrand's home for sailors in *Ghosts*; these things have a life of their own and then a life behind that life, a double existence that is the essence of Ibsen's art, and which they could never have if he were not writing "confessionally," on two levels. Whatever one calls the technique, "confessional," "allegorical," or "symbolist," it gives depth to a stage action, satiric indirectness to the author's point of view, and, at its best, immense vitality to the characters on the stage.

It is in terms like these that we ought to consider Ibsen, as Mr. Krutch (*Theatre Arts*, October, 1956) asks us to consider him, "a poet." The poetry is to be found, not in the flatulent and often obscure Germanic symbolism of the last plays (Miss McCarthy rightly calls it "corny"); not in fine writing, of which the best plays of the middle period are entirely and ruthlessly denuded; not in inventive frolics of wit and fancy, such as Ibsen showed himself capable of in *Peer Gynt*. It lies in an extraordinary gift of perfectly quiet, perfectly lucid double vision, hidden behind the polished façade of an amazingly supple and indirect dialogue.[3] There is nothing more to it, really, than placing a blank short perspective next to an infinitely lengthened one, and making a counterpoint of the two. Some subtlety went into the writing of this counterpoint; it is rich in hints, innuendos, silences, avoidances, half-admissions. There is also something perfectly impeccable and cold about Ibsen's long vision, an austerity bespeaking long and almost inhuman discipline. But the essence of the effect is simplicity, not trickery; Ibsen's is an art of seeing into something and through it, not of raising hackles on the audience by promoting an intense reaction for or against it. Only contrast the Victorian-domestic treatment of adultery in a popeyed melodrama like James's *Portrait of a Lady* with the cool, understated handling of the same theme in *Rosmersholm*; it is the moral difference between *Sandford & Merton* and *Liaisons Dangereuses*. But, cold and remote as Ibsen's best perspectives often are, I do not think he uses them, even in *Hedda Gabler* (or at least never before then), to make dramatic conflicts an occasion of histrionic display. His view of life is bifocal and perhaps a little mad; but it is hardly ever stagy. Late photographs of Ibsen show a curious quality of the man's physical features; one eye focusses on the camera, the other looks fiercely through it, through the miserable photographer and the whole miserable nineteenth century, fastened on an infinite and perhaps a purely private perspective.

He was, in fact, a perfectly destructive author; the critics have shied away from saying it, and the explanatory writers of the early

3. There is a story that the Norwegian novelist Jonas Lie, trying to learn about dramatic technique from Ibsen, asked him: "How long is a character in a play allowed to prattle?" He was aware, Lie said, that a general's lady could be permitted to talk all the nonsense she wished; but what about lesser personages? Ibsen's reply is not recorded, but Eric Bentley's analysis of Ibsen's celebrated "natural conversation" nicely measures the naïveté of the question:

An Ibsenite sentence often performs four or five functions at once. It sheds light on the character speaking, on the character spoken to, on the character spoken about; it furthers the plot; it functions ironically in conveying to the characters (and it is not merely that the characters say things which mean more to the audience than to them, but that they also say things which, as one senses, mean more to the characters than to the audience); finally, an Ibsenite sentence is part of the rhythmic pattern which constitutes the whole act. The naturalistic prose, then, is not there for its own sake. It is not there to display Ibsen's ability to write "natural" conversation. It is as rich in artifice as the verse of *Peer Gynt*. Its very naturalness is the final artifice, the art that conceals art. . . .

Quoted from *The Playwright as Thinker* (New York, 1946), p. 82 [Editor].

century thought it an impeachment to be repelled at all costs. But the long string of suicidal endings in the last plays (from *Rosmersholm* on, with the exception of *The Lady from the Sea*) tells its own story. Ibsen's satire of human beings was based on a discontent with the human condition itself. In his mind the very act of creation was a bringing of the soul to doom-judgment, a release of poisonous hatreds, a conditioned reflex keyed to personal torture. Modern opinion tends dimly to associate Ibsen as a late-nineteenth-century post-romantic with John Stuart Mill, Emile Zola, and chromos of "The Man With the Hoe" in dark wood frames. We shall probably be a good deal closer to the truth if we try for a while putting him with Jonathan Swift, Gustave Flaubert, and Franz Kafka as one of the great negative voices in literature. "Der Jasager und der Neinsager"[4]—it is an old dispute and a trite one; but it is not clear that the respectable party has yet established any inherent superiority or even temporary advantage. Let us hope it never will. If anything, we make too little of our sceptics; and, by trying to huddle all authors together under the same umbrella of a liberal-Christian democratic-individualist commonplace, render them perfectly innocuous and undistinctive.

In death as in life, Ibsen resists absorption. First and foremost he was a moralist, perhaps the last and certainly the hardest-minded of the stage-moralists. He was also a poet, but a poet who had to bury his poetry under the very prose of prose in order to make it live. He was a realist who thought nineteenth-century reality the most fantastic and improbable set of disguises ever devised by man. Finally, he took toward human existence as a whole a complex and austere viewpoint which is hard to communicate, difficult to appreciate, and impossible, really, to enjoy—which lays claim, in fact, to only one merit, that of embodying some part of a bitterly uncomfortable truth. Since our age has no concern whatever with truth, but only with adjustment, integration, motivation, and acceptance, Ibsen is evidently obsolete. Indeed, given all the handicaps which he chose or was furnished, it must always be more surprising that Ibsen once attained widespread popularity than that he has presently lost it.

Of course he is not, in a textbook phrase, the Father of Modern Drama. Such wholesale paternity would disgust him. Even Peer Gynt was asked to father only one troll-brat—why must Ibsen be saddled with responsibility for Tennessee Williams? The *Streetcar*, that primordial Williams' play which is every year transposed into a different key under a different title, clearly derives from *Madame Bovary*—a novel which is also said, in its way, to be confessional. Perhaps Clifford Odets has a dramatic parent; if so, who can it be but Chekhov? Eugene O'Neill was begotten by Strindberg. And so

4. "The yea-sayer and the nay-sayer."

it goes. If Ibsen has present-day successors, one of them is no doubt Arthur Miller. This is no more Ibsen's fault than it is to his credit. So long as we have a middle-class, we shall probably have dramas which discuss middle-class problems in a middle-class milieu. But if Ibsen's bourgeois décor and personal allegory lead somewhere near Arthur Miller, one must also add that his satiric vision and ethical insights point toward Bert Brecht. Brecht's epic theater is something other than Ibsen's ethical theatre largely because of Brecht's rueful, comic personality. But its core is the transformation of the audience from audience to something better, to the role of participant in the action or judge of it. The drama of Brecht invites us to sit in doom-judgment on a soul, a nation, a society, a condition of life; like Ibsen's drama it refuses the happy ending, in fact, the ending of any sort. Whatever its ultimate value, the theater of Brecht is certainly the largest and most impressive structure on the contemporary theatrical horizon.

And even if we insist upon visiting the sins of the sons on the fathers—an odd undertaking at any estimate—the chances are that Ibsen will not stagger under the burden. How many playwrights whose best work was done before 1890 are the fathers of anything or anyone these days? If Miss McCarthy is found beating Ibsen in the columns of *Partisan Review*, it can only be because he stands out among the windrows of dead and stacked dramatists as a figure still instinct with life, if not with health. He has long outlived the first generation of his offspring, Pinero and Jones, as well as his contemporaries, Scribe, Sardou, *et al.*; he is remembered now, when Christopher Fry is as dusty as Elmer Rice, and I make bold to think he will still be a subject of discussion when Ionesco and Beckett have taken their places among the fashionable obscure. No one will mistake him for a dramatist of the order of Sophocles or Shakespeare; but it will take a long perspective and some little purity of motive to account for him in the end.

MAURICE VALENCY

[*The Wild Duck*]†

In 1869, in a poem addressed to "My friend, the revolutionary orator," Ibsen * * * defended himself against a charge of political passivity by saying that there had been but one thoroughgoing revolution in the history of the world—that was the deluge; but even

† From Maurice Valency, *The Flower and the Castle* (New York: The Macmillan Company), pp. 168–76, 379–80, 382–83. Copyright © 1963 by Maurice Valency. Reprinted with permission of The Macmillan Company.

that was bungled, since Noah had survived it. "The next time," he concluded, "I shall put a torpedo under the ark." This oft-quoted brag was quite in character for the young Ibsen of thirty-one. *The Wild Duck* shows how completely opposed he was, at fifty-five, to any disturbance of the peace.

Ibsen spent rather more than a year thinking about this play; then he wrote it quickly. In June of 1883 he had written to Georg Brandes that he was contemplating a new play in four acts. A year later he wrote to Theodor Caspari: "I have just finished a play in five acts, that is to say, the rough draft; now comes the elaboration, the more energetic individualization of the persons and their mode of expression." At the beginning of September, 1884, he sent the manuscript to Hegel for publication, with a letter expressing his belief that he had done something new: "This new play in many ways occupies a place of its own among my dramas; the method is in various respects a departure from my earlier one. I do not want to say any more about this for the present. The critics will, I hope, find the points; in any case, they will find plenty to quarrel about, plenty to misinterpret . . ."

He was disappointed in his expectations. Although it was hissed a little at the opening performance in Copenhagen, the play was successful enough in the Scandinavian theatres; but the critics made little of it one way or the other. It was applauded in Berlin, howled down in Rome, received with indifference in Paris, and with frigidity in London. In a review of a series of Ibsen's plays, published in 1889, Edmund Gosse echoed, with characteristic acumen, what many had already said of *The Wild Duck*: "This is a very long play, by far the most extended of the series, and is, on the whole, the least interesting to read . . . There is really not a character in the book that inspires confidence or liking . . . There can be no doubt that it is by far the most difficult of Ibsen's for a reader to comprehend." But Bernard Shaw wrote in 1897, "Where shall I find an epithet magnificent enough for *The Wild Duck!*"

It is not immediately apparent in what way *The Wild Duck* seemed to Ibsen to mark a new departure in his method. Its style seems to be a development of the technique of *Ghosts*, and it resembles that play in more than one respect. Like *Ghosts* it involves a tragic action played, in part, by comic characters, and its effect is similarly strange. Structurally, it falls into the familiar mold of Second Empire drama. It is, in some respects, a *pièce à thèse* which demonstrates the advantages of domestic life, and the folly of destroying the home because of some supposed flaw in its moral foundation. As this thesis involves the idea that the paramount concern of the parents is the happiness of the children, it seems well out of line with the doctrine we associate with A *Doll's House*.

Up to a certain point, *The Wild Duck* was a rearrangement of materials that had already seen service. The chambermaid who was palmed off with a dowry upon the carpenter Engstrand in *Ghosts* becomes here the chambermaid Gina Hansen, who is bestowed in similar fashion upon Hjalmar Ekdal. Captain Alving's illegitimate daughter Regina has her equivalent in Hedvig, who inherits, like Osvald, the paternal infirmity, in this case a tendency to blindness. Haakon Werle appears to be a version of Consul Bernick in *Pillars of Society* and, like him, he has permitted his friend to expiate a crime he himself committed. Gregers Werle is in the nature of a vindictive Osvald come home to confront his father with the sins of his past.

The plot of *The Wild Duck* hangs upon a situation of the utmost banality. A husband discovers that his wife was pregnant by another man when he married her fifteen years before; in righteous anger, he casts her off and disowns his child, who thereupon kills herself. The death of the innocent child reunites the family in sorrow. The moral of the play is then announced by the family doctor: "It is best not to stir up old troubles." The English reviewer in *The Athenaeum* for May 12, 1894, commented: "The play must be a joke . . . it is a harmless, if not very humourous piece of self-banter, or it is nothing."

One might be excused for considering *The Wild Duck* a clumsy travesty. The play has a proper undercurrent of sentimentality, but the plot is all askew. The outraged husband is caricatured to the point of clownishness; the faithless wife is the mainstay of the family; they are all living on the proceeds of the sin on which their establishment is based; and the canonical scenes of accusation and reproach are all comic. Only the child suffers; and the introduction of a tragic note into a distinctly comic situation might well seem an unpardonable incongruity. At any rate, the melodramatic elements of the familiar play of transgression and retribution are obviously deformed in accordance with a new and radical concept. The figures and the design of the narrative are all recognizably traditional, but the manner of their representation goes somewhat beyond the demands of realism. One's first impression is of a familiar scene viewed in a distorting mirror. In fact, the technique is analytical in a manner that suggests the post-impressionists; and it is perhaps to an innovation of this sort that Ibsen referred in his covering letter to the publisher.

It is interesting to see how Ibsen arrived at the novel effect of *The Wild Duck*. He began with a theme on which he had already played several variations. Driven by an exaggerated sense of guilt, the idealistic Gregers comes as a savior to set the Ekdal family free through the truth. In precisely this manner, Julian came to liberate the world, and Brand to save it. The Ekdal family, however, has no use for the truth. It has managed in its misery to find a way of life which approximates happiness, and it would prefer to be left in peace. As old Ekdal demonstrates, the human soul has considerable ingenuity; it can construct a forest in an attic; it can build, if necessary, a world in a shoebox. The illusion serves quite as well as the reality so long as it is not disturbed. Consequently, nobody thanks Gregers for his idealistic efforts. On the contrary, his meddling results only in irreparable misfortune.

The doctrine that Dr. Relling, the *raisonneur* of the play, makes explicit in *The Wild Duck* is thus seen to be the same that was implicit in *Brand* and in *Emperor and Galilean*, and which was advanced cynically in *An Enemy of the People*; it is quite opposed to the idea we associate with the Ibsen of *Ghosts* and *Pillars of Society*. In these two plays it is Ibsen's position that felicity must be based on health, and that health, from the social standpoint, depends upon truth. The superstructure, however elaborate, that is raised on a false foundation must sooner or later topple: a house built on a lie cannot stand. If one is to have stability, the lie must be uprooted, the house must be rebuilt; and the event that brings about this outcome, no matter how disagreeable, is prophylactic and providential. *The Wild Duck*, however, depends on a less heroic concept. Dr. Relling in effect reiterates the words of Agnes[1] when she exclaims at the folly of exacting All or Nothing from the human race in its poverty. In a world miserably patched together of lies and fancies, it is best to let things alone. Men have no use for truth: illusion alone makes life tolerable. "Rob a man of his life-lie," says Dr. Relling, "and you rob him of his happiness." Unlike Gregers, who pins his faith on the surgical efficacy of truth, Relling devises opiates for the incurable. Gregers demands All or Nothing; Relling speaks for the spirit of compromise which is the practical aspect of *deus caritatis*.

To illuminate these ideas in the situation of *The Wild Duck* it was necessary to destroy the theatrical conventions relating to the play of the deceived husband. Dumas would have done this through argument. Ibsen did it through laughter. Gregers reveals his secret to Hjalmar with theatrical impressiveness, and Hjalmar reacts as people do in plays, assumes the appropriate postures and speaks the time-honored lines. But it is clear that he is going through the necessary formalities of the outraged spouse without real conviction, and the resulting scenes are broadly comic. In the midst of a situation that rapidly becomes ridiculous, the action is

1. In *Brand* [Editor].

brought up sharply by the sudden death of Hedvig, and the play acquires abruptly another dimension. The action has proceeded unobtrusively along several levels of reality simultaneously; all at once it is seen that what had no reality for some evidently had terrible reality for others. For Hjalmar, the deception that has shaped his life has not even as much validity as the forest primeval in the attic. His sufferings are largely histrionic. But for Hedvig, his sufferings are supremely real, and she must buy them with her life. The conclusion is plain: in this world it is necessary to look out above all for those who are capable of suffering. These are the sensitive children of life, the nobility of the race, and their lot is tragic. The rest are drugged to the point of insensibility. To expect of them a tragic response to life is to invite absurdity; and this truth is in its implications, perhaps, more poignant than the conventional tragedy of the theatre.

The development of *The Wild Duck*, like that of Turgeniev's *A Month in the Country*, or Chekhov's *Uncle Vanya*, is of the order of a chemical reaction. Into a situation which appears calm and limpid, a reagent is introduced. At once hidden tensions are released, the thing seethes, rages, and gives off fumes. There is a precipitation. Then equilibrium is re-established. Once again calm descends upon the scene, and it is as if nothing had happened; yet everything is changed. It is a simple and effective way of arranging a dramatic action, and quite different from the Scribean contest of intriguers.

The eruption of Gregers into the tranquil world of the Ekdals is very skillfully managed. There is the charming family scene reminiscent of a contemporary genre-painting—the father playing a Bohemian dance on the flute, the mother and daughter grouped happily about him. We are vaguely aware of discordant elements in this scene; nevertheless, it is a tableau suitable for framing. Now comes Gregers, a disagreeable man, advancing "the claims of the ideal," and he reveals their life for what it is—a patchwork of lies and pretenses, a tissue of illusion as pathetic as the imitation forest in the attic.

His motives are decidedly more questionable than Dr. Stockmann's in *An Enemy of the People*; but they are of the same order. Ostensibly he is interested only in truth and justice. In reality, he is a sadistic busybody, and he has personal reasons, besides, for wishing to embarrass his father. Whatever his inner motives may be, however, he has rationalized them in terms of his missionary zeal. He thinks of himself as a rescuer of fallen souls, "a really absurdly clever dog; the sort that goes in after wild ducks when they dive down and bite themselves into the weeds and tangle" at the bottom of the sea. It is in the furtherance of this mission, with its attendant requirements of All-or-Nothing, that he asks little Hedvig to sacrifice the thing she loves most in order to show Hjalmar how much she loves him:

> Ah, if only you had had your eyes opened to what really makes life worthwhile! If you had the genuine, joyous, courageous spirit of self-sacrifice . . .

This is the final stage of the progressive vilification of Brand which marks Ibsen's middle period. In *Pillars of Society* the idealistic Hilmar is merely obnoxious with his *ugh* of disgust at the squalor of the world; in *An Enemy of the People*, Dr. Stockmann is funny and lovable in his futility; but Gregers is hateful. It is interesting that he is cast in the first instance as the *raisonneur* of the play.

In *The Wild Duck*, the *raisonneur* of the conventional *pièce à thèse* suffers an interesting transformation. The *raisonneur* of Second Empire drama was traditionally the author's representative, and was therefore intended to inspire respect and admiration. Gregers, however, is unsympathetic. He has, moreover, a rival *raisonneur* in Dr. Relling, who is very likeable. Neither, of course, is trustworthy. Of the two manipulators of the plot, the one is fanatic, neurotic, sadistic, and perhaps mad; the other is a drunkard and a disgrace to his profession. These two angels battle for the soul of the hero, which is worthless:

> GREGERS. Hedvig has not died in vain. Didn't you see how grief brought out what was noblest in him?
>
> RELLING. Most people feel some nobility when they stand in the presence of death. But how long do you suppose this glory will last in his case?
>
> GREGERS. Surely it will continue and flourish to the end of his life!
>
> RELLING. Give him nine months and little Hedvig will be nothing more than the theme of a pretty little party piece . . . We can discuss it again when the first grass grows on her grave. Then he'll bring it all up, all about the child so untimely torn from the loving father's heart! Then you'll see him wallowing deeper and deeper in sentimentality and self-pity.

Dr. Relling was destined, unhappily, to become a theatrical cliché, and in conceiving him as he did, Ibsen did what he could to dissociate himself from his doctrine. But there can be no doubt that this estimable quack speaks for that side of Ibsen which had by now supplanted Brand as the Ibsen "of his finest moments," an Ibsen who viewed the world from a standpoint somewhere between contempt and compassion, but always with a certain amusement. This is the Ibsen we see in his plays henceforth; until we are confronted suddenly with the agony of *The Master Builder*.

The Wild Duck, like its relatives and descendants, *Il berretto a sonagli*,[2] *The Playboy of the Western World*, and *The Iceman Cometh*, indicates the uses of illusion in a world of unbearable realities, but we cannot conclude from this that Ibsen advocated self-deception as a panacea for the ills of humanity. The play is contemplative, not demonstrative. It has the form, in general, of a *pièce à thèse*, but it is not a thesis play so much as a play of antitheses. It proves nothing: it invites us to think. The mood is meditative, lyrical, a mood of despair. In *The Wild Duck* the priest is drunk, the soldier is broken, the idealist is mad, the doctor is ill. They have all sunk, metaphorically, into the ooze at the bottom of the sea. Here, as in Gorki's *Na dye*,[3] there is the comfort of hopelessness: bad things happen and it makes no difference. There is no indication that out of these experiences will come a better life; on the contrary, the expectation is that after this brief period of turbulence, life will go on precisely as it did before, and in this realization Ibsen finds an authentic source of emotion. Despair, for Kierkegaard, is the terminal phase of each stage of the progress of the soul toward God. In *The Wild Duck* nobody is capable of going beyond the initial stage; but even in the climate of despair it is possible to create a world in which one can live in something like joy.

Of this nature, it is intimated, is the sphere of art, the last refuge of aesthetic man, as pathetic a substitute for nature, perhaps, as a chicken coop in an attic, but very dear nonetheless, and well worth defending. In the absence of God, there is no plausible way of making life seem other than a pointless mummery. Maximus says at the end of *Emperor and Galilean*, borrowing, to express his discontent, a phrase out of Schopenhauer: "What is life worth? All is sport and make-believe. To will is to have to will!" It is evident that in the mood of these plays is prefigured the despair of the existentialist; but Ibsen had no faith in the redeeming power of engagement. In the power of fantasy, however, to find in chaos a home for the soul of man, Dr. Relling sees something godlike. At any rate, this is as close to God as he can come.

In *The Wild Duck* all the characters are formulated in terms of despair; but the source of emotion is the despair of the author, not the despair of the characters. The characters do not complain. It is the author who, by implication, bewails them. The pleasure of the play derives, accordingly, not from the identification of the audience with the protagonist, as in tragedy, but from a feeling of intimate communion with the author in the contemplation of the action, a feeling akin to the pleasure of poetry. As the spectator is never asked to surrender his autonomy, he is afforded an individual

2. *Cap and Bells* (1917), Luigi Pirandello. [Editor].

3. *The Lower Depths* (1903) [Editor].

experience which is contrapuntal to, but quite distinct from, the emotions experienced on the stage. This technique differs materially from that of Dumas, for example. Dumas, through his *raisonneur*, is often on the stage as presenter and commentator, but the action is always intended to be a realistic demonstration, in academic terms, with a total illusion. Ibsen is never on the stage; but the entire action is portrayed impressionistically, so that we are constantly aware—as in impressionist painting—of the individuality of the author's perceptions. *The Wild Duck* thus marks a subtle, but important step away from the illusionism which especially characterizes realist drama, and it points the way toward a conception of theatre in which the author, rather than the characters, becomes the center of attention, a conception which Strindberg and, after him, Pirandello developed rapidly in the next decades.

The immediate effect of such plays as *Ghosts* and *The Wild Duck* was to stimulate in various quarters artistic currents such as the contemporary naturalistic dramatists had not succeeded in propagating. *The Wild Duck* had influence everywhere, save in France and England, and particularly on Russian drama. These plays, moreover, had interesting consequences of a non-dramatic nature. It was by breaking down the accepted stereotypes of the theatre that Ibsen revitalized the drama of his time, and very likely this is all he meant to do. But the social reflex was inevitable. The revaluation of the clichés of the theatre in time brought about a revaluation of the clichés of real life, which the stage ordinarily reflects and defines. Thus Ibsen, to his embarrassment, found himself once again a leader of public opinion, a position which flattered him, but caused him acute discomfort. As he felt the impulse to be extremely aggressive, yet desired to offend nobody, he was much concerned to resist definition, tacked constantly, changed direction from play to play, and while maintaining a certain general orientation, became exceedingly difficult to follow.

* * *

In the latter half of the nineteenth century it was sensible to give one's ideas a scientific turn. It was sensible also to follow the example of the most successful dramatists of the time in directing attention to social and moral questions in the theatre. But Ibsen, as he himself said repeatedly, had no great interest in such matters: it was as a poet that he viewed the facts of life. There was, accordingly, no contradiction in his mind between the impressionist's interest in the sensual aspects of the world and the symbolist's desire to see into the soul. His tendency toward symbolism had been perceptible even before the time of *Brand*, and with *Brand* he established a style which was useful to him all the rest of his career. In the drama, clearly, he was a symbolist some years before the symbolists.

*   *   *

The symbolism of *The Wild Duck*, more widely imitated than that of any other of Ibsen's plays, comes somewhat closer to the method of the medieval allegories, but it is not the same. The elusiveness of the Wild Duck as a symbol is different from that of the Pearl in the poem of that name, or of the Eagle of the *Paradiso*. The forest in the attic resembles only superficially the forests of error or of illusion in which it is customary for knights to lose themselves in Renaissance *romanzi*. What distinguishes the modern from the medieval symbol is not merely its ambiguity, but its capaciousness, its amplitude.

The Eagle of the *Paradiso* yields to no symbol in point of ambiguity; no one has succeeded in fixing its meaning. But the possible limits of interpretation are more or less fixed, and the symbol challenges the reason as an enigma which is entirely amenable to rational interpretation. The Wild Duck, on the other hand, like the White Horses of *Rosmersholm*, or the Rat-Wife of *Little Eyolf*, completely eludes this sort of approach: it prefers not to be defined. As a metaphor, the wounded bird serves to characterize the lives and souls of almost all the characters in the play from Old Ekdal to Gregers Werle; it refers to Hedvig in still another way; and it is used emblematically to describe in general the therapeutic role of illusion in life. In the end, the Wild Duck serves to unify in a single figure the entire action of the play: so much meaning radiates from this symbol that anything that serves to define it, serves also to restrict its efficacy. From Chekhov's *The Seagull* to Graham Greene's *The Living Room*, no device has been found more useful in searching out the poetic core of a dramatic action than a metaphor of this sort. One might imagine that in using it as he did, Ibsen had in mind the prescription of Mallarmé, published, however, some seven years later, in 1891:

> C'est le parfait usage de ce mystère qui constitue le symbole: évoquer petit à petit un objet pour montrer un état d'âme, ou, inversement, choisir un objet et en dégager un état d'âme par une série de déchiffrements.[4]

4. Huret, Enquête, in *Oeuvres de Mallarmé* (ed. La Pléiade), p. 869.
"It is the perfect use of this mystery which constitutes the symbol: little by little to evoke an object in order to show a state of soul, or, conversely, to choose an object and to extricate a state of soul from it by a series of unveilings" [Editor].

DOUNIA B. CHRISTIANI

Notes on Interpretation

I do not, in these pages, purpose to add a systematic study to those already before the reader but rather to submit various observations based on these and on works of criticism not reprinted in this volume, as well as on the original text of *The Wild Duck* itself. Usefulness is the sole *raison d'être* of my remarks and their sole unifying principle. "First," as James E. Kernans has said, "we accept as one of the primary tests of value in any essay in dramatic criticism the question, 'How does it interest anyone who is to produce or perform in the play?'" Second, I would add, how does it interest anyone concerned with dramaturgy in general? For however little esteem the well-wrought play may currently enjoy, dramatic art is not achieved independently of craftsmanship any more than architecture, which Ibsen on one occasion called his "profession," subsists independently of engineering. And we are dealing here with the acknowledged masterpiece of the master builder. In *The Wild Duck*, Ibsen's command of his craft makes such virtues of necessity that even the keenest analyst of the play is apt to overlook basic problems of dramatic structure.

Thus, in the process of demonstrating the symbolic appropriateness of the actions in Ibsen's plays to their meaning, one critic cites the mess which Gregers makes in his room at the Ekdals' as "a sequence for the sole purpose of making an allusion of this kind [a secondary evocative function]," that is, as a sketch in little of Gregers and an epitome of his role in the play. "Gregers' mishap with the stove does nothing to forward the plot . . ." No; but without planting this mishap early in Act III, Ibsen would have had no realistic justification for setting the later brief but essential private confrontation between Gregers and his father in the Ekdal studio.

Again, in a psychological study of Ibsen's characters, it is stated that not only does Hjalmar exhibit signs of homosexuality but that he is "clearly impotent—married fifteen years, and Hedvig not his daughter." Now, medical questions aside, how should Ibsen have managed a number of young children in the cramped Ekdal apartment? Unlike the Helmer offspring in *A Doll's House*, they could not be sent off with a nursemaid or otherwise accounted for during daytime scenes. As a matter of fact, Ibsen did originally plan to give Hjalmar and Gina younger children; he presumably dropped them as soon as he started to construct the play, for they are already absent from the first draft. One has only to consider the irrelevancies they would have introduced, and the loss of poignancy in Hedvig's death, to see how necessary it was to omit them.

"As for symbolism," William Archer writes in "Ibsen as I Knew Him,"

> he says that life is full of it, and that, consequently, his plays are full of it, though critics insist on discovering all sorts of esoteric meanings in his work of which he is entirely innocent. He was particularly amused by a sapient person in *Aftensposten* who had discovered that Manders in *Ghosts* was a symbol for mankind in general or the average man, and, therefore, called Manders. He also spoke of some critic who had found the keynote of *Emperor and Galilean* in Makrina, a character of no importance whatever, introduced because it happened that Basilios had, as a matter of fact, a sister of that name.

One cannot quarrel with the scholar who sees in Hjalmar's borrowing Molvik's tailcoat a symbol of his borrowed ideas—although it would seem to do service enough as an indication of Hjalmar's social and economic abasement and as the occasion for a display of puerile vanity as he reassumes his own "style" (just as Gregers, by a parallel change of clothes, reassumes his). But when this exegete notes a visual symbol in the contraption of canvas and fish net between the attic and studio, can we not hear Ibsen demanding: "How else, in a realistic drama, am I to show the audience an attic ostensibly hopping with poultry and rabbits?" And when we have impressed upon us the significance of the fact that "Ibsen shows Hjalmar only retouching [improving on reality], Gina photographing [reproducing prosaic reality]," Ibsen's own metaphor of "photography" for his realistic dramas comes to mind, and one is confused by the clash of symbols. Besides, Hedvig too is shown retouching; Gina learned to retouch first of all, and presumably still does it; while Hjalmar apparently avoids the actual business of photographing not only from general laziness but because he feels it to be beneath him to deal at first hand with "a lot of nobodies." And has not Ibsen, in any case, fully exposed Hjalmar's relation to reality by way of the great "invention"?

Indeed, Ibsen has been criticized for underscoring his points all too well—a charge which might be valid could he have counted on an ideal performance of the play before an ideal audience. In the study, it must be admitted, this pointing often does seem excessive. Hjalmar's "Don't touch the pistol, Hedvig! One of the barrels is loaded; remember that" is like a flashing traffic signal. There has been no objection to his climactic speech to Gregers, "If I then asked her: Hedvig, are you willing to turn your back on life for me? [*Laughs scornfully.*] Thanks a lot, you'd soon hear the answer I'd get"—immediately followed by the pistol shot—but one deplores the need to make even a self-dramatizing egoist like Hjalmar express such an outrageous notion in order to provide Hedvig with a direct cue to pull the trigger.

Still, although Hjalmar's remark in the same scene to the effect that Hedvig is a little pitcher with big ears indicates that she is eavesdropping on the conversation, and although Gregers hears the wild duck "scream" just as he has promised Hjalmar proof of Hedvig's devotion, and although Relling later makes it clear that Hedvig's death was no accident, explicators disagree about Hedvig's intentions upon going into the attic, about just when she decides to die, about what causes the duck to cry out. (Does she attempt to shoot it and fail? Does she wring its neck?) So it seems that even the diagrammatic sequence of cue and action leaves room for that baffled speculation which in actual experience suicide always evokes.

The critics' most serious reservations about *The Wild Duck* concern Gregers' overestimation of Hjalmar. As Otto Reinert puts it, "It is hard to accept Gregers Werle's continuing faith in the greatness of a man who almost without stop reveals his phoniness (sincere phoniness though it is). Gregers may be sick, but he is not supposed to be stupid." And indeed, if Gregers' misguided determination to enlighten that egregious ham is the basic action of the drama as well as its principal business, the very structure of the play is open to criticism: Act I, already censured for its trite expository opening, becomes a mere prologue.

But suppose now we shift the focus from Gregers' concern for Hjalmar to his passionate hatred for his father? Or rather—since the interpreter's right to shift the focus may be debatable—suppose we look beyond Gregers' involvement with Hjalmar to its underlying motivation. This approach might perhaps confute the major objections to the play. For if the primary action is the revenge of the son on the father, revenge in which his "best and only friend" (whom Gregers has not kept in touch with for some seventeen years!) serves not only as a handy tool but as the only available one, then Gregers' continuing faith in Hjalmar is not so much stupidity as a stubborn refusal to give up what serves his ends. In this light, Gregers' homecoming is no prologue, but the true *erregender Moment* of the action. And Hedvig's death becomes the tragic climax of the primary struggle, the accomplishment of an insane reckoning, rather than the ricochet of a fumbling idealist's misaimed fire. "I knew it. Restitution would come through the child," says Gregers when the shot in the attic disposes of Hjalmar's doubts; Hedvig is no accidental victim.

I am not qualified to explore the psychological depths broached by this suggestion, but I make it first of all because it seems to me that a full awareness of Gregers' motives is essential to a just and effective interpretation of *The Wild Duck*. To give full value to the force of Gregers' will on Hedvig—subconscious though his aim may be—should not only settle all doubts about the relevance and realism of Hedvig's suicide but minimize her rather dated innocence as well. For while it is evident that Hedvig *is* wise to Hjalmar (Ibsen makes it abundantly clear that she knows Hjalmar to be the baby of the family, to be soothed and indulged), her ignorance of the so-called facts of life is rather difficult to believe, in these days of elementary school sex education. My students, at any rate, are put off by Hedvig's "childishness," although I add to the general observation that her incipient blindness cuts her off from her contemporaries the further suggestion that the shadow of disgrace over the family and her anomalous situation (as the child of a former servant girl and a declassed gentleman) would in any case limit her social contacts. Her insight into Gregers is the clearest evidence of her fine intelligence—evidence which has the advantage that it can be conveyed in a performance of the role.

This is not to say, of course, that her talk about being "found" is disingenuous, that her rejection by Hjalmar is any less devastating even if she sees through him, or that her suicide is a conscious submission to Gregers' will. But on the other hand, is she so naïve as not to suspect, however dimly, some connection between her birthday gift from Werle senior and Hjalmar's immediate repudiation of her? To admit the possibility of Hedvig's dawning suspicion that she is Gregers' half sister into an interpretation of the role would not only rescue the fourth-act scene between them from the danger of mawkishness but communicate its power, not to say horror. It might quicken audience response to the sublime orchestration of Act IV—surely without equal in realistic drama.

It has always seemed to me that Gregers' shaking horrors upon Hedvig's death attest to his inward recognition of what he really wished of her when he suggested that she sacrifice the wild duck; but that Hedvig should intuit this wish, unrecognized at the time even by Gregers, was perhaps a daring hypothesis, if an attractive one. In preparing this edition, however, I came across a Norwegian study of Ibsen and modern psychology which confidently advanced this view as early as 1931. Hedvig understands that she is the wild duck, writes Ingjald Nissen, "she guesses instinctively that Gregers wants to kill her because she is his father's child. . . . Being an idealist, he naturally does not do it himself, but kills symbolically." According to Nissen, already the "depths of the sea" scene in Act III shows that he conceives of Hedvig as a wild duck, and by his demand of the sacrifice Gregers shows that she is *the* wild duck, for "the child understands symbolism."

Squaring accounts with his father, Gregers destroys the only vulnerable extension of Werle's self (incidentally proving himself to be his father's son, for now he too has "shattered a life"). At the same time, Hedvig plays the last act in "the Tragedy of the House of Ekdal"; she fires the pistol by which, according to Hjalmar, his father was too cowardly to die and he himself too brave. According to the Norwegian scholar Daniel Haakonsen, Hedvig thereby redeems Hjalmar, who never really returned to life after his suicide attempt and never got over the shame of accepting the false and diminished existence which his father's archenemy provided for him. The point Haakonsen develops is that Hjalmar is consciously playing a role to cover up his guilt—which would make him a deeper character than the surface caricature suggests; and indeed, Ibsen wrote that "his sentimentality is genuine, his melancholy charming in its way—not a bit of affectation."

But if Hjalmar has accepted a sort of rebirth from Håkon Werle, then he is not only his victim but also in a sense his son. And Ekdal *père*: did he not cripple Hjalmar's life, even as Gregers accuses Werle of crippling his? Haaksonsen makes the pregnant observation that Hjalmar evidently resents his father's failure to expiate his crime (it was *his* duty to redeem the family honor) and that in his emotional turmoil after the catastrophe Hjalmar must often have wished him dead. But to Gregers, one might add, Ekdal is his father's blameless victim; he compares Hjalmar's desolation on his father's imprisonment with his own upon the death of his mother—the first and archetypal victim of that terrible man. His deference and consideration for old Ekdal are singularly touching, coming from a blind idealist who in all his other human contacts exhibits a total lack of compassion, an only son who absented himself during his mother's last illness, not even coming home for her funeral.

Although I question the widespread assumption that Mrs. Werle's "tragic failing" was drink, since Gina says that she had "*fysiske raptusser*" ("physical fits," but Gina means psychic ones) just like Gregers', the son's feelings for his mother, whether of contempt or pity, were nowhere so strong as his fear of his father. From the exchange between Gregers and Werle in Act I, it appears that this fear was implanted in him by his mother; Gregers arrived at his "idealism"—the recognized sublimation of an aversion to sex—by the exemplary route.

What is behind the blind determination with which he sets about "purifying" the Ekdals' marriage? It does not seem too far-fetched to suggest a man who finds his very name a cross to bear, who loathes it (himself?) so that he "could spit on a man with such a name," would like to undo his own begetting if he could. In this, of course, he can *only* act symbolically; Werle's sins must never be forgotten and all his gifts must be rejected—including, and perhaps especially, the gift of life. At this level of interpretation, Gregers' stubborn faith in Hjalmar ceases to be unrealistic, serving as it does a passion beyond the reach of reason. And Hedvig's death no longer looks like "a meaningless and uninteresting little pat of blood"[1] unrelated to the central action, a contrived intrusion of specious pathos. Her suicide becomes the vicarious fulfillment of Gregers' repudiation of his father, as in Haakonsen's view it redeems Hjalmar's treachery toward his.

A relatively minor objection is raised by Brian W. Downs to Old Ekdal's repeated phrase about the revenge of the forest; and it must be admitted that if one regards this character as "despicable and ludicrous as he is pitiable," then truly the "expression is [not] at all consonant with his usual speech and is either farcically inappropriate or else cloudily portentous." But for Haakonsen, Old Ekdal is neither comical nor pitiful in the scene where he speaks the portentous phrase for the last time; to him, the old man's childishness and cowardice fall away in the moment he shuts himself in the attic after Hedvig's death: now the fiction in which he hides from reality must in any case include death. A reconciliation of these divergent views should perhaps be sought through a closer look at Old Ekdal's *usual* speech, especially since Ibsen made the point that each of the characters in the play has his own special, individual way of speaking.

This statement, which appears in a letter to a would-be translator of *The Wild Duck*, concerns the individualized speech as an index to the various characters' degree of education (which would require an intimate knowledge of the Norwegian language) and does not, of course, exhaust the subtleties of the dialogue. Ibsen not only individualized his characters' speech but even took into account the observation that the same person speaks differently at different times of the day. It should be noted that Old Ekdal uses the portentous phrase in Act I, at night and in a state of inebriation, and in Act V, under the stress of great emotion. Professor Reinert, furthermore, directs our attention to the old man's habitual avoidance of the pronoun "I"—which, I take it to mean, signifies Ekdal's terror of being singled out, perhaps accused and punished. If this is so, then it is neither ludicrous nor despicable for him to respond to Hedvig's death by an immediate resurgence of dread.

But it would be a mistake, it seems to me, to accommodate a portrayal of Old Ekdal to this uncharacteristic line. In *The Wild Duck*, as Maurice Valency observes, "the characters do not complain"; they must not be made to seem aware of their own condition. I should therefore like to add that Ekdal's omission of "I"

---

1. See "Contemporary Reception," p. 216.

may also suggest an affectation of the clipped speech of a former officer and a laconic old sportsman. One of the most delectable turns in his characterization is his familiar condescension to Gregers the moment he learns that he is not to be feared. This is somewhat obscured when the *far* ("old chap," "old man") he uses in addressing Gregers is translated as "sir."

As to Gina's diction, although Ibsen writes that whenever she speaks "one can immediately hear that she has never learned any grammar and that she is a product of the lower classes," there seems to be a universal desire to promote her a little, and it is impossible to settle on a degree of vulgarity which will not offend some readers. Not that vulgarity need diminish her in the least; to Shaw, "All Shakespear's matrons rolled into one, from Volumnia to Mrs. Quickly, would be as superficial and conventional in comparison with Gina as a classic sybil by Raphael with a Dutch cook by Rembrandt." Gina's dialogue in the Archer translation, near-standard English peppered with impossible distortions (Would a woman ignorant of the word "divert" say "pervert theirselves"?) and mispronunciations lifted unchanged from the Norwegian (Who would say "pigstol" for "pistol" in English?), has given Gina the false reputation of a second Mrs. Malaprop. But her outlandish expressions are the reverse of Mrs. Malaprop's ambitious sallies, those "select words so ingeniously *misapplied*, without being *mispronounced*." Gina does not overreach herself, she simply has no ear. And couldn't care less, obviously.

It seems to me too that Hedvig's frequent use of the word "Daddy" for *far*, "father," though quite satisfactory in a British version, may strike Americans as childish or sentimental. The easy monosyllable *far*, a contraction of *fader*, is used at every age level and almost every degree of formality. What to choose—Father, Papa, Dad, Daddy—that will be appropriate for the nineteenth century and yet not sound too formal to us? I have imagined that Hedvig has for some time called her parents Father and Mother, but that she says Daddy whenever she tries to ingratiate herself with Hjalmar, and occasionally when she regresses to little-girlhood.

"Like *Hamlet*, *The Wild Duck* can be interpreted by each man in his own image," writes Muriel C. Bradbrook. "One day it will be read as a tragedy, the next as the harshest irony; parts of it are clumsy, in other parts are embedded old controversies of that time. So searching yet so delicate is the touch, that these flaws and vagaries seem in themselves to strengthen the work. In this play . . . Ibsen perfected his own special power . . . to infuse the particular, drab, limited fact with a halo and a glory."

Why, for all the brilliant roles it affords—the self-dramatizing

Hjalmar, the baleful Gregers, the disenchanted, witty Relling, to say nothing of Old Ekdal (What could not a brogueless Barry Fitzgerald make of that part!), Gina, Hedvig—why is *The Wild Duck* more honored in the study than on the boards? A recent telecast of a rehearsal suggested one reason: all the players in the scene (Hjalmar's return from the Werle party, Act II) were uniformly wistful and noble—as though overawed by the halo and glory above their heads. I was prompted to remark that were I ever to direct the play I would do everything in my power to keep the literary stature of *The Wild Duck* a dark secret from the actors.

Critical Views

[Contemporary Reception]†

People had got used to the idea that Ibsen's dramas should engage in controversial issues, and when *The Wild Duck* came out, 11 November 1884, the public was utterly bewildered. ALEXANDER KIELLAND found the book odd and was annoyed by "these everlasting symbols and hints and crude emphases." BJØRNSON called the whole play "disgusting," and thought its psychological foundation false: "The plot is based on the assumption that the fourteen-year-old martyr believes her father, who can hardly say one true word. Now, we know that nobody is quicker than children to observe if the promise of the person they depend on is to be trusted. She was wise [to him] from the time she was four years old." In Denmark the majority of the press and of the Copenhagen theatergoing public was unable to grasp what Ibsen had intended by making such a "humoristic *genre* painting where, just in one corner of the floor, there lies a meaningless and uninteresting little pat of blood." But AUGUST STRINDBERG was most displeased of all; he imagined that Hjalmar Ekdal was intended as a caricature of himself, in revenge for the satire which, in "Married," he had recently directed against the viewpoints in "A Doll's House." A few years later, Strindberg gathered up his antipathy to Bjørnson and Ibsen, and especially to the line of reasoning in "Ghosts" and "The Wild Duck," in a pregnant dramatic speech: "Give back joy to us, you preachers of the joy of living! Give us the cheerful little spirit of compromise and send the Old Men of the Mountains back where they belong! They came from their misty heights and made life dark and frightful. Give back the sun to us, just a little bit of sunshine, so one can see that the old celestial body still sits there in its old heaven."

HAVELOCK ELLIS: [The Least Remarkable]‡

"The Wild Duck" is, as a drama, the least remarkable of Ibsen's

† From Francis Bull, *Norsk Litteraturhistorie*, Volume IV (1937), pp. 18-19. Reprinted by permission of H. Aschehoug & Co. Translated by Dounia B. Christiani.

‡ From Havelock Ellis, *The New Spirit*, p. 166. Reprinted by permission of The Society of Authors as the literary representative of the Estate of the late Havelock Ellis.

plays of this group. There is no central personage who absorbs our attention, and no great situation. For the first time we also detect a certain tendency to mannerism, and the dramatist's love of symbolism, here centered in the wild duck, becomes obtrusive and disturbing. Yet this play has a distinct and peculiar interest for the student of Ibsen's works. The satirist who has so keenly pursued others has never spared himself; in the lines that he has set at the end of the charming little volume in which he has collected his poems, he declares that, "to write poetry is to hold a doomsday over oneself." Or, as he has elsewhere expressed it: "All that I have written corresponds to something that I have lived through, if not actually experienced. Every new poem has served as a spiritual process of emancipation and purification."

BERNARD SHAW: [Spellbound by Ibsen]†

I need hardly go on to explain that Ibsen is at the back of this sudden explosion of disgusted intolerance on my part for a style of entertainment which I suffered gladly enough in the days of the Hare-Kendal management. On Monday last I sat without a murmur in a stuffy theatre on a summer afternoon from three to nearly half-past six, spellbound by Ibsen; but the price I paid for it was to find myself stricken with mortal impatience and boredom the next time I attempted to sit out the pre-Ibsenite drama for five minutes. Where shall I find an epithet magnificent enough for The Wild Duck! To sit there getting deeper and deeper into that Ekdal home, and getting deeper and deeper into your own life all the time, until you forget that you are in a theatre; to look on with horror and pity at a profound tragedy, shaking with laughter all the time at an irresistible comedy; to go out, not from a diversion, but from an experience deeper than real life ever brings to most men, or often brings to any man; that is what The Wild Duck was like last Monday at the Globe. It is idle to attempt to describe it; and as to giving an analysis of the play, I did that seven years ago, and decline now to give myself an antiquated air by treating as a novelty a masterpiece that all Europe delights in. Besides, the play is as simple as Little Red Ridinghood to anyone who comes to it fresh from life instead of stale from the theatre.

RAINER MARIA RILKE: [A New Poet]‡

. . . But the most remarkable part of this very long day was the

---

† From Bernard Shaw, *Our Theatres in the Nineties*, p. 138. Reprinted by permission of The Society of Authors.

‡ From Rainer Maria Rilke, *Selected Letters of Rainer Maria Rilke*, translated by R. F. C. Hull, p. 95. Reprinted by permission of Macmillan & Co., Ltd.

evening. We saw Ibsen's *Wild Duck* at the Antoine. Excellently re-hearsed, with a great deal of care and shaping—marvellous. Of course, by reason of certain differences in temperament, details were distorted, crooked, misunderstood. But the poetry! Thanks to the fact that the two female characters (Hjalmar Ekdal's wife and the fourteen-year-old Gina) [sic] were simple, without French frippery, all its splendour came from the inside and almost to the surface. There was something great, deep, essential. Last Judgment. A finality. And suddenly the hour was there when Ibsen's majesty deigned to look at me for the first time. A new poet, whom we shall approach by many roads now that I know one of them. And again someone who is misunderstood in the midst of fame. Someone quite different from what one hears. And another experience: the unprec-edented laughter of the French public (albeit very low in the pit) at the softest, tenderest, most painful places where even the stirring of a finger would have hurt. Laughter—there!

Henrik Ibsen: A Chronology†

1828   March 20. Henrik Ibsen is born in Skien, Norway, a town of two thousand inhabitants about sixty miles southwest of Oslo. Henrik is the second child born to Knud and Marichen Ibsen. The older child, born in 1826, dies less than a month after Henrik is born. Four more children are born between 1830 and 1835.

1832   or 1833. The Ibsen family moves to a more expensive property in Skien, the Hundevad estate.

1834   Knud Ibsen finds himself in increasing financial difficulties, and in 1836 is declared bankrupt.

1835   The family moves from Skien to Venstøp, a small town a short distance away in the parish of Gjerpen.

1843   October 1. Ibsen is confirmed in the Gjerpen church. The family moves back to Skien and lives in a house bought by Knud Ibsen's half brother. Immediately after Christmas, Henrik leaves Skien for Grimstad.

1844   January 3. Ibsen arrives in Grimstad and begins his apprenticeship as an apothecary.

1846   Ibsen becomes the father of a son by a housemaid who is ten years his senior. For the next fifteen years Ibsen has to contribute to the support of the child.

1847   His earliest extant poem, "Resignation," probably dates from this year.

1848   Studies Latin in order to prepare for university examinations.

1848–49   Winter. Writes his first play, *Catiline*.

1849   September 28. "In the Autumn," Ibsen's first poem to be published, appears in *Christiania-Posten*.

1850   April 12. *Catiline* published in an edition of 250 copies, of which all but fifty are later disposed of as waste paper. The cost of printing is paid for by Ole Schulerud. This is the first play to be published in Norway since Wergeland's *The Venetian* in 1843.

    April 13. Leaves Grimstad for Christiania [Oslo] and

† From *Ibsen: Letters and Speeches*, edited by Evert Sprinchorn. Copyright © 1964 by Evert Sprinchorn. Reprinted by permission of Hill and Wang, Inc., New York, and MacGibbon and Kee, Ltd., London.

probably pays a short visit to his family in Skien. This is the last time he sees his parents.

April 29. Arrives in Christiania to cram for the university entrance examinations. Takes the examinations in the autumn, failing in Greek and mathematics, and passing the others.

Writes a one-act play, *The Warrior's Barrow* (*Kjæmpehøjen*) and nearly completes two acts of a romantic comedy, *The Ptarmigan in Justedal* (*Rypen i Justedal*). On September 26 at the Christiania Theater, *The Warrior's Barrow* becomes the first play by Ibsen to be staged. *The Ptarmigan in Justedal* is later reworked as *Olaf Liljekrans*.

1851 Engages in various journalistic activities. Edits a student paper. Contributes articles to *The Worker's Union Paper*, edited by Theodore Abildgaard. Serves as one of three contributing editors of a short-lived satirical journal, known at first as *The Man* and later as *Andhrimner*. Writes *Norma, or A Politician's Love*, a political squib, based on Bellini's opera and published in *Andhrimner*.

November. Ibsen is engaged as playwright in residence at the newly organized National Theater in Bergen.

1852 April to September. Studies the theater in Copenhagen and Dresden.

1853 January 2. Ibsen's *Midsummer Eve* (*Sancthansnatten*) is performed at Bergen.

1854 January 2. *The Warrior's Barrow* performed at Bergen. To fulfil his obligation to provide the theater with a new play each year Ibsen had completely rewritten the work.

1855 January 2. *Lady Inger of Østraat* performed at Bergen.

1856 January 2. *The Feast at Solhaug* performed at Bergen. Ibsen's first success in the theater. Performed at the Christiania Theater, March 13. Published March 19.

1857 January 2. *Olaf Liljekrans* performed at Bergen.
September 3. Assumes his duties as artistic director of the Norwegian Theater in Christiania.

1858 June 18. Marries Suzannah Thoresen.
November 24. Produces *The Vikings at Helgeland* at the Norwegian Theater in Christiania.

1859 Writes the poems "On the Heights" ("Paa Vidderne") and "In the Picture Gallery."
December 23. Son Sigurd is born, the only child of the marriage.

1861 Writes poem "Terje Vigen."

1862 May. Awarded a grant from the University of Christiania to compile folk songs and tales. Travels extensively in Norway.

   Summer. The Norwegian Theater is forced to close.

   December. *Love's Comedy* published.

1863 January 1. Becomes literary adviser to the Christiania Theater.

   May 23. Receives another grant from the university to collect folk songs in the country. Stays in Christiania.

   September 12. Awarded a travel grant by the government.

   October. *The Pretenders* published.

1864 January 17. *The Pretenders* performed at the Christiania Theater.

   April 5. Leaves Christiania for Copenhagen and Rome.

   April–May. Travels to Italy, staying over at Copenhagen, Berlin, and Vienna.

1865 November 14. Receives publishing contract from Frederik Hegel, head of the Gyldendal publishing firm in Copenhagen.

1866 March 15. *Brand* published.

   April 30. Is voted a travel grant of 100 specie-dollars ($100) by the Royal Norwegian Science Association.

   May 12. Is voted an annual stipend of 400 specie-dollars by the Storting (the Norwegian parliament).

   June 28. Another travel grant of 350 specie-dollars is awarded to him by the Storting.

1867 November 14. *Peer Gynt* published.

1868 October 1–2. Moves to Dresden.

1869 June 3. Ibsen's mother dies.

   July 3. Receives a grant from the Norwegian government to study in Sweden.

   July. Goes to Stockholm as delegate to the Nordic orthographic conference. Receives the Vasa Order from King Charles XV.

   September 30. *The League of Youth* published. Performed October 18 at the Christiania Theater.

   October–November. Attends the opening of the Suez Canal as the representative of Norway.

1870 July 19. The Franco-Prussian War is declared. Ibsen stays in Copenhagen from July to October.

1871 May 3. Publishes his *Poems.*

   Works on *Emperor and Galilean.*

   January 24. The Dannebrog Order conferred on Ibsen.

1872 Works on *Emperor and Galilean.*

1873　June–July. Serves as judge at the International Art Exhibit in Vienna.

July. Made a Knight of St. Olaf at the coronation of King Oscar II of Sweden and Norway.

October 16. *Emperor and Galilean* published.

November 24. *Love's Comedy* performed at the Christiania Theater.

1874　July–September. Spends two and a half months in Norway. In August he attends an international conference of archeologists in Stockholm.

September 10. Honored by Norwegian students in a torchlight procession.

1875　April. Moves to Munich for the benefit of the education of his son, Sigurd.

May 1. Settles in his apartment in Munich.

1876　February 24. *Peer Gynt* performed with music by Edvard Grieg at the Christiania Theater.

April 10. *The Vikings at Helgeland* performed at the Court Theater in Munich, the first of Ibsen's plays to be produced outside Scandinavia.

June. Is guest of honor at the court of the Duke of Saxe-Meiningen, who decorates him with the Ernestine Order.

1877　Ibsen's father dies.

September 6. Honorary doctoral degree conferred on Ibsen at the University of Uppsala, Sweden.

October 11. *The Pillars of Society* published.

November. *The Pillars of Society* performed in the Danish provinces and at the Royal Theater in Copenhagen.

1878　Autumn. Moves to Rome, returning to Munich a year later.

1879　December 4. *A Doll's House* published.

December 21. Première of *A Doll's House* at the Danish Royal Theater in Copenhagen.

1880　Autumn. Moves to Rome when his son finishes his education in Munich.

1881　December. *Ghosts* is published.

1882　May. World première of *Ghosts* takes place in Chicago.

July. University of Rome confers degree of Doctor of Law on Sigurd Ibsen.

November 28. *An Enemy of the People* published.

1883　Revises *The Feast at Solhaug*.

January 13. *An Enemy of the People* performed at the Christiania Theater.

August 28. First European performance of *Ghosts* produced by August Lindberg in Helsingborg, Sweden.

1884   Sigurd Ibsen takes a position in the consulate in Christiania.

November 11. *The Wild Duck* published.

1885   Sigurd enters the Swedish-Norwegian diplomatic service as attaché at the Swedish Department of Foreign Affairs.

January. First performances of *The Wild Duck*, in Bergen, Christiania, and Stockholm.

March 24. The New Theater in Stockholm stages *Brand*.

June–September. Ibsen visits Norway.

June 14. Delivers speech to the workers in Trondhjem.

October. Moves from Rome to Munich.

1886   November 23. *Rosmersholm* published.

December 22. Ibsen is the guest of Duke Georg II of Meiningen for a production of *Ghosts* by the Meiningen Players.

1887   January 17. First performance of *Rosmersholm* staged by the Bergen theater.

July–mid-October. Visits Denmark and Sweden.

December. Ibsen's publisher, Frederik Hegel, dies.

1888   November 28. *The Lady from the Sea* published.

1889   February 12. *The Lady from the Sea* performed by the Christiania Theater and the Court Theater in Weimar simultaneously.

March 3–15. Ibsen is feted in Berlin and Weimar.

Summer. Meets Helene Raff and Emilie Bardach while vacationing in Gossensass in the Tyrol.

1890   Sigurd Ibsen leaves the diplomatic service.

December 16. *Hedda Gabler* published.

1891   January 31. Première of *Hedda Gabler* at the Munich Residenz-Theater.

April. Ibsen feted in Vienna and Budapest.

July. Leaves Munich to settle in Norway.

July 16. Arrives in Christiania. Goes on a tour of the North Cape.

August 17. Returns to Christiania and settles in his apartment on Victoria Terrace.

August. Meets the young pianist Hildur Andersen.

1892   October 11. Sigurd Ibsen marries Bjørnson's daughter Bergliot.

December 12. *The Master Builder* published in Scandinavia. Published in London, December 6.

1893   January 19. Première of *The Master Builder* in

Trondhjem.

July 11. Ibsen becomes a grandfather.

1894 December 11. *Little Eyolf* published.

1895 January 12. *Little Eyolf* performed for the first time at the Deutsches Theater in Berlin.

1895 July. Moves to 1 Arbin Street.

1896 December 15. *John Gabriel Borkman* published.

1897 January 10. Première of *John Gabriel Borkman* in Helsinki, closely followed by performances in Germany and Norway.

April 29. The University of Christiania refuses to offer a professorship to Sigurd Ibsen.

1898 March. First volumes of the collected edition of his works published in Denmark and Germany.

March 20—April 16. Seventieth-birthday celebrations. Ibsen honored in Christiania, Copenhagen, and Stockholm; receives the Grand Cross of the Dannebrog Order in Denmark, the Order of the North Star in Sweden.

1899 July 14. Sigurd Ibsen appointed head of the Norwegian Foreign Office.

September. Attends the opening of the new National Theater in Christiania, the first modern theater in Norway.

December 19. *When We Dead Awaken* published in London; published in Scandinavia and Germany, December 22.

1900 January 26. First full production of *When We Dead Awaken* given by the Stuttgart Court Theater; play also staged in Copenhagen (January 28), Helsinki (January 29), Christiania (February 6), and Stockholm (February 14).

1900 March. Ibsen ill with erysipelas.

Summer. Spends the summer at a sea resort undergoing a cure for his illness.

1901 Suffers his first stroke in Christiania.

1903 Suffers another stroke that leaves him unable to write or walk.

1906 May 23. Dies in Christiania.

A Selected Bibliography

The present translation is based on Volume VI, pages 163–269 of *Henrik Ibsen, Samlede Værker*, 8 volumes, Gyldendalske Boghandel—Nordisk Forlag (Kristiania og København, 1914), checked against Volume VII of the 1900 edition of the collected works by the same publisher and against Ibsen's manuscript.

The Oxford *Ibsen*, translated and edited by James Walter McFarlane, is replacing Archer's *The Collected Works of Henrik Ibsen* as the standard English edition. Koht's *The Life of Ibsen* remains the definitive biography.

Selections reprinted in this volume are not listed below, nor does the bibliography include general histories or studies of drama except for Hettner's *Das Moderne Drama*, a vital influence on Ibsen, and several works which cast particular light on Ibsen's achievement.

Aall, Anathon. *Henrik Ibsen als Dichter und Denker*. Halle, 1906.

Adler, Jacob H. "Ibsen, Shaw, and *Candida*." *JEGP*, Vol. LIX, No. 1 (January 1960), University of Illinois Press.

Antoine, André. *Mes Souvenirs sur le Théâtre-Libre*. Paris, 1921. *Memories of the Théâtre-Libre*, trans. Marvin A. Carlson, ed. H. D. Albright. Coral Gables, Florida, 1964.

Archer, William. Introduction to *The Wild Duck, The Collected Works of Henrik Ibsen*. 12 vols. London, 1906 ff., vol. 9, pp. xvii–xxv.

———. "Ibsen as I Knew Him." *The Monthly Review*, Vol. xxiii (April–June 1906).

Arup, Jens. "Narrative and Symbol in Ibsen." *Discussions of Henrik Ibsen*, ed. James Walter McFarlane. Boston, 1962.

Bentley, Eric. *The Life of the Drama*. New York, 1965.

———. *The Playwright as Thinker*. New York, 1946.

Boyesen, Hjalmar Hjorth. *A Commentary on the Works of Henrik Ibsen*. London, 1894.

Bradbrook, M. C. *Ibsen the Norwegian*. Hamden, Conn., 1966.

Brustein, Robert. *The Theatre of Revolt*. Boston & Toronto, 1962.

Courtney, W. L. *The Idea of Tragedy in Ancient and Modern Drama*. New York, 1900.

———. *Studies at Leisure*. London, 1892.

Dobrée, Bonamy. *The Lamp and the Lute*. London & Edinburgh, 1964.

Downs, Brian W. *Ibsen: The Intellectual Background*. Cambridge, 1948.

Eitrem, H. *Ibsen og Grimstad*. Oslo, 1940.

Ellis, Havelock. *The New Spirit*. Boston & New York, 1929.

Elster, Kristian. *Illustreret Norsk Litteraturhistorie*. 2 vols. Kristiania, 1923.

Fergusson, Francis. *The Idea of a Theatre*. Princeton, 1949.

Fjelde, Rolf, ed. *Ibsen: A Collection of Critical Essays*. Englewood Cliffs, New Jersey, 1965.

Gassner, John. *Form and Idea in the Modern Theatre*. New York, 1956.

———. "Shaw on Ibsen and the Drama of Ideas." *Ideas in the Drama*, ed. John Gassner. New York & London, 1964.

———. *Theatre at the Crossroads*. New York, 1960.

Gosse, Edmund. *Ibsen*. London, 1907. New York, 1907.

Guthke, Karl S. *Modern Tragicomedy*. New York, 1966.

Haakonsen, Daniel. *Henrik Ibsens Realisme*. Oslo, 1957.

Hans, Dr. Wilhelm. *Ibsens Selbstporträt in seinem Dramen*. München, 1911.

Hettner, Hermann. *Das Moderne Drama*. Berlin & Leipzig, 1924. (First appeared in 1850.)

Høst, Sigurd. "Henrik Ibsen, Drøm og Daad." *Edda*, IV (1915), 328–341.

———. *Ibsens Digtning og Ibsen Selv*. Oslo, 1927.

Huneker, James. *Iconoclasts: A Book of Dramatists*. New York, 1905.

Ibsen, Bergliot. *The Three Ibsens: Memories of Henrik, Suzannah, and Sigurd Ibsen*, trans. G. Schjelderup. London, 1951.

Jaeger, Henrik. *Henrik Ibsen: 1828–1888. Ein litterarisches Lebensbild*, trans. Heinrich Zschalig. Dresden & Leipzig, 1890.
———. *Henrik Ibsen: A Critical Biography*, trans. C. Bell. London, 1890.
Johnston, Brian. "The Metaphoric Structure of *The Wild Duck.*" *Contemporary Approaches to Ibsen*, ed. Daniel Haakonsen. Oslo, 1965.
Kerans, James E. "Kindermord and Will in *Little Eyolf.*" *Modern Drama*, ed. Travis Bogard & William Oliver. New York, 1965.
Knight, G. Wilson. *Henrik Ibsen*. Edinburgh, 1962.
Koht, Halvdan. *Henrik Ibsen: Eet Diktarliv*. 2 vols. Oslo, 1954.
———. *The Life of Ibsen*. 2 vols. New York, 1931.
Krutch, Joseph Wood. *Modernism in Modern Drama: A Definition and an Estimate*. New York, 1953.
Lavrin, Janko. *Ibsen and His Creation: A Psycho-critical Study*. London, 1921.
Lee, Jeanette. *The Ibsen Secret: A Key to the Prose Dramas of Henrik Ibsen*. New York & London, 1907.
Lucas, F. L. *The Dramas of Ibsen and Strindberg*. New York, 1962.
MacCarthy, Desmond. *The Court Theatre* 1904–1907. London, 1907.
McFarlane, James W. *Ibsen and the Temper of Norwegian Literature*. London, 1960.
Nissen, Ingjald. *Sjelelige Kriser i Menneskets Liv: Henrik Ibsen og den Moderne Psykologi*. Oslo, 1931.
Northam, John. *Ibsen's Dramatic Method: A Study of the Prose Dramas*. London, 1953.
Paulsen, John. *Samliv med Ibsen*. København & Kristiania, 1906.
Peacock, Ronald. *The Poet in the Theatre*. New York, 1960.
Raphael, Robert. "Illusion and Self in *The Wild Duck.*" *Scandinavian Studies*, XXXV (Feb. 1963), 37–42.
Reinert, Otto. *Modern Drama: Nine Plays*. Boston & Toronto, 1961.
Roberts, R. Ellis. *Henrik Ibsen, A Critical Study*. London, 1912.
Shaw, George Bernard. *Our Theatres in the Nineties*. 3 vols. London, 1932.
———. *The Quintessence of Ibsenism*. London, 1913.
Tennant, P. F. D. *Ibsen's Dramatic Technique*. Cambridge, 1948.
———. "A Critical Study of Ibsen's *Vildanden.*" EDDA XXXIV (1934), 327–354.
Thompson, Alan Reynolds. *The Anatomy of Drama*. Berkeley & Los Angeles, 1946.
Weigand, Hermann J. *The Modern Ibsen: A Reconsideration*. New York, 1925.
Zucker, A. E. *Ibsen, the Master Builder*. London, 1929.

NORTON CRITICAL EDITIONS

MACHIAVELLI *The Prince* translated and edited by Robert M. Adams
MALTHUS *An Essay on the Principle of Population* edited by Philip Appleman
MELVILLE *The Confidence-Man* edited by Hershel Parker
MELVILLE *Moby-Dick* edited by Harrison Hayford and Hershel Parker
MILL *On Liberty* edited by David Spitz
MILTON *Paradise Lost* edited by Scott Elledge
MORE *Utopia* translated and edited by Robert M. Adams
NEWMAN *Apologia Pro Vita Sua* edited by David J. DeLaura
NORRIS *McTeague* edited by Donald Pizer
Adrienne Rich's Poetry selected and edited by Barbara Charlesworth Gelpi and
    Albert Gelpi
The Writings of St. Paul edited by Wayne A. Meeks
SHAKESPEARE *Hamlet* edited by Cyrus Hoy
SHAKESPEARE *Henry IV, Part I* edited by James J. Sanderson
    Revised Edition
Bernard Shaw's Plays selected and edited by Warren Sylvester Smith
Shelley's Poetry and Prose edited by Donald H. Reiman and Sharon B. Powers
SOPHOCLES *Oedipus Tyrannus* translated and edited by Luci Berkowitz and
    Theodore F. Brunner
SPENSER *Edmund Spenser's Poetry* selected and edited by Hugh Maclean
STENDHAL *Red and Black* translated and edited by Robert M. Adams
SWIFT *Gulliver's Travels* edited by Robert A. Greenberg *Revised Edition*
The Writings of Jonathan Swift edited by Robert A. Greenberg and
    William B. Piper
TENNYSON *In Memoriam* edited by Robert Ross
Tennyson's Poetry selected and edited by Robert W. Hill, Jr.
THOREAU *Walden and Civil Disobedience* edited by Owen Thomas
TOLSTOY *Anna Karenina* (the Maude translation) edited by George Gibian
TOLSTOY *War and Peace* (the Maude translation) edited by George Gibian
TURGENEV *Fathers and Sons* edited with a substantially new translation by
    Ralph E. Matlaw
VOLTAIRE *Candide* translated and edited by Robert M. Adams
WHITMAN *Leaves of Grass* edited by Sculley Bradley and Harold W. Blodgett
WOLLSTONECRAFT *A Vindication of the Rights of Woman* edited by
    Carol H. Poston
Middle English Lyrics selected and edited by Maxwell S. Luria and
    Richard L. Hoffman
Modern Drama edited by Anthony Caputi
Restoration and Eighteenth-Century Comedy edited by Scott McMillin